The
Squatters

Also by Barry Stone

Secret Army (2017)
The Desert Anzacs (2014)
The Diggers' Menagerie (2012)
The Almost Complete History of the World (with Joseph
Cummins and James Inglis, 2012)
Scandalous (2012)
Mutinies (2011)
Great Australian Historic Hotels (2010)
History's Greatest Headlines (with James Inglis, 2010)

The Squatters

THE STORY OF AUSTRALIA'S PASTORAL PIONEERS

BARRY STONE

ALLEN&UNWIN

SYDNEY·MELBOURNE·AUCKLAND·LONDON

Allen & Unwin
83 Alexander Street
Crows Nest NSW 2065
Australia
Phone: (61 2) 8425 0100
Email: info@allenandunwin.com
Web: www.allenandunwin.com

 A catalogue record for this
book is available from the
National Library of Australia

ISBN 978 1 76029 153 2

Internal design by Midland Typesetters Australia
Set in 11.5/15 pt Sabon by Midland Typesetters, Australia
Printed and bound in Australia by Griffin Press

10 9 8 7 6 5 4 3 2

 The paper in this book is FSC® certified.
FSC® promotes environmentally responsible,
socially beneficial and economically viable
management of the world's forests.

Dedicated to Yvonne, Jackson and Truman.

My beautiful family.

CONTENTS

Workers outside their bark hut, Queensland c.1870.
Richard Daintree, State Library of Queensland

INTRODUCTION

'I remember a ball at the local town hall, where the scrub aristocrats took one end of the room to dance in, and the ordinary scum the other.'

—Henry Lawson, 'The Hero of Redclay', 1900

In July 1789, a Cornish farmer turned convict named James Ruse came to the end of his term of imprisonment. Guilty of the theft of two silver watches and other assorted property, he had been transported to New South Wales with the First Fleet a year and a half earlier, on board the three-masted cargo ship *Scarborough*. Four months after his term expired Governor Arthur Phillip, realising the importance of self-sufficiency for the new colony, permitted Ruse to work an acre of cleared land at Rose Hill near Parramatta. Having no animals, Ruse was forced to hoe the ground himself, into which he sowed bearded wheat and maize. In the absence of manure, he energised his soil with potash from the timbers he burned, and composted it with its own weeds and grasses. He produced such a healthy, albeit small, harvest that in February 1791 he declared himself self-sufficient. A few weeks later he was awarded a grant of 30 acres, a grant that became known as 'Experiment Farm'. It was the first land grant in Australian history.

Food production was a constant preoccupation for the early British settlers. Arriving with no knowledge or experience of Australian soils, the land around Sydney Cove was thought to be only a shade shy of barren compared to the fertile English soils they'd left behind. By the Christmas of 1791, however, arable lands either side of the Parramatta River, including the land under cultivation at the Rose Hill farm, were increasingly being worked by emancipists (pardoned convicts) who were offered land grants so they could grow their own food and help lessen the colony's dependence on government stores.

Initially tents were the settlers' most common form of accommodation, but these soon gave way to slab huts, which in turn were replaced by dwellings of sandstone and clay. The colony's first track, from Sydney to Parramatta, was finished in 1791, and three years later a road was laid to the Hawkesbury River and an early unsuccessful attempt to cross the Blue Mountains was made. Port Stephens was surveyed in 1795, and the following year came another try at crossing the seemingly impenetrable Blue Mountains, this time by the explorer George Bass.

The colony was growing with the arrival of every ship. Growing, too, was its need for food.

There were seven horses, 87 chickens, eighteen turkeys, nineteen goats, 35 ducks, 29 geese, five rabbits and 44 sheep on the First Fleet when it arrived in January 1788. Brought over solely as a food source with no thought given to the significance of their fleeces, the sheep were killed. Other factors combined to make the food situation in the new colony progressively more tenuous. In September 1788, the first crops failed to germinate because the seeds had overheated on the long sea journey. Beef and pork rations had already been cut, and fish was increasingly being used as a substitute source of nutrition.

In October 1788, HMS *Sirius* was sent to Cape Town in South Africa for more supplies. The ship arrived back in May 1789 with 56 tons of barley, flour and wheat. But by the end of the year rations for 'every Man, from the Governor to the Convict' had to be reduced by two-thirds, although extra rations were given to gamekeepers and fishermen, those whose job it was to procure food. Work days were scaled back to a mere six hours of toil. The colony was edging perilously closer to famine.

There were also cattle on the First Fleet, but when a de-horned bull, a bull calf and four cows purchased in South Africa during the voyage—the new colony's entire stock—wandered off from their yardage in what is now the city's Botanic Gardens, their disappearance was considered nothing less than a calamity. And not only for the luckless Edward Corbett, the convict hired to guard them who was later hanged for the theft of a smock. The itinerant beasts were not seen again until 1795, when a scouting party, spurred on by Aboriginal rock drawings depicting a familiar, de-horned animal, forded the Nepean River at Camden, climbed a small hill near Menangle, and to their astonishment saw a contented herd of 40 grazing cattle. By 1801, that same herd, now wild, had grown to between 500 and 600 head, and by 1804 had swelled to several thousand. Over time the herd disappeared, either having been slaughtered or blended with privately owned stock brought on later ships.

In 1801, that great pioneer of the Australian wool industry, John Macarthur, sailed to England to convince British wool manufacturers that New South Wales' merino fleeces were the equal to the best in the world, which at the time were coming from Spain. His timing was fortuitous, as he arrived when wool manufacturers were fighting to repeal laws prohibiting the use of water-powered spinning and weaving machines. Macarthur's promise of fresh supplies of fine-grade wool led to those laws being abolished, paving the way for a serious ramping up of production—and demand. In the age before refrigeration, meat was unable to be exported and cattle were raised only for domestic consumption, so Macarthur was in no doubt as to which industry the colonists in New South Wales should be developing.

The land was beginning to forge a new identity. In 1804, the name 'Australia' was used for the first time by Matthew Flinders. Three years later came Macarthur's first wool exports to England. In April 1809, Scottish colonial administrator and British Army officer Lachlan Macquarie was appointed governor of New South Wales, and under his eleven-year rule the colony transitioned from a penal colony to a free settlement. Soon after his appointment Macquarie announced the establishment of five new towns—Richmond, Castlereagh, Pitt Town, Wilberforce and Windsor. Even then, whatever lay beyond the 'Great Divide' of the Blue Mountains remained a mystery to the colonists.

Eventually the dry savannah-like interior, so different to the rock-encrusted humid environment of Sydney Cove, was found and opened up, and to those early settlers—both squatters and moneyed-up pastoralists—it must have seemed extraordinary. They had left England, where lands had been passed down through generations of landowners, and now found themselves in a new world that was so vast and fertile that all you needed to do to start a new life was to pack your belongings onto a bullock dray, journey beyond the reach of Sydney's meddlesome authorities, mark out a parcel of land, claim it for yourself and your descendants, populate it with sheep or cattle, and forge a future. Little could they have known that within a few decades they would not only be building a life for themselves, but collectively they would be providing the foundation for a nation's prosperity.

Through hard work and enterprise these early pastoralists—a mix of free settlers and penniless and moneyed-up squatters—would create a rural equivalent of the English aristocracy, a 'squattocracy', a new ruling elite, a pioneering migration to the land that would, in just a few generations, provide for many an enviable lifestyle.

In his short story 'The Hero of Redclay', Henry Lawson disparagingly referred to this new rural elite as 'scrub aristocrats', and by the mid-1800s they had developed many of the unsavoury trappings of a privileged class. Country dance halls had chalk lines drawn on their floors to separate landholders from commoners. Pastoral families gathered together in gilded dining rooms while white employees ate in the kitchen—and Aborigines on the benches outside. Grazing families intermarried to maintain control of property. A few even owned their own artillery batteries, in the unlikely event there should ever be a proletarian revolt.

Settlers spread out across south-eastern Australia, occupying an area the size of Western Europe, and forever changed the landscape adding windmills and fence lines, dry-stone walls and storehouses, livestock yards and droving routes that you can still see etched into the earth today if you know where to look. It's all still there—faded markers leading to abattoirs, railway sidings, sale yards, riverbank wharves. They brought the concept of ownership to a continent whose original inhabitants owned nothing except their weapons and who saw creatures such as sheep and cattle as every bit the product of nature as the arrival of migrating birds. To them it was a preposterous notion that any animal could be the property of a person, so they would spear sheep and cattle—and later suffer the consequences. Even those few squatters fair-minded enough to accept that their land claims were tenuous, were in no doubt as to who owned the livestock. Conflict, and bloody murder, were inevitable.

Setting land aside for Aborigines began in 1826 with grants to missionaries on the shores of Lake Macquarie. Large scale reserves began to appear in the late 1800s but were often far removed from their traditional country, and were seen by the government as more of a means to keep Aborigines separate from settler communities.

The so-called 'peaceful' colonisation of Australia has long been exposed as the myth it always was. Indigenous Australians *did not* passively accept the loss of their lands; they *did not* 'mutely die' in confronting armed settlers as some anthropologists once suggested. They fought back, and died in battle for control of their traditional lands. And the story of the European settlement of Australia cannot be told without reminding ourselves of the fact that many settlers who ventured into the great unknown in search of a livelihood did so with blood on their hands.

The subjugation of the continent was achieved without having to overcome many of the economic obstacles that would have had to be confronted if the same were attempted in England. Australia had a far more temperate climate than England, which meant the need to construct outbuildings and expensive winter housing to provide shelter for livestock was not as pressing. Land was so plentiful that there was no need for fencing to keep your livestock separated from your neighbour's, who more often than not was so far away you couldn't see his land anyway. Allotments being so large also meant there was no struggling with economies of scale—you could start with large numbers of stock if you had the means to purchase them.

Forests did not need clearing because initially there was enough open grassland for everyone, and last but not least, the land was, of course, 'free'. Cheap convict labour was assigned to early settlers, and sheep multiplied all on their own, and rapidly, without any injection of capital, meaning an expansion of the wool output. Rarely in the first, faltering steps of an emerging society had so many factors combined to so readily facilitate the creation of wealth.

And there were the faceless ones whose names we will never know who saw it all happen. There were the swagmen, itinerant workers who might spend a day or two on a station before moving on, habitual wanderers whose only desire was to see a bit of country; the horsemen who considered themselves a cut above the 'swaggie', who rode their own horse with their supplies heaped onto a second but who really weren't as different from the man with the swag as they thought they were; and the sundowners, those who'd arrive at a station as the sun went down with no intention of working, just in time for a meal and a bed. Labourers, wanderers, opportunists. The drifting ghosts of our heritage.

What follows is an account of how vast wealth and privilege was eked out of a capricious and uncompromising landscape, the bounty of which can still be seen today, a world invaded, shaped and tamed by a rare breed of pioneer who created a new and powerful mythology.

And in the process, forged a nation.

Meal break for teamsters and horses.
Powerhouse Museum

1

THE LIMITS OF LOCATION

'After a seclusion of twelve months in the bush the young squatters come down for a little amusement and relaxation, and a hundred pounds is gone before they know where they are— so avoid Sydney as much as possible, and you avoid one of the dangers on your road to advancement.'

—Christopher Hodgson, *Reminiscences of Australia*, 1846

By the mid-1780s there were more than 100,000 men and women crammed into Britain's prisons, a situation brought about by the inability to send any more convicts to America in the wake of their victory against the British in the War of Independence in 1783. America had been a dumping ground for convicts since the 1600s, but now, with their options suddenly limited after other colonies in Africa and elsewhere were ruled out as impractical for one reason or another, the British government decided to jettison tens of thousands of convicts to a little-known outpost of the empire. The decision was purely and overwhelmingly one of economy. It cost the government £26 a year to keep a criminal in a British cell; the cost of transportation was a modest £20.

It was never anticipated the destination would eventually evolve into a colony. No thought was given to the notion or creation of a 'society'. The exercise was purely a mechanism designed to solve a persistent and increasingly troublesome convict problem. Little thought was given to precisely how the people would survive beyond the vague assessment that Australia was known, through various voyages of exploration, to be a vast land, and so it was assumed that it had to be capable of supporting millions of people. Somehow they would find the means to survive. There were no plans for land distribution, nor were there any plans for what convicts might do with themselves once their terms expired. There would be no regard given to sending crop seeds, or recruiting free men who had farming experience. No recourse would be made for a freed convict's eventual return to Britain. There was not even any thought given to how the new colony might communicate with other established British interests in the region.

With such a pervasive sense of abandonment felt by all, most of whom would eventually gain their freedom and look to new horizons, is it any wonder when they transitioned from convict to settler then to squatter, that few would take any notice of laws forbidding the pegging out of runs on Crown lands? Convicts, and even free settlers, knew from the moment they left England that they would be on their own.

Fine then, they thought. Let it be so.

It was Captain Henry Waterhouse, a midshipman who joined HMS *Sirius* in 1786, and Lieutenant William Kent of HMS *Supply*, who joined the navy at the age of ten and rose to the rank of lieutenant at 21, who imported the colony's first merinos, in 1796, after being sent to the Cape of Good Hope by Governor John Hunter to bring back much-needed provisions. Waterhouse and Kent returned with five rams and a number of ewes, privately purchased from the widow of the former Dutch military commander of the Cape, Colonel Robert Gordon, who had taken his own life the previous year when the British took over the Dutch colony.

The merinos were part of a flock originally given to the Netherlands' Prince William of Orange by King Carlos III of Spain. In 1789, the Prince had dispatched two rams and four ewes to the Dutch colony in South Africa to be looked after by Colonel Robert Gordon, who returned the original breeding animals in 1791 when ordered by the Dutch government to do so. He did, however, keep their offspring. After his death, Gordon's wife inherited the sheep and a year later sold them to Waterhouse and Kent for £4 per head.

The flock was split between HMS *Reliance* and HMS *Supply* for the journey to Australia. Poor weather almost doubled their time at sea, however, and more than half the sheep perished on the journey. Captain John Macarthur, who was then an officer in the New South Wales Corps, offered Waterhouse 15 guineas a head for the remaining sheep on the condition he could purchase them all. Waterhouse refused and instead grazed his sheep at The Vineyard, his 140-acre property on the banks of the Parramatta River that he purchased on his return from the Cape.

Waterhouse kept his new merino flock segregated, making certain that they bred only with each other, and as his flock grew he sold some to John Macarthur, the Reverend Samuel Marsden, Captain Thomas Rowley and Lieutenant Kent. When Waterhouse returned to Britain in 1800, William Cox, the English-born road maker and builder who purchased Brush Farm from John Macarthur in 1800, bought the majority of the flock which included several of the original sheep purchased by Waterhouse and Kent. The remainder went to Macarthur, and from these sheep the colony's merino industry was developed. Pastoralism quickly became the main driver of our expanding settlements, and in time would underwrite our prosperity. Its profits and promise were such that even as late as 1861, six out of every ten people still lived in rural areas.

While Macarthur pursued purity and fineness of fibre, it was the farmer and churchman the Reverend Samuel Marsden who became interested in crossbreeding with a view to producing a breed that would better withstand harsh Australian conditions, and it was Marsden's wool that first convinced England that the fibre had a future in the colonies. Marsden was born in Yorkshire in 1765 and arrived in Sydney Cove in March 1794 to take up a position as assistant to the Anglican chaplain of New South Wales. While committed to his role within the Church, Marsden also found himself increasingly committed to farming, despite having no prior experience. By 1802, he had accumulated 201 acres in grants, and acquired 239 acres from settlers. Some 200 acres of his lands had been cleared, and he was grazing close to 500 sheep. By 1805 his farm near Parramatta ran some 1000 sheep, 44 cattle and 100 pigs. Between 1803–05 Marsden reported to Governor Philip King and Sir Joseph Banks on the future of sheep-breeding and wool-growing—by this time he'd gained a reputation as one of the colony's most productive farmers. In August 1804, eight samples of the very first wool produced in Australia—from Marsden's sheep—were sent to Governor King, who in turn sent them to England where they were presented to King George III and helped to prove the viability of the nascent Australian wool industry.

Marsden was praised for his work on soil studies and its relationship to the colony's climate. He concentrated his efforts on developing muscular, heavy-framed sheep like the Suffolk breed, which were valued more highly in the colony than John Macarthur's Spanish merinos. In 1812, more than 1814 kilograms (4000 pounds) of Marsden wool was sold in England for 45 pence a pound. Marsden's contribution to breeding and marketing may have been less influential than John Macarthur's, but there is no doubt he was an important promoter of the wool staple at a time when the wool industry was desperately looking to establish itself in the markets of Britain.

On 16 January 1793, the first free settlers—five men, two women and six children—arrived in Sydney Cove. A few weeks later, on 7 February, they became the first free settlers to receive land grants, establishing themselves in the Liberty Plains area to the south-west of Parramatta. The settlers and their servants cleared the land and grew wheat and corn. One of those granted a lease, Samuel Crane, was killed in 1794 when a tree fell on him. His farm was subsequently put up for sale, with a 'comfortable hut, four acres planted to corn, and half an acre to potatoes'.

In Van Diemen's Land in the early 1800s, the term squatter was first used to describe a class of settler considered at best frontiersmen, and at worst bushrangers, who gathered their herds together by whatever lawful or unscrupulous means necessary. In faraway London, their infamy knew no bounds. In 1815, squatters were denounced in the House of Commons and generally considered to be instigators of crime, receivers of stolen property, and prone to harbouring runaways and bushrangers. In New South Wales, they were looked upon a little less severely, mostly as vagabonds and vagrants. In Victoria, the pastoralist and author Edward Curr painted one squatter in particular as 'wild and indestructible' in his acclaimed homage to the days of his own youth, *Recollections of Squatting in Victoria*:

> . . . he wore habitually Hessian boots and spurs, of which it was uncertain whether he ever divested himself; that he was much given to emu and kangaroo hunting; had constant encounters with hordes of blacks . . . lived solely on tea, mutton and damper, and enjoyed, when in the saddle, a perfect immunity from fatigue . . .

Our earliest photographs of squatters, taken in the 1860s, however, show people who are well fed and well dressed, strong and proud. They were clothed in fine jackets, some even wore tie pins, and their expressions suggested authority and even aloofness. Of course not all squatters were so presentable. Only the successful, after all, would allow themselves to be photographed.

And while they were invariably disparaged as bandits only able to survive by bartering stolen goods and spirits, the reality, even from the very beginning, was far different. The squatters did what any pioneer would do to survive. They built their huts, established and stocked their pastures, and forged a living in fertile, hostile environments, only to be pilloried for their efforts by an officialdom that was foolishly prejudiced against them. These men and women were the vanguard of a new civilisation, but one whose dreams were often thwarted by officials with military backgrounds for whom whatever was not an order was very much *out* of order. Disciplined backgrounds don't easily bend to accommodate opportunists and dreamers. Anyone who took up a squat anywhere in an unoccupied space put himself, at the same moment, at loggerheads with authority.

It must have seemed extraordinary to those squatters who first dared to venture into our broad horizons, to be confronted with a land that was so abundant it could be acquired by anyone of limited means, armed with not much more than determination and audacity to go and claim distant grazing lands that had little intrinsic value, their worth deemed to be only as great as the amount of stock one could afford to place upon them.

Incidents of conflict between squatters during these formative days were surprisingly rare, considering that sheep stealing in the days prior to branding was not difficult, and boundaries were often defined only by natural features, such as a river or a line of hills, rather than precise lines of demarcation such as fencing. One reason for this was that hut-keepers were often employed in order to enforce ownership of a parcel of land and, together with shepherds, keep a watch over flocks. There is also written evidence of many early squatters entering into agreements that referenced what they considered to be their *de facto* rights, rights that included a mutual respect for the declared boundaries of their neighbours. Squatters also proved adept at managing their own disputes, and by so doing kept meddlesome and suspicious authorities at bay.

◄O►

While much is made of Australia's early European explorers regarding their discovery and opening up of the country's interior, exploratory parties were few and far between. It was our indomitable squatters who made lands unknown to Europeans, known, who were lured and teased towards golden horizons without any help from a government whose legislators wanted to facilitate an environment that was conducive to settlement and expansion, but who repeatedly failed to provide anything in the way of practical assistance to help make it all happen.

When new runs were marked out, any sense of elation soon gave way to more pressing needs, such as to secure a water source, build shelters, and transform the land so it could provide an income. And forget the mythology; there was nothing altruistic about the squatter. He was in it for the money. He was not there to create a colonial mythology, nor to act as the leaven between the Aborigine and the military authorities, nor even to be a vanguard for others who were to follow. He was there to make a profit.

Making a profit was a bulwark to being driven from the land by any number of circumstances, and even that was no guarantee of success. It only increased the odds. The only markets for meat were local ones, with prices set at the whims of the wholesalers who may or may not have quietly colluded with one another to pay the least amount possible. So squatters running cattle walked them to sale yards and took what prices they could get. Not the most ideal of circumstances, but payment at least came quicker than for those who ran sheep, and were exporting their wool to England.

The degree to which a squatter could create a liveable environment for himself depended upon what he brought with him on his journey. Stock, if he had any, would have remained behind on an agistment until he found land; if he had no bullock or dray he'd have had to return to buy them so he could carry supplies. Trees had to be felled to build huts, although camping under a dray was good enough shelter for most to start with.

Bark huts became a common sight, and the stripping of trees for their bark was a skill most squatters fast acquired. Using axes, shapes were cut into the trunk and the bark then peeled away with the help of a spade. Some were more adept at the technique than others. Some sought out stringybark trees over a metre wide, dried the bark over a fire and placed weights on it to make it flat. The higher up a tree the cut was made, the larger the sheet. Aborigines had long used this method to make a humpy, or *gunyah* (tent)—shelters made of bark laid over saplings—and these proved adequate for many squatters while a more substantial dwelling could be built. Some huts were so well built that they lasted for decades, their bark sheets kept in position by using a combination of pegs and the untanned hides of animals, tied to rafters and securing them to ridge poles using lengths of fibrous stringybark.

An improvement on the bark hut was the more substantial slab hut, dwellings made from split or sawn timber. Trees were felled, then sawn into the required length, then split down their length using a maul and a wedge to create a single 'slab' of timber. Slab huts became churches, schools, even homesteads, and were so widespread in south-eastern Australia that they became an intrinsic part of our bush heritage.

Where timber was scarce, layer after layer of wet earth became the construction material of choice. Placed within a wooden frame, the earth would be compacted and dried, a process of rammed earth construction known as *pisé*. The frame was then moved along the ground and the process repeated, until a length of wall was formed, with gaps left for doors and windows. Ideally the soil was one-third clay and two-thirds sand and had to be wet enough to prevent the formation of cavities. The walls were then sealed with a whitewash and linseed oil mix or, alternatively, with a mixture of water, lime and mortar.

There seemed to be no in-between for the adventurous and the foolhardy who set about this great exodus with barely a thought given to the consequences. You either succeeded and flourished, or withered away in the harsh and often unforgiving landscape. This nationwide quest for self-sufficiency began innocently enough, with patchy forays into the land around the Hunter and Hawkesbury rivers, expanded beyond the Blue Mountains when they were finally crossed in 1813, and expanded anew in 1824 when explorers Hamilton Hume and William Hovell reached the shores of Port Phillip Bay at the end of their epic journey south from New South Wales. Districts were settled the moment they were founded. Squatters were everywhere, either buying land if they could, or where they were unable to buy it, simply claiming it. Occasionally they even indulged in 'wedging'—the practice of establishing a run on unoccupied land in between two existing properties.

The one criteria was that the land must have a permanent supply of water. Waterholes were welcomed, but their source might be problematic. Creeks and rivers were preferred, but even then poor knowledge of the land meant no one knew if the rivers were 'high' or 'low'. Was the water level of a creek or river seen for the very first time at its highest—or at its lowest?

The land should also be relatively clear of trees in order to save clearing them later, but have enough timber to build with. Mature trees, particularly yellow box, were a sign that the soil was healthy, while land with immature, smaller trees indicated that it was poor. Squatters also looked to their animals when judging the land: did they survive in the weeks following their arrival, or lose condition?

To many, though, these new lands held great promise. Charles Browning Hall, an early squatter in Victoria's Wimmera region saw creeks that were lined with reeds and shrubs and water-loving gum trees, with the surrounding land abounding in turkey, quail and wild fowls. Another early arrival to Victoria, John Casterton, wrote of thickly forested lands that encircled Portland Bay, a world so verdant and full of promise that he could think of nothing else.

◄O►

By the end of 1788, a miserly 20 acres of crops had been planted, and convicts were proving more adept at stealing food rather than growing it. To encourage free settlers to emigrate, Governor Phillip promised grants of 100 acres to any non-commissioned Marine Officers, and the following year he wrote to the British government requesting they send more settlers, primarily those with farming experience who could cultivate the land. In the 1790s, land grants also began to be made to free settlers, former convicts and women. The first woman in the colony to be granted freehold land was Ellenor Frazer, who was granted 20 acres in the Concord district, her rent being one shilling a year beginning after ten years. A prudent settlement policy meant that by 1821 less than 2590 square kilometres of land in New South Wales had been officially allocated. Unofficially, however, by that time much of the land within a 320-kilometre radius of Sydney had been occupied by either graziers or farmers, and increasingly by squatters—none of whom were deterred by the prospect of self-imposed isolation.

Government efforts to explore the lands that lay beyond established boundaries only served to undermine their own arguments that limits should be imposed. As early as 1817, the then–New South Wales' Surveyor-General John Oxley led two expeditions into the Hunter Valley and discovered the rich pasture lands of the Liverpool Plains, separated from the coast by the wall of the Liverpool Ranges, which initially acted as an impediment to settlement. But not for long. Once news reached England of the quality of the soil there, the queue to migrate to Australia, especially among those who harboured pastoral aspirations, quickly lengthened.

The Australian Agricultural Company (AAC) was incorporated in London in 1824 and given a million acres of unsettled land on the New South Wales' north coast around the sites of present-day Newcastle, Port Stephens and along the banks of the Manning and Karuah rivers. Its task was to improve the colony's stocks of fine merino wool as well as certain crops such as tobacco and flax for export to England. The eyes of many in the colony were beginning to be turned to northern New South Wales. It was just another reason why limits on where settlers were permitted to venture would never be taken seriously. By 1826, the AAC was grazing 2000 sheep and 1000 head of cattle. Within three years the number of sheep had grown to over 17,000, and by 1828 the region was a vital, thriving community with over 600 farms and gardens interconnected by a vast network of roads.

It's hard to imagine what the pace of early settlement might have looked like had there been sufficient numbers of the one animal Europeans had always taken for granted—the horse—and that lack undoubtedly slowed the rate of expansion. Only two of the seven horses that came over on the First Fleet survived, the others being consumed by starving settlers. At the end of 1791 a livestock inventory—*A Complete Account of the Settlement of Port Jackson*—by Captain Watkin Tench, a British Royal Navy marine officer from Cheshire, tells us there were just ten horses in the settlement at that time: two stallions, six mares and two colts. Though the number didn't include privately owned stock, the number of horses in those early years that came here on subsequent voyages is generally accepted to have been no more than twenty. Numbers began to increase from 1795, however, when the *Britannia* arrived via the Cape of Good Hope with one stallion, 29 mares and some fillies.

A sustained approach to breeding followed, however, and by 1802 there were hundreds of horses in the colony. The first stray horses were noted in 1804, and by 1810 the colony had the numbers it needed for ploughing, haulage and transportation over a landscape still bereft of roads. Thanks to the horse, exploration at last sped up, and the vast interior, with its tantalising promise of pastures and wealth for all, became all the more attainable.

When explorers Gregory Blaxland, William Wentworth, William Lawson, their three convict servants, a local Aboriginal guide, four pack horses and five dogs navigated their way over the Blue Mountains in 1813 and became the first Europeans to gaze upon the vast plains beyond, Lawson was so impressed he described it as 'the best watered Country of any I have seen in the Colony'. It took just six days for them to return with news of what they'd seen. And it didn't take long after that for settlers to begin making some trails of their own.

Nevertheless, it was a bad year for the fledgling colony. A persistent drought had led to the loss of an estimated 5000 sheep and 3000 horned cattle, four out of five newborn lambs died because their starving mothers were unable to feed them, and new pastures were desperately needed. There had been droughts before, notably in 1803 and again in 1804, which resulted in poor harvests and hardships for man and beast alike, but animal numbers had been fewer then, and so they were better nursed and attended to. This time, the losses were on a far more devastating scale.

In December, the surveyor George Evans, flush with the success of his earlier surveys of the Illawarra and the shoreline around Jervis Bay, was tasked by Governor Macquarie to go beyond the furthest point reached by Blaxland, Wentworth and Lawson—Mount Blaxland—and continue west. This he did, naming the O'Connell and Macquarie plains and reaching the site of present-day Bathurst. Macquarie had sent Evans over the Blue Mountains in the hope of finding healthy pastures for the colony's increasing numbers of cattle, which is confirmed in a letter he wrote to Colonial Secretary Earl Bathurst in 1816:

> I am induced to grant permission to several of the great Stockholders in the Colony to send their Horned cattle across the Blue Mountains to Graze in the New discovered Country and I also sent some herds of the Government cattle thither as an Experiment.

George Evans was a true pioneer. He spent a brief period in 1814 living in Tasmania on a 1000-acre land grant given to him by Governor Macquarie, but by 1815 he was back in New South Wales. He became the first European to enter the Lachlan Valley, and in June 1815 reached Eugowra on the Lachlan River, by far the most westward point then reached by a European. Evans's descriptions of the land around Bathurst must have sounded heaven-sent to those east of the 'Great Divide', eking out a living in the Sydney Basin's substandard soils. Evans described what he called the Bathurst Plains as having the best grasses he had ever seen. And so it proved to be. Within just four years of the Bathurst Plains being settled, more than 11,000 sheep had been sent westward over the mountains.

In 1820, after more than thirty years of colonising this 'new' land, remarkably little was known of the continent the settlers were so determined to conquer. One of the many attempts to chart the coastline was undertaken on a series of four voyages from 1817 to 1822 by Phillip Parker King, a naval officer and hydrographer. From Arnhem Land in the north to King George Sound on the south coast of Western Australia, as well as large swathes of the Queensland coast, King filled in many of the blanks left by James Cook and Matthew Flinders. King's voyages saw him chart 32,000 kilometres of coastline, and his maps were of great assistance in determining the paths of settlement in remote areas.

But maps, however useful to governments and legislators, had little relevance for settlers and squatters. A squatter didn't need a map to tell him where the horizon was. In fact he didn't much care for 'paperwork' at all. An opportunistic squatter considered 'proof of ownership' to be the fact he was there. In 1821, the governor of New South Wales, Thomas Brisbane, expressed his frustrations that settlers considered 'the smallest scrap of paper containing the promise of a grant to be equivalent, if not superior, to the best title from the Crown'.

There was never any shortage of muscle in the ploughing of new fields and the establishing of pastures. Men greatly outnumbered women from the earliest days of settlement, a sobering statistic that left those women in Britain wanting to emigrate looking upon a four-month voyage to the Antipodes with disdain bordering on fear. The settlement had become synonymous with depravity and dysfunction, and by 1836 in New South Wales there were still more than twice as many men as women. While such an imbalance might have been good for agricultural expansion, it was hardly the sort of thing that attracted would-be female emigrants across the seas for the reward of becoming the partner of a convict.

Bathurst, the nation's first inland settlement, was proclaimed a town on 7 May 1815, although the first land grant in the area preceded the proclamation by a year—a thousand acres given to Maurice Charles O'Connell of the British 73rd Regiment, presumably as a result of his marriage to the daughter of Governor William Bligh. Bathurst was a city of firsts. It had Australia's first jail, first court house, and first mounted police headquarters. In 1823, the town's first windmill, and so the first windmill west of the Blue Mountains, was erected by the Bathurst District's first coroner, Thomas Hawkins, an event not lost on the *Sydney Gazette*:

> To see a windmill on the plains of Bathurst will certainly be a novel as well as a cheering sight; and be extremely welcome to the population of some hundreds who have now to use the fatiguing common steel mill.

The first white child born west of the Blue Mountains was born in Bathurst in 1819 to Richard and Ann Mills (the sixth of nine children), who lived in a four-room thatched sod house modelled after Ann's family home in England. Located on the Kelso side of the Macquarie River, it had 45-centimetre (18-inch) thick walls, a brick bread oven and a water well. The house was extended years later with the addition of a laundry, and in 1831 it became a pub—the King William Inn, one of three inns in town.

Bathurst, the town, was thriving. So too, were its pastoralists. As 1826 drew to a close there were an estimated 25,000 head of cattle and 70,000 sheep in the Bathurst area, though many of the region's original squatters, despite possessing as much as £10,000 worth of land and stock, still lived in their original dwellings of rammed earth.

The taking up of land and the riches that would, in the minds of many, inevitably follow had become *the* topic of conversation by the mid-1820s. There was nothing that could compare to the possibilities that might arise from getting oneself into 'good stock'. In 1824, Henry Dangar, a surveyor and pastoralist who emigrated to New South Wales as a free settler in 1821 and who was made responsible for the drawing up of plans for a new settlement called King's Town (present-day Newcastle), became the first settler to explore the upper reaches of the Hunter Valley, eventually discovering the confluence of the Goulburn and Hunter rivers. Squatters were locating their runs in what Dangar described as 'primitive' places in order to avoid detection. In his *Index and Directory to Map of the County Bordering Upon the River Hunter*, published in London in 1828, he wrote:

> . . . from the early part of 1822 to the end of 1825, all parts of the colony made extraordinary advances in settlement. It is difficult

to determine which division of the colony, during the time, made the greatest progress.

People were dispersing faster than the government could keep track of them, particularly to the south and west following the region's principal rivers, and entire communities everywhere were becoming fixated with one overriding idea: how best to rapidly acquire a fortune by gaining land and rearing sheep and cattle.

On 5 September 1826, in an attempt to prevent or at least slow the exodus, Governor Ralph Darling introduced limits on land grants. New grants would now only apply to the already settled areas around Sydney and Parramatta. On 14 October 1829, those boundaries were increased to take in the established Nineteen Counties, an area stretching from the Manning River in the north to its source in the Mount Royal Range, then south to the Moruya River, west through Orange, Cowra and Yass, beyond the mountains to Wellington on the junction of the Macquarie and Bell rivers, along the Liverpool Range, and south to Bateman's Bay. A large swathe of land to be sure, but even a compromise on this scale would ultimately prove inadequate, if only because the search for good grazing land knows no boundaries. In a letter home to his family in Scotland, George Ranken, who arrived with his wife Janet from Britain in 1821 and settled on the Bathurst Plains, described the unrelenting nature of this early expansion:

A state of affairs arose which was unprecedented, unrecognised by authority, and was totally unintelligible according to all official and business authority—the population was expanding, and the sheep and cattle were increasing still faster. Impelled by a common impulse, the pioneers headed for the boundary. Shortly they were pouring across the frontiers in scores, north, south and west—the Governor could not have prevented this because all the police and military in Australia could not have guarded an open frontier of 500 miles. The trespassers had found a new name for themselves . . . they called themselves squatters.

(George and Janet Ranken's coach, which they brought out with them from Scotland and is known today as the 'Ranken Coach', is one of Australia's oldest surviving horse drawn vehicles. Donated to the Royal Australian Historical Society it was pulled across the Sydney Harbour Bridge when it opened in 1932, and returned to Bathurst in 1940 to mark the city's 125th anniversary. It is now on display at the National Museum of Australia in Canberra.)

Darling's intention to set limits on the colony's expansion was made visible in a single document, a topographical map of the Nineteen Counties created by the New South Wales Surveyor-General, Thomas Mitchell. The map was, and remains to this day, a triumph, a cartographic masterpiece. Depicting the state's divisions into its various parishes and counties, it was the state's first triangulation survey, begun in April 1828 with the establishment of two baselines at Botany Bay that extended from a small hill at the bay's southern end to Sydney Lighthouse. The hill offered views south to the summit of Mount Jellore in the County of Camden, and west to Mount Tomah and Mount Hay in the Blue Mountains. Teams of surveyors and draughtsmen under Mitchell's guidance were away for as much as six months at a time, plotting their work in the field and sending their results to Mitchell by dray and by horse. A gifted engraver, John Carmichael, was employed to engrave the copper plates from which the map would be drawn.

The final product was described by Granville Stapylton, assistant to the Admiral of the Royal Navy, as 'a gem, and not to be equalled in any Colony belonging to Her Majesty's dominions'. The former Surveyor-General of New South Wales, Alfred Chesterman, called it a 'memorial to the zeal and assiduity of one of Australia's best known explorers', adding that it depicted the Nineteen Counties with an almost 'microscopic fidelity'. Now all that remained to be seen was whether or not this extraordinary map would have any effect in stemming the tide of the landless.

Details surrounding Darling's new law, the Limits of Location, were published in the *Sydney Gazette and New South Wales Advertiser*. Applications for land within certain areas could be made and, if the application were successful, land would be granted at the rate of £500 per 2.6 square kilometres (1 square mile), with a maximum grant of 10.4 square kilometres (4 square miles) to those with £2000 of assets that included 'stock of every description, implements of husbandry, and other articles that may be applicable to agricultural purposes'. In other words, only the wealthy need apply. It was hoped that placing a high price on settling new lands would result in a slowdown in migration. But these hopes, too, were soon dashed, and in the years that followed the acquisition of land sped up to a pace few could have foreseen.

The approach used for acquiring land during this period often went something like this: there would be an initial rush to claim and peg out runs, followed by a period of trench-like warfare over the precise location of boundaries that would remain unresolved until one of the thirteen commissioners arrived to adjudicate disputes. Prior to their arrival a number of commonly held principles, the origins of which no one could say for sure, held sway and maintained a semblance of order, such as the idea one could run stock *anywhere* within a 5-kilometre radius of their homestead—a reasonable-enough proposition although no one could say where they'd ever heard it upheld in a court or made plain in a government document. Boundaries may have been illegal and arbitrary, but agreements crafted by neighbouring squatters to keep the peace were often surprisingly precise. One such agreement signed by two squatters in the Bathurst district described their boundary as only they could:

. . . following Mr Whyte's ploughed line as far as a rock described by Mr Grant as situated about 350 yards from a tea-tree spring, then a straight plough furrow to be drawn to the intersection of Mr Henty's plough furrow.

In the end, of course, New South Wales was a vast colony—so vast that the majority of it wasn't surveyed and mapped until the 1890s. For the first hundred years of settlement, no matter where its boundaries were drawn, no matter what constraints were imposed upon its settlers, there was always land beyond the limits of any map drawn or authority imposed. There was no end to the potential for new lands to be illegally squatted.

The eventual closing of the frontier, the day when there would effectively be nothing left for Europeans to discover, was still generations away.

'The Pioneers Wife': a selector and his wife burn forest trees on
a newly marked block of land, late nineteenth century.
George Bell, Powerhouse Museum

2

EVER WESTWARD

'The mountains saw them marching by;
They faced the all-consuming drought,
They could not rest in settled land,
Their faces ever westward bent
Beyond the farthest settlement,
Responding to the challenge cry,
Of 'better country further out'.
Could braver histories unfold
Than this bush story yet untold—
The story of their westward march.'
                —A. B. 'Banjo' Paterson, 'Song of the Future', 1889

In 1847, a new book appeared in bookstores in Sydney and Melbourne: *Settlers and Convicts, or Recollections of Sixteen Years' Labour in the Australian Backwoods*. It was written by the little-known London-born atheist, womaniser and deserter Alexander Harris, who had arrived in New South Wales in 1825, lured by the prospect of higher wages and the chance to turn around his own flagging fortunes after a hoped-for career in publishing failed to materialise. Alas, his fortunes only continued to spiral downhill, and after an uneventful number of years spent as a labourer and cedar-getter in the Australian bush, Harris returned to London. And began to write of his old colonial days.

Harris's keen eye painted a vivid picture of colonial life before he even set foot upon his new home, observing Sydney across the water from his ship's approaching bow and describing it as 'a waterside town scattered wide over upland and lowland, and if it be a breezy day the merry rattling pace of its manifold windmills, here and there perched on the high points, is no unpleasant sight'. His accounts of the living conditions on the pastoral frontiers of Australia were similarly detailed and vivid. The sheep stations on which he found work were invariably 'two yards side by side, made of heavy boughs piled and interwoven'. Huts were 'made with split slabs and having a roof of bark', consisting of one large room with a fireplace at one end and a sleeping area at the other, where shepherds and workers would 'spread their beds on sheets of bark'. Near to the hut were piles of sheep dung cleaned out of the yards and left to dry in the baking sun. Shepherds would take the sheep out by day, and the hut-keeper would watch over them by night. The flocks, often as many as 800-strong, were far too numerous for the shepherd to effectively manage. It was the same routine every day: eat, drink, clean the pens, don't lose any sheep, sleep on a bark bed at night.

Harris spent much of his time in the colony as a cedar-getter along the coastal fringes of New South Wales. Cedar was a valuable commodity, fragrant, easy to work, and with a beautiful rich red grain that saw it felled almost to the point of extinction. Cedar-getters often found themselves employed in areas of true wilderness, alongside squatters who were working runs beyond the purview of the authorities.

Both were in constant contact with local Aborigines who, according to accounts, were rarely troublesome. Harris would sometimes recount local Aboriginal legends, including one in particular that gave pause to some early squatters in the

Illawarra region south of Sydney, a tale describing a 'great, tall animal' that resembled a man, but which had its feet turned backwards and was excessively larger in stature. The creature, Harris wrote, recounting what local Aborigines had told him, was 'covered in hair', and wandered the bush making a 'perpetual, frightful noise'. Most squatters in the region felt the stories were simply made up in order to frighten them away, but nobody really knew for sure. Harris said he'd spoken to other cedar-getters who swore they'd seen shadowy images in the bush at night, and heard noises the like of which they'd never heard before or since.

The pastoral potential of New South Wales was quick to be realised. By the mid-1820s most of the primary lands in the Canberra–Yass–Goulburn region had already been settled. The 38,000 acres that would one day make up Richlands Estate, an outstation in the Southern Tablelands a day's ride west of Camden and part of the vast Macarthur pastoral empire, was first settled by John Macarthur in the mid-1820s. The Hunter Valley was opened to settlement in 1821, with most of its river frontages taken up by 1825. On the south coast of New South Wales, Alexander Berry and Edward Wollstonecraft took up 14,000 acres in the Shoalhaven in 1822. When explorers Hamilton Hume and William Hovell found a route south from Yass to Port Phillip Bay in 1824 they were astounded by what they described as verdant, well-watered lands of 'immense downs and forests partially wooded'. In 1829, Charles Sturt traced the Murrumbidgee River through the Riverina all the way to Spencer Gulf in South Australia, and in the 1830s a wave of Scottish pioneers swept through the tablelands around Armidale and Tenterfield. Everywhere that pastoral expansion spread, and word filtered back of Eden-like places, settlement soon followed.

The need for the early colonists to develop a sense of 'place'—to gain an understanding of where they needed to migrate to best facilitate their prosperity—presented one select group of settlers with a daunting set of challenges: the surveyor. Surveying was a vital tool in the art of empire building, yet here was a land that was mostly unexplored, and unusually flat and eroded, a topographical challenge which meant trigonometric measurements were not always accurate. Many of the surveyor's tools—barometers, chronometers, telescopes, sextants, azimuth compasses, pendulums and thermometers—were delicate instruments and easily broken. Their internal mechanisms expanded and contracted in the heat and humidity of both voyages through the tropics and days spent in the field under a summer sun, environments they were not designed to withstand. Add to that the fact that the New South Wales colonial government was poorly funded, which made it difficult to attract those with the best skills. Instead, draughtsmen were employed as surveyors, as was anyone with even the most rudimentary mathematical skills. As late as 1840, qualified surveyors were still hard to find, meaning settlers, even when wanting to comply with the law, sometimes established runs on unsurveyed lands.

Sir Thomas Mitchell was appointed the New South Wales Surveyor-General in 1828 and, more than any other person, produced a legacy of maps and documents that detailed and gave life and dimension to a new land. An old army man, Mitchell was used to uncomplicated hand-held pocket sextants commonly used by reconnaissance patrols in battle and preferred them to the instruments needed in a full-scale trigonometric survey. Mitchell also drafted the first useable map of the Nineteen Counties, complete with coastlines, hills and lines of meridian.

But what Mitchell achieved over the course of his surveyor's life was more than just map-making; he created an image of a new and vibrant land, even though the details of his maps did not always please all who read them. The Birmingham-born writer and illustrator Louisa Meredith—author of *Notes and Sketches of New South Wales,* 1844, and an early settler in the

Bathurst region—was particularly annoyed at his tendency to make roads appear as straight as possible, regardless of terrain:

> I could not avoid noticing that Major Mitchell's roads, wherever originally marked by him, was almost invariably carried over the summits of hills whilst level valleys lay within a few hundred feet; and as we proceeded I looked but for the highest peaks ahead of us, knowing by experience that the surveyor's road would lead us over them.

Criticisms of the trajectories of his roads, however, did little to stem the tide of settlers and squatters who lost no time in mustering large numbers of stock and taking them along his well-marked routes. And when they began to settle their land, settlers did with their boundaries precisely what Mitchell had done with his roads, with runs established using straight longitudinal and latitudinal lines that almost never paid heed to the prevailing terrain.

Still, the work of defining boundaries pressed on. Bullocks and carts were used to transport surveyors and their equipment, and fresh convicts were continually requested to replace those who absconded. From 1827, surveyors had to complete newly printed standardised forms detailing their work, which was a marked improvement over earlier methods of recording: a combination of stakes in the ground and marks etched into trees and onto rocks. Yet despite this important work, the job of a surveyor was anything but secure, particularly in lean times when government coffers neared empty. Poor job security was a constant worry, mostly for those claiming to possess mapping qualifications that they did not in fact possess.

Our popular conception of squatters as disreputable opportunists needs some revision. As early as 1831, even Governor Richard Bourke, an avowed emancipist who opposed the continuance of New South Wales as a penal colony, considered just occupying land inferred at least some rights upon the one who was squatting there. And by the 1830s, those who had taken up runs on Crown land were not only squatters in a traditional sense, but increasingly were people of respected families such as William Lawson and John Blaxland. The ranks of the 'scoundrel squatter' had been infiltrated by emigrants from England, by merchants from Sydney, adventurous colonial youths and demobilised military officers. No longer just social outcasts or former convicts, they had risen to the lofty status of 'unauthorised occupants'. Bourke told the Colonial Office in London their hopes of opposing their dispersal were doomed to fail. 'Not all the armies of England', he wrote, 'not a hundred thousand soldiers scattered through the bush, could drive back our herds within the limits of the Nineteen Counties'. And even to attempt to do so, he ventured, would be 'a perverse rejection of the bounty of Providence'.

By the early 1830s, elegant homesteads such as Kippilaw on the banks of the Wollondilly River near Goulburn, home to the pioneering Chisholm family, were becoming common-place. Established as a cattle station in 1832, its owners soon turned their attention to sheep, wheat and maize. Kippilaw had extensive lawns and gardens and from a distance must have seemed a rural version of the governor's residence in Sydney. The shingle-roofed stone house had four wings surrounding a central courtyard, rows of shuttered windows, a verdant creeper-draped verandah, and outbuildings that included a small stone church, servants' quarters, a blacksmith shop, a butcher and stables.

Entrepreneurial settlers continued moving well beyond the limits of location in two primary pincer movements—one heading south-west towards western Victoria and the region around Port Phillip, and the other northwards through New England and the Darling Downs. It was a land grab of gar-gantuan proportions, with contempt shown to both Aboriginal territorial claims and Crown rights, an expansion that can be traced in the gazetting of the continent: Northern Districts and New England in 1839, the Clarence River and Moreton Bay in 1842, the Darling Downs in 1843, Wide Bay in 1847 and so on. Explorers got all the press for their high profile expeditions, but in reality the continent was explored by squatters, fanning out at the rate of over 300 kilometres every year.

The mid-1830s saw the movement of settlers and squatters to outlying regions, resulting in increasing tensions between the legitimate settler and the opportunistic squatter. Both camps had their sympathisers. A Legislative Council report in 1835 spoke of the 'nefarious practises' of squatters, vagabonds who 'lived off their neighbours', while Supreme Court judge William Burton thought them 'improper occupiers of waste lands' and questioned their acquisition of wealth which, he wrote, 'must lead every reasonable man to the conclusion they did not get it honestly'. Governor Bourke, however, took issue with Burton's assessment. It seemed to him that squatters were only following in the footsteps of wealthier settlers whose own questionably attained lands were, he considered, 'held by no better title'.

Squatters in many cases could not have made their mark in the Australian landscape were it not for the labour supplied to them by convicts. In 1835, Bourke permitted landholders one convict for every 160 acres under pasture and one for every 40 acres under cultivation, with a limit of 173 acres—a limit few achieved. Convicts were used to tend and keep watch over sheep, to lead them to greener pastures and to guard over them at night. Despite the fact the squatter could not have done without them, it nevertheless meant that he had to provide each man 5.5 kilograms of wheat and 3 kilograms of meat per week, and clothe them as well. Though an additional burden, some managed not only to provide their workers with the bare minimum but gave generously from what they could spare of tobacco, tea and sugar, and convicts were quick to acknowledge their lot was considerably better on a station than at the hands of the government.

Many squatters observed station life bring an end to the typical convict's more pervasive vices—drunkenness and theft—a change due in no small part to a general absence of alcohol and any possessions worth pilfering. In any case, kindness proved more productive than punishment; anything that kept the local magistrate at bay was better for squatter and convict alike. And when the time came for the convict to receive his ticket of leave—a document of parole given to convicts who had shown they could be entrusted with a measure of freedom—there was a greater likelihood he'd stay with his employer, as convicts were seen as far more adept at station life than free immigrants. Few migrants bothered to venture beyond the 'safety' of the cities.

And, you might say, for good reason. For the squatter and traveller alike, simply moving through rural Australia in the 1830s was a hazardous undertaking. By the end of the decade there were only five police stations between Melbourne and the Murray River, a dearth of law and order so profound that many who needed to travel long journeys preferred to do so by sea. The theft of mail became so rife that people sending cheques tore them in half and posted each half a week apart, and the theft of valuable horses from their stations was a major concern for pastoralists. Bushrangers—those who chose to live off the land and engage in the armed robbery of free settlers— were quick to appear on the colonial landscape. John Donohue was the first to be widely celebrated, thought of (wrongly) as a 'robber of the rich and powerful' after a series of raids on the Sydney to Windsor road in 1827. Historians estimate there to have been over 1200 bushrangers Australia-wide between 1788 and the murder trial of the Kenniff brothers, Patrick and James, 'Australia's last bushrangers', in Queensland in 1903. More than enough outlaws, you might think, to give one pause before setting out on unfamiliar trails.

◄〇►

The central west of New South Wales was also subject to the unrelenting spread of settlement, with itinerant pastoralists beginning to infiltrate the area as early as 1817. Thomas Mitchell, on his journeys of exploration, noted Aborigines' casualness at their encounters, suggesting they'd already become used to the presence of Europeans.

Squatting in the Parkes region may have been illegal prior to the *Squatting Act 1836*, but that didn't stop squatters risking all to occupy the area's rich grazing lands. In the Parkes region the first License to Depasture, the right to place animals on grazing lands, was offered in 1839 and taken up by Thomas Kite, a former convict found guilty of the theft of bank notes, his death sentence commuted to life on account of prior good character.

Kite's story was one of triumph over adversity. Transported to New South Wales in 1813, in 1818 he received a conditional pardon after working on the construction of the road over the Blue Mountains. Kite was selected by Governor Macquarie to be one of the first ten settlers of the Bathurst region and was granted 50 acres at Kelso on the Bathurst Plains. He was also given a convict servant, a cow and a measure of seed wheat. He married a woman named Sarah Bayliss and they had nine children. Over the years he expanded his pastoral holdings relentlessly, buying land in Bathurst, Orange, Wellington, Molong, Lachlan and Parkes. He built a house in Sydney and the Club Hotel at the corner of Hunter and Castlereagh streets, and by 1851 owned in excess of 200,000 acres and 14,000 head of sheep and cattle.

Another of Bathurst's 'First Ten' was William Lee, born in 1794 on Norfolk Island to convict parents. He came to New South Wales in 1805 with his stepfather William Pantoney. After living for a time in Windsor, the two worked on the road over the Blue Mountains in 1815, the construction of which would later be described in the *Lithgow Mercury* of September 1905 as 'an object of the first importance to the future prosperity of the colony'. At the conclusion of his labour in 1816, young William received a grant of government cattle, and in 1818 he was granted 134 acres of land at Kelso near Bathurst and awarded a ram for the industriousness he had shown in bettering his position. And when Governor Sir Thomas Brisbane increased his original grant to 300 acres, William Lee was on his way to becoming one of Bathurst's wealthiest landowners. Over the years his holdings increased to include 2430 acres at Larras Lake and stations on the Lachlan and Castlereagh rivers.

Often the only trails linking one station to another, or to a town, were the tracks the station hands or owners themselves had made. For a recently arrived settler to suddenly ride off into the great unknown was almost unheard of. As roads began to appear, travelling in general became easier. But this took time. As late as 1861, over seventeen days the road from Wagga Wagga to Junee saw only seven teams of horses, a handful of stagecoaches and, last but not least, four teams of bullocks.

The cities had horses, and the outback camels, but many regions of inland Australia wouldn't have been properly settled as quickly as they were were it not for the bullock. Bullocks did far more than simply haul carts and provide a means of transport. They cleared land, hauled logs for building, were cheaper to acquire than horses and were more useful into old age. A team of bullocks was as essential to the success of a station as machinery is today. Everything was weighty, from wool bales to fencing wire to the everyday supplies one had to get from the nearest town. Occasionally river transport helped, such as that which sprang up along the length of the Murray River, but for most even the simple task of replenishing the things they could not grow themselves, such as tea, sugar and tobacco, relied upon the arrival of the bullock and the 'bullocky'.

Bullockies and their teams remained a feature of rural life even after the expansion of the railways in the 1890s, and were highly visible, unlike shearers and drovers who were often out

of sight in remote locations. Rachel Henning, who left England
for Australia in 1854, only to return homesick in 1856, and
then return to Australia permanently in 1861, eventually settled
on a property near Appin in New South Wales. In a series of
letters to her family in England she described her impressions
of a typical bullocky:

> The bullock drivers are almost the best-paid men on the place.
> They get 40s a week, as much a year as some clerks and curates
> have to live on at home. It requires a great deal of skill and practice,
> though, to make twelve or fourteen bullocks all pull together.

Bullocks were harnessed according to their size, with the largest
at the front and the smaller behind, and were driven by a combination of commands and the bullocky's prized whip, usually
made from plaited lengths of hide. A team might consist of as
many as twenty beasts, and they were guided by the bullocky
not from a seat on the wagon, but as he walked by their side,
using nothing but his voice and whip. When heavy rains could
make a dray sink up to its axles and bring a team to a stand-
still, is it any wonder the bullocky was known for his colourful
language? It was dangerous work. It wasn't uncommon for a
bullock team to haul 120 bales of hay weighing more than
12 tons, or dozens of kegs of rum, the contents of which could
easily be pilfered along the way.

For city dwellers, travelling inland carried a different set
of risks. There was the possibility of having to ford swollen
streams, a risky feat if riding in a buggy with an inexperienced
driver—a single error of judgement could see the buggy swept
downstream with horses and passengers flailing about in tow.
Spending nights in the bush also meant staying overnight in
country inns, establishments designed to drain as much money
as possible from the pockets of all who entered them.

The advent of coach travel in the 1850s and 1860s eventually made long-distance travel more pleasurable. By the early
1870s, Cobb & Co were putting more than 6000 horses a day

under harness in Victoria, New South Wales and Queensland, pulling their American-designed Concord coaches along more than 40,000 kilometres of emerging rural roads every week.

After 1829, the taking up of Crown lands beyond the Nineteen Counties continued unabated, and by the early 1830s flocks and herds shepherded by innumerable settlers were being taken south-west along the banks of the Murrumbidgee River and north into the Liverpool Plains. In 1833, in yet another failed attempt to stem the flow, Governor Bourke—who spoke despairingly of settlers spreading out in every direction—again tried to prevent the sort of unauthorised occupations he feared would inevitably spill over into a firestorm of disputes with future legitimate titleholders, and proclaimed another ineffectual Act: 'An Act for protecting the Crown Lands of this Colony from Encroachment, Intrusion, and Trespass'.

The Crown Lands Encroachment Act 1833, which sought to prevent the unauthorised taking up of Crown lands through 'intrusion or trespass', provided for the appointment of thirteen (part-time) commissioners of Crown lands to enforce the Act's provisions. But the squatters still could not be stopped, and the grab for land continued. By 1836, it was clear it was no longer feasible to attempt to remove the growing numbers of entrenched squatters from their stations, and so the Squatting Act 1836 was made law. If the government couldn't prevent the settling of lands beyond the Nineteen Counties, it could at least do something to prevent their unauthorised occupation, and gain a little revenue along the way.

Squatting at last became a legitimate pursuit.

The Squatting Act—asked for in part by an increasingly vocal and organised cadre of landed squatters who wanted to be distinguished from what they saw as unscrupulous opportunists—allowed anyone to claim all the land they could afford, for an annual fee of £10 and a halfpenny for every head of stock.

Additionally, those who had already gone beyond the limits of location could now legalise their holdings by paying the same fees. The sole purpose of the Act was to permit the lawful taking up of Crown land. A new wave of settlers and squatters went out in search of land, and it was this new migration of pioneers who gave the term squatter its much longed-for respectability.

Some were even calling themselves by a new title: Gentleman Squatters.

The new fees meant that to be a squatter, one now required a degree of wealth. A squatter had to pay for his land and pay for each animal he grazed upon it, as well as navigating all of the usual currents involved in the running of a business. Demand for stock predictably increased along with the demand for new lands, and as a result so did the cost of each animal. If the squatters were grazing sheep, not only would they have to have enough cash to pay their workers, they'd have to survive on what cash reserves they had for up to a year before they could be paid for their wool. Those with little behind them fell away, but those with money or who were able to afford the periodic selling of livestock to cover costs, survived.

Prior to the Squatting Act, the absence of any coherent land policy and so much land well out of sight of government, meant that squatting Crown land was always destined to happen— the plains beyond the Great Dividing Range were seen as fair game to the landless and dispossessed. It was absurd to attempt to restrain settlement when grasslands that stretched for who knows how far were there for the taking. 'You may as well have attempted', New South Wales Governor George Gipps wrote with hindsight in 1840, 'to confine Arabs within a circle traced on sand'.

In their book *Class Structure in Australian History*, authors Robert Connell and Terence Irving argue that in the late 1830s the majority of these 'landed squatters'—who came largely from wealthy middle-class British families and went on to develop traditionally hierarchical, structured rural societies—did so only in three distinct regions of their adopted country: Van Diemen's Land, western Victoria and Queensland's Darling Downs. Outside those three areas, the phenomenon of the squatter actually prevented any aristo-cratic rural elite from evolving. In the vast majority of areas settled, young squatters wanted nothing to do with creating a privileged establishment. Any ideas of a nationwide, heredi-tary aristocracy would by stymied by the realities of a brash, earthy brand of colonialism.

Even the New South Wales region of New England, consid-ered in the late 1830s to be one of the more aristocratic parts of the state, was in reality far from it, despite many of its new inhabitants arriving from Oxford and Cambridge. Most were more of a get-rich-quick breed of middle-class aspirants, who believed that capitalism, free enterprise and old-fashioned hard work would lead to an egalitarian, prosperous society with enough wealth for all.

As for the influx of so-called 'landed squatters', most had one thing in common, quite apart from their ancestry: they knew little or nothing about farming sheep and cattle. In *Australia Visited and Revisited* (1853) authors Samuel Mossman and Thomas Banister observed:

> Nine out of ten of these squatters are therefore only amateur wool growers and graziers, men who never bred a ewe or an ox in their lives before they set foot in Australia. No doubt they have gleaned sufficient knowledge of cattle breeding and sheep farming from books and other sources . . . but very few of them have been regularly bred to the business. The fact is, that a knowledge of the management of livestock in Australia is so easily acquired, that any educated man possessed of common shrewdness may be qualified in the course of twelve months to superintend a sheep or cattle station. So if you are desirous of establishing yourself as a squatter on the waste lands of Australia, it is of greater

importance that you should go into the market with a heavy purse than with skill and experience.

Squatters were rarely the landless peasants of popular myth. Although all ten of the first free settlers that headed to Bathurst in 1818 were ex-convicts or native-born, the truth is by the 1820s only a small percentage of the white population fitted that description. By 1825, the majority of settlers had come here of their own volition, and with considerably more money than freed convicts could ever hope to acquire. Almost all of those who became squatters were the children of people who had already established a measure of financial independence. Access to capital, that one indispensable requirement for anyone wishing to stock grazing land with sheep and cattle, was all but unattainable for a prospective peasant squatter. Swept aside by an incoming tide of well-to-do new arrivals, the best livelihood most convicts could hope for was as a station hand. By the 1840s, two out of every three bushies were either native-born Australians, or serving or ex-convicts.

Whether a migrant from of Britain's wealthy urban class succeeded here depended not so much upon the thickness of their wallet but on their ability to adapt. While most were educated, few had any experience at overseeing a pastoral run. The colony soon became littered with the broken dreams of educated city people who knew little of the life that existed beyond the cobbled alleyways of London and Manchester, and failed to make a successful transition to antipodean farmer. One of the more notable examples of an educated man who was an abject failure as a pastoralist was Edward Bell.

Bell arrived in Sydney in 1839. On the voyage over he had taken the opportunity to devour every book on Australia he and his shipmates had in their possession, including James Lang's *New South Wales* and Thomas Mitchell's *Three Expeditions into the Interior of Australia*, but he'd never actually clapped eyes on a living cow in his life. His knowledge of sheep and cattle and the tending thereof was, in his own estimation, imperfect, freely admitting to anyone who'd listen that he could barely tell a wether from a ewe, nor a bull from an ox.

Soon after arriving in Sydney he began travelling south through New South Wales, with the intention of settling in Victoria. Along the way, he purchased a thousand head of cattle near the alpine town of Tumut. The problem was, the cattle had already spent quite some time on the run, and had become rather accustomed to it. Despite Bell having an unspecified number of hired hands, the cattle flatly refused to be moved from the run where they were so content. (Until the 1830s, cattle were seen as little more than 'walking larders', mobile food that developed slowly as a domestic commodity but certainly not ripe for export the way wool was.)

Discouraged, Bell abandoned all thoughts of moving to Victoria and decided instead to keep his cattle at a nearby station. After a year he had a change of heart, sold his cattle, moved south, and devoted his time to sheep farming along the banks of the Broken River in north central Victoria. When a large number of his flock was lost to catarrh—the excessive build-up of mucus in a sheep's airways and cavities—he tried to cross over into the newly discovered Gippsland region. When that also failed, he sold his sheep to local butchers, packed his bags, and made his way to Glenelg in South Australia before returning to Melbourne, where he finally found his place in the new colony: as private secretary to the superintendent of the Port Phillip District of New South Wales, Charles La Trobe.

Even those who successfully transitioned to life on the land still had to contend with all of the usual hazards, like bushfire. The first squatters soon realised they were in a climate that presented an almost constant fire threat. If excessive rains produced too much feed for stock, what wasn't consumed became tinder dry and spread across an entire run. If it caught alight the fire was impossible to stop. Natural water sources were the squatter's only defence, but where were the means to utilise them? In 1845 in Victoria a series of bushfires burned for three months, sweeping everything before them. Forming guards around buildings and advancing on a fire and trying to beat it down was the only recourse, and hopelessly ineffective.

Conflict with Aborigines, droughts, floods, diseases such as anthrax and the respiratory infection pleuro-pneumonia led to the loss of a million head of cattle in Victoria and New South Wales in 1858. And then there were the rabbits.

There were rabbits on the First Fleet but they were mostly eaten and failed to multiply. It wasn't until Thomas Austin, an English settler, imported twelve breeding pairs of wild rabbits in 1859 and set them loose at his Barwon Park property at Inverleigh in Victoria that the seeds for a relentless invasion were planted. Within just a few years his property had been laid waste, despite Austin himself killing more than 20,000 of the creatures. By the end of the 1860s rabbits were in the Wimmera, by 1872 they had reached the banks of the Murray River and by the mid-1890s they had reached the Western Australian border. They were the pastoralist's malevolent scourge, reducing the carrying capacity of a property by anywhere from half to virtually nothing.

In the early 1840s came another scourge that had affected economies the world over but had seemed a world away in a new country full of optimism and awash with capital: recession.

It began with a bad drought in 1839 that saw wool prices fall sharply. Debts began to be called in, and sheep that were increasingly thin and gaunt were all but worthless. The nation had been laid prostrate by the winds of adversity. Insolvencies in every trade soared with settlers and pastoralists suffering more than anyone. The value of each sheep fell to 6 pence, and so they were boiled down to produce tallow (mutton fat), used in turn to make soap and candles which could be sold on the streets of London for between £2 and £3 per 50 kilograms. Tallow production went a long way towards saving the emerging sheep industry. Purpose-built factories rose up to cope with the demand: over two years a million sheep—the product of years of grazing and nurturing—were slaughtered in commercial boiling vats.

On 9 January 1831, the New South Wales government brought an end to free land grants and instead sold it by auction, a move it hoped would raise prices and stifle the rush to settle new lands. But no such stifling occurred, and the rush continued unabated. By 1839, there were 649 sheep farms located beyond the Nineteen Counties, and the New South Wales Legislative Council, in addition to a £10 annual licensing fee, began to tax the squatter for the number of animals he owned: 1 pence per annum for each sheep, 3 pence for horned cattle and 6 pence for every horse. The growth in numbers of both sheep and squatters, and the increased value of wool exports, saw the squatters evolve from a sub-group illegally occupying Crown land into a powerful constituency. By 1848, the number of squatters in New South Wales totalled 1865. They owned 5.5 million sheep and 882,000 cattle, and occupied over 220,149 square kilometres of pastoral lands—around 29,160 acres per squatter.

By the 1840s, the importance of the squatter class in New South Wales was acknowledged by all who didn't have a personal axe to grind. The bulk of the state's wool production was from their hands, and rather than coming from the least-educated classes, they were among the most educated, talented and wealthiest men in the colony.

At the same time, as if in some kind of mocking opposition to this emerging aristocracy, there were also the first stirrings of the larrikin Australian, seen in that first generation of Australian-born bushmen who delighted in lauding their own innate bush skills over the educated 'foolishness' of recently arrived settlers. 'He is the biggest chuckle-headed ass God ever created, he is going back to England and a good job, too', one bushman said when he met an Englishman at a homestead near Goulburn in June 1844. He'd better 'fasten a bell round his neck', he said, or 'he'll lose himself as sure as God made little apples'. The dominance of these early colonial Australians over subsequent arrivals of free, cashed-up settlers continued only in the bush. The cities quickly became outposts of urban sophistication. But the bush had larger shoes to fill, creating myths involving stockmen and drovers and shearers and jackaroos, all of the things that said *this out here* was the *real* Australia, and if you wanted to find it, you'd need to leave the safety of the cities and open yourself up to a world of wool, wheat and cattle.

Within a couple of generations of the arrival of the First Fleet, the look and feel of Australia's early pastoral stations were well defined. Stations generally had grown from having just one or two outbuildings to comprising as many as a dozen or more, the furthest of which might be located 6 kilometres or more from the homestead. Those squatters and settlers who could afford it tended to hire overseers, whose knowledge of farming and animal husbandry would hopefully prevent the owner from making any calamitous mistakes.

Flocks of sheep might number anywhere from a few hundred to as many as a thousand, and were looked over by shepherds who did little else but take their flock out to graze each day and return to their huts with them in the evening. The shepherd's life might seem idyllic, but it was far from it. Many were badly treated by their squatter employers, and both free and convict shepherds could be brought before the courts or refused wages if they lost their sheep. Their life was a lonely one, a fact embraced by some but which turned others mad. Typically they were dirty, unshaven, and clad in rags with sheepskin slippers; a mix of street-sweeper and castaway.

In the 1850s, the lure of the (mostly southern) gold fields saw huge numbers of shepherds abandoning their flocks to seek their fortunes along creeks and riverbanks, an exodus that brought about the demise of the shepherding era, but also saw squatters realise, as they watched their flocks continue to contentedly graze in the shepherds' absence, that their usefulness had been, to say the least, markedly exaggerated. The demise of the shepherd saw the rise of the boundary rider, men whose job it was to ride along the fence lines, checking their status, making repairs, driving sheep from poor ground and laying baits for predators, mainly dingoes. The boundary rider's routine rarely changed, and in many ways his life was every bit as lonely and detached from society as that of the shepherd before him.

Loneliness wasn't a stranger to the squatter, either. Edward Curr spoke of how time 'hung on the squatter's hands' with long periods where there was little else to do but watch over a flock or herd. 'We read a good deal', he said, 'but after one has done enough of that sort of work for the day, a weary portion of the twenty-four hours still remains to be got through'. Conversations suffered due to a lack of fresh subjects. 'Around us were the same everlasting gum-trees basking in changeless sunshine, whilst the rarely varied meal of tea, mutton and damper made its appearance on the table three times a day with such dyspeptic regularity that I used to loathe the sight of it'. In time, however, the gradual increase in the colony of one vital new ingredient altered the squatter's often pessimistic disposition: women.

As more women arrived the imbalance between the sexes began to be righted, and the squatter started to marry. While this led not only to better and more varied meals, it also saw the construction of more substantial homesteads, not to mention an improvement in personal cleanliness, as comforts that once were done without now increasingly became *de rigueur*. With marriage also came a spur to improve one's living quarters and general well-being. Homestead exteriors also improved: now plastered with mud and with flower gardens.

Soon came woolsheds and stockyards, workshops for artisans such as blacksmiths and millers, carpenters and harness makers. It wasn't uncommon for a squatter in the 1840s to employ 50 or 100 people. Squatters were doing more than merely building stations—they were creating communities.

Considering the hardships that awaited them it's remarkable women ventured into the bush at all. The 1841 New South Wales census reveals that in and around Sydney and Parramatta women represented 42 per cent of the population, but only 17 per cent in the squatting districts beyond. (In the early 1850s in the Burnett district of central Queensland the ratio was one woman to every seven men!) And by the time young squatters had established themselves and acquired enough comforts so that they could practically think of marriage, they were no longer young. Many were in their late thirties or early forties by the time they married.

For some fortunate women like Mary Deane, wife of William Pitt Faithfull of Goulburn, now a thriving rural town in 1844, her home the day she first arrived looked more like an estate than a station. Some lamented the dearth of fashion in the bush. In another of her letters back home, Rachel Henning described Sydney fashion being months behind that of London, and in the bush another twelve months still. 'We get hold of a fashion when we go to Sydney', she wrote. 'And wear it till we go down there again'.

Other women had little time for fashion; widowed women had to take over the running of the station.

The daily lives of many women, though, was predictable—and depressingly routine. Scottish-born Mary Braidwood Mowle began a diary in 1850 after the birth of her third child, and painted a vivid picture of her rural life:

The same old story, get up, dress the children, feed the poultry, breakfast, go to work, feed the chickens, work till sunset, feed

chickens, stroll about till dark, put Kate to bed, have tea, undress
the others—play (piano) for an hour, my chief solace, work till
eleven, go to bed and rise next morning to recommence the same
routine.

By 1840, there were over 670 runs throughout New South
Wales, and increasingly sheep were the dominant animal: 1.25
million sheep as opposed to fewer than 360,000 cattle. This
was reflected in the workforce engaged to look over them:
in 1846 there were over 15,000 shepherds and hut-keepers
spread over the mainland colonies, but only 6000 stockmen,
though fewer men were needed to tend sedentary cattle than
wandering sheep.

Considering the pace of settlement, there were remarkably few disputes over boundaries, which always became the
dominant point of discussion whenever squatters laid claims to
new lands. Often landmarks were used to denote a boundary,
such as a river. River frontages were, of course, keenly sought
after. The young New South Wales–born pastoralist James
'Hungry' Tyson, who would go on to become Australia's first
self-made millionaire, owning more than 5.3 million acres over
three states by the time of his death in 1898, ventured west to
the Murray River in 1844 only to find all of the river frontages
had already been claimed or occupied. He later remarked on
how his presence was far from appreciated:

> A new man coming along in search of land at this stage was looked
> on by most of the squatters as worse than a highwayman, and he
> could seldom obtain information as to the boundaries of the runs.

Sheep were preferred by the squatter because they produced
income in the form of wool without having to be slaughtered,
they did less damage to the edge of vital creeks and streams
and they required less water.

Cattle, however, had their benefits, too. They were hardier, could roam over greater distances looking for food and water, could better look after themselves and had few predators. They were not perceived to require supervision, and hence the squatter saw less need to construct outstations. Feeding grounds were established for herds of usually around 200, and they rarely wandered from them, in fact becoming so accustomed to their 'patch' they could be hard to remove if sold. And the cattle remained very much wild beasts, huge creatures whose horns could inflict severe wounds if one wasn't careful. Many who were bred in isolation might not even have seen a human until the time came to muster them. Unlike shepherds, it took a special breed of man to work them.

Stockmen quickly became aware of the special place they were carving out in the Australian landscape. Unlike shepherds, whom they invariably despised, a stockman could ride a horse and his livelihood depended upon his skill as a rider. Stockmen rode on saddles with deep seats and elevated knee pads, which meant their horses were able to be ridden comfortably for long periods. Saddles were one of the few things a stockman claimed to own, and were greatly prized, as were their whips. Horses did much of the work on cattle stations, but on sheep stations the dog was most useful.

The first dog breeds to be tried with sheep were collies and smithfields, but their temperaments were far from ideal. In the 1830s, drovers began experimenting with crossbreeding. Smithfields were crossed with dingoes, greyhounds with collies, and dingoes with merles that produced a breed called Hall's heelers. But they were undisciplined, refusing to turn a herd when required and prone to intimidating horses and bullocks alike. Eventually, of course, it was the kelpie that proved ideal for the job. According to the myth, they were bred in Scotland by a gypsy who crossed a collie with a pet fox. The kelpie was a tireless worker and its exploits in mustering sheep soon became the stuff of legend.

Moving sheep and cattle from station to station was the work of the overlander or drover. Drovers were mostly independent contractors who worked for a set fee or a share of the profits on the sale of the stock they'd moved. They owned what they called their 'plants': horses, wagons, packs, riding and cooking gear, and rations. As droving became more commonplace, regulations were enacted to make sure squatters and pastoralists were not being taken advantage of by drives that took longer than necessary. Sheep and cattle had to be moved a minimum distance each day unless prevented from doing so by flood or fire.

One of the greatest dangers for the drover was, ironically, water. If none had been found for days, cattle would stampede at the smell of it. In north-west New South Wales, 600 out of 1300 bullocks were stampeded and drowned at the Wonna-mitta waterhole. Sheep fared even worse than cattle when it came to a lack of water. In 1859, one drover lost 800 sheep on a drive through Gilgandra. Drovers had to guard against sheep gorging themselves to death on green fields, or from over-heating on blisteringly hot days. Crossing rivers also had its dangers. A rope would be tied around the lead sheep's horns in the hope the others would simply follow it across. And most of the time they did. But not always.

Sheep were easier to drive than cattle, and just as stockmen tended to look down upon shepherds, so did those who drove cattle look down upon those who drove sheep. Sheep also had much less endurance than cattle and so when it came to the great long drives of Australian history, they were made with cattle.

By 1854, the suburbs of Sydney were spread out over countless promontories. There was a railway, but it only extended as far as the foot of the Blue Mountains. The great pastures to the west, explored and taken up long ago by squatters and pastoralists, were still unfenced and only partially stocked, mostly with cattle as the great days of the 'golden fleece' were still to come. The Great Artesian Basin, that hidden ocean of water beneath the land, was still to be found. The Riverina and the Liverpool Plains were not yet secured, vineyards were still to be planted in the Hunter and the shepherd still held sway over the boundary rider.

In the 1860s, the large influx of migrants that had arrived during the gold rush began looking to establish new careers as agriculturalists and farmers, thus putting pressure on land distribution. In response it was decided to unlock lands throughout New South Wales and Victoria that were perceived as 'idle' and unproductive, lands that were held by a few hundred sheep and cattle pastoralists, and then sell them off in smaller parcels to 'selectors', new settlers who would live in closer proximity to one another and who would, it was hoped, help develop sustainable regional communities. Large pastoral runs continued to be offered, but they were not immune from being surveyed, divided up and sold off. This 'squatter–selector' conflict was a pivotal episode in the settlement of Australia, as squatters did all they could to preserve the best lands for themselves in the face of a series of government 'selection acts'.

As the push for selection increased, so too did the possibility that lands claimed for selection might inadvertently include part of squatting properties. As expected, squatters used their wealth wherever possible to nullify reallocation attempts, and loopholes in the legislation made such actions relatively straightforward. One such practice, known as 'dummying', made it possible for squatters to enter into contracts with agents— who were often under their own employ—to select a part of their own land, use a false name to register the claim with the Department of Lands, and simply sell it back to the squatter at a later date for a small fee. Squatters could also select their own land using a family member's name. It's estimated that in New South Wales, eight out of every nine selections reverted back to the land's first white owners.

The prospect of establishing homesteads on New South Wales' settled lands held an alluring appeal, and large stations such as Goonoo Goonoo (313,298 acres) near Tamworth and Warrah (249,600 acres) on the Liverpool Plains were teasing representations of this idealised pastoral life, with flocks increasing in profusion, free flowing income, and self-sufficiency in vegetables, meat and fruit. Many homesteads grew to be so influential that they were the epicentre of the far-flung communities that surrounded them. When a railway extension through to Tamworth was completed in 1868, Goonoo Goonoo played host to the governor of New South Wales Sir Hercules Robinson, and a kangaroo hunt was organised for his entertainment. The homestead, which has since been remodelled and renovated many times, has managed to retain the core of its initial design, as reported in the *Newcastle Chronicle* on 22 October, 1870:

> The residence at Goonoo Goonoo is a good, substantial two-storey brick building, surrounded by trees and shrub. It stands on an elevated position, and has a comfortable as well as a pleasing appearance and is, certainly, a much better residence than any of the squatters, even the richest of them, possess. There are, of course, a store, and other necessary buildings near the dwelling house, and there is also an accommodation house for travellers, and a post office.

Throughout New South Wales, stations like Goonoo Goonoo quickly became the centre of life in otherwise poorly populated landscapes. In 1827, the New South Wales–born pastoralist William Pitt Faithfull was granted 1280 acres of prime, well-watered grazing land on the Goulburn Plains. There he established Springfield Merino Stud, which he stocked with ten rams purchased from Sir William Macarthur's flock in Camden Park. The main residence wasn't built until 1857 and was known as the 'Big House', and the property contained such a myriad of outbuildings and workers' cottages that from a distance it seemed more village than station.

◄○►

At the beginning of the 1850s two out of every three dollars of New South Wales' export income came from wool, and the quest for land sent the pastoralists ever westward, into regions closer to Adelaide and Melbourne than Sydney Cove. One such station was owned by a true pioneer of the Australian sheep industry—George Peppin.

Peppin, his wife Harriet and two sons George and Frederick, sailed from England in 1850, and by mid-1851 had settled near Mansfield in central Victoria. In 1858, the Peppins purchased South Wanganella Station and its 8000 sheep, with the aim of fattening them up and selling them in Melbourne. The station, not far from Deniliquin in the Riverina district, was later expanded with the purchase of neighbouring Boonoke and Moraga stations. The following years, however, brought little rain and conditions were hard. After placing the station on the market but failing to attract a buyer, the Peppins instead turned their attention to producing a tougher breed of merino, sheep that would be able to cope with long walks to water sources, and that would be more robust with a heavier wool that would withstand dust and the heat of the Riverina sun, and hopefully thrive in one of Australia's hottest, driest and flattest farming landscapes.

After selecting their finest 200 ewes and acquiring a further 100 from the nearby Riverina station Canally, then adding rams from France and Germany and densely fleeced rams from Vermont in America, the Peppins established a stud at South Wanganella in 1861—and went on to breed the famous Peppin strain in just seventeen years. The Peppin merino was the product of the station's stud masters—they weren't afraid to cull or to let the climate and environment have a say in which sheep survived. Their sheep produced a very long and lustrous fleece that effectively doubled the fleece weight per sheep that was being achieved as recently as the 1850s.

In 1878, the 75,000-acre Boonoke Station and half of its stock was purchased by a partnership that included Franc Falkiner, who continued to use the principles employed by the

Peppin family. By the mid-1900s it is estimated that almost nine out of ten of the sheep at all the merino studs in Australia could be traced back to the Peppin–Falkiner bloodlines.

As the 1870s drew to a close, the New South Wales colony was becoming stable and self-assured. The last British troops had returned to England, an increasingly confident police force working in tandem with local militias was maintaining law and order, and a once-feared outbreak of class conflict in the wake of the gold rush, as penniless prospectors returned with broken dreams to the cities, failed to materialise. But there were tensions. The free traders in Sydney railed against protectionist-minded Victoria, and an abiding rivalry between the continent's two largest colonies that saw the Victorian government establish entry points along the Murray River, stood in the way of national unity.

But all that was politics, and hardly mattered a jot to pastoralists in the 1880s who were busily pumping water up from the Great Artesian Basin and stocking previously waterless lands with sheep. Great Britain was happily taking the bulk of our exports, and the Australian economy was growing as fast as that of the United States and vastly out-performing Britain.

The pastoral industry had every reason to look to the 1890s with unbridled optimism. Strikes in the shearing and maritime industries? A bank and building society crisis that would leave the banking system in ruins? A depression? Of course, no one could possibly have foreseen any of this. As the 1880s drew to a close, all were certain the prosperous times would surely continue.

Sheep Shearers at Canowie Station, South Australia, c.1880.
National Library of Australia

3

THE WASTELAND
OF THE CROWN

'We have found our paradise.'
—Robert Rowland Leake, pastoralist, 1844

The first Europeans to arrive in South Australia were the crew of the American brig *Union*, who were set down on an estuary by Pelican Lagoon, which has been known as American River ever since, on Kangaroo Island and wintered there for four months in 1803. Ten thousand years earlier, during the last Ice Age, rising sea levels set Kangaroo Island adrift from the Australian mainland, marooning on it a small number of Aborigines who died out or left the island between 2000 and 4000 years ago. When explorer Matthew Flinders and his crew sailed along the South Australian coast on HMS *Investigator* and arrived on its shores on 21 March 1802, they became the first humans in thousands of years to set foot on the island the Aborigines called *Karta*, the 'Island of the Dead'.

From 1803, the waters of the Southern Ocean were fished by whalers and sealers who occupied the island, together with a lawless rag-tag mix of ships' deserters and escaped convicts.

They collected seal skins and whalebone and whale oil, which would, in time, become the future colony's first exports. (Up until around 1825 it was sealers, not squatters, who were the driving force behind territorial expansion in the colonies, from Kangaroo Island to the islands throughout Bass Strait, and the export value of seal skins continued to be many times greater than all other exports—including wool—until well into the 1820s).

Aboriginal women were taken to the island from Tasmania, and the men fathered children with them. It was hardly a sanctioned colony, of course, and three entire decades passed until 27 July 1836 when the arrival of the three-masted *Duke of York* in Nepean Bay brought the island's first official settlers. And when they disembarked, instead of finding an orderly encampment occupied by people who'd maintained their civility, they encountered wild-looking men, their hair matted and coarse, their bodies draped in the hides of kangaroos and wallabies. One 1819 report on the island said the inhabitants, who seemed more like castaways than settlers, looked like 'complete savages' and smelled 'like foxes'. It must have appeared a dystopian scene.

There's no shortage of conjecture when it comes to who may have been the first person to wade ashore at Nepean Bay, Kangaroo Island, and so become the first free settler to set foot on the new colony of South Australia. One story goes that the second mate of the *Duke of York*, Robert Russell, rowed to shore with two-year-old Elizabeth Beare, daughter of Thomas Hudson Beare, aged 48, and his wife Lucy, aged 32, and Russell lowered little Elizabeth onto the sands of Nepean Bay. This is courtesy of an interview with Elizabeth's brother William, given to the *South Australian Register* in July 1886 when he was 82 years old. It's a romantic and tempting version, and one beloved by today's island residents. But the fact is it's rare for historians to come down on the side of family memories and personal recollections. Reminiscences require careful assessment, particularly when other, more contemporary and reliable sources paint another picture.

The other picture, in this case, is less romantic but very likely the story of what really happened. The diaries of Captain Robert Morgan, the methodical, rational commander of the *Duke of York*, and Samuel Stephen, the manager of the South Australian Company, are in agreement that, after anchoring in between five and seven metres of water at around half past ten in the morning, they lowered a boat and, together along with several of their crew, rowed ashore. In neither of their accounts do they mention the presence of a toddler, or of Robert Russell, in any boat. The plausibility of their accounts is hard to argue with, especially when you consider the unlikely scenario that both men allowed second mate Russell to spirit tiny Elizabeth away ahead of an official landing party.

Still, the story that Elizabeth's little feet were the first white female feet to touch the edge of the new colony persists. Elizabeth was one of four children, the only children who took passage on the *Duke of York*. Lucy Beare arrived pregnant with their fifth child, who died after just two days, and the following year Lucy herself passed away after giving birth to Mary, who survived. Thomas and his children moved to the mainland in 1827. Elizabeth was burned to death in a house fire at the age of twelve.

The *South Australia Act 1834* authorised the establishment of a province covering an area of 802,511 square kilometres, the entirety of which was considered 'Wasteland of the Crown' with vacant possession for all, waiting to be occupied. The following year the South Australian Company was formed and given the task of setting the new colony on a sound financial footing through the raising of funds from the sale of new lands. The company would determine the site of the new capital, and be responsible for the surveying and sale of its land, £35,000 of which had to be sold before any settlement would be permitted. The first group of settlers and administrators, a total of 636 people, including little Elizabeth Beare sailing with her parents on the *Duke of York*, departed England in February 1836 in nine vessels and arrived on Kangaroo Island with the view of forming a permanent settlement. One of those ships, the *Rapid*, carried as a passenger Colonel William Light. Light, a former army officer, surveyor and avid painter, would be given the task of surveying the new lands and deciding the location of its capital.

Light was determined that the Province of South Australia would be a very different place to the eastern colonies that preceded it. His vision was of a self-sustaining colony free of religious persecution, one that offered free emigration for any who were able to make the journey, and who would be employed by landowners and given the means to one day become landowners themselves. The site for the capital Adelaide was chosen by Light in 1836, and a survey of the land was completed the following year and the first 1-acre allotments were made. No rural lands were opened for selection until the first quarter of 1838.

This new socially and politically progressive colony would also be convict-free, a beacon of enlightenment in a faraway land. In fact, there was so much optimism regarding the crime rate, or lack thereof, that there wasn't even the provision for a jail in William Light's 1837 plan for Adelaide. There would be no Port Arthurs or Norfolk Islands, no 'convict stain', no dependence upon a slave workforce. Settlers were coming to South Australia on the understanding it would be guaranteed exemption from 'convictism', a revolutionary approach to colonisation that would be fiercely pursued by the state's founders. (The Swan River settlement in Western Australia was technically convict-free too, but was heavily dependent upon convict labour.)

South Australia was to be a social and political experiment unlike any before, a place where wealth could be properly gained through business and honest trade. But there was still the unmistakable whiff of privilege in the air. Just as Britain in the 1830s was a society riddled by class, wealth and rank, so too would its antipodean protégé colony reflect a society replete with rank and station, maintained through complex social conventions, and which many thought were not only quite proper but a reflection of Divine Providence itself, as seen in these now oft-omitted lines from the popular hymn 'All Things Bright and Beautiful':

> The rich man in his castle.
> The poor man at his gate,
> God made them high or lowly,
> And ordered their estate.

Aristocratic ideas persisted, ideas that were held by many but which, over time, coalesced around a singular personage: Edward Wakefield. A London-born politician and colonial promoter, Wakefield saw South Australia as a template and wanted to transplant all of Britain's hierarchical class structure into her newest colony. There would be an end to the chaotic granting of free land and the two problems it inevitably led to: a dependence upon convicts and a shortage of labour. 'Wakefieldian' principles were born out of an alarm that mere convicts could not only exercise an unhealthy unwillingness to work for landowners, but also aspire to be landowners themselves! His solution? To restrict the availability of land by bringing to an end the practice of land grants. Land should be purchased, not given away, and concentrated for sale not over wide and disparate areas but in controlled and planned settlements. Such an approach would ensure more land became available to be sold by the government at a uniform price, high enough to fund further emigration, and calculated to ensure a 'proper' balance of labourers and landowners. The sale price would also be sufficiently high as to make it very nearly certain that common labourers wouldn't have the audacity to gravitate to the status of landowner *too* quickly.

In the end, it's difficult to know how much actual influence Wakefield had on the shape of the new colony. A poor speaker in public but persuasive in private, his name appears only rarely in official documents, and he spent much of his time during South Australia's early years in Europe. By the time he returned to Adelaide his commitment to the new colony was on the wane and he began to actively distance himself from it, while vociferously disagreeing with the low price set for land sales.

The first sheep to arrive in South Australia were six merino and Leicester rams brought over on the *John Pirie*, a tiny 19-metre-long schooner built in Scotland in 1827 and one of the initial nine ships that sailed to the colony from England in early 1836. Also part of the cargo of that 'first fleet' were horses, ducks, rabbits, goats, turkeys, pigs, fowls and hogs, most of which were loaded in England but some of which were purchased along the way at various 'restaurant ports'. Seventy head of sheep came later that same year from the grazing lands of Tasmania, and in 1837 more followed from South Africa. But it would be the overland drives of thousands of sheep and cattle from New South Wales in the late 1830s that firmly established the colony's pastoral industry.

In January 1838, in response to a series of reports that the emergent colony of South Australia was on the brink of famine, the pioneers Charles Bonney and Joseph Hawdon, in what turned out to be one of the great Australian droving tales, left Goulburn in New South Wales with 300 head of cattle. They drove them via Albury and along the Murray River, guided only by maps prepared by the region's explorers Charles Sturt and Thomas Mitchell. Bonney and Hawdon arrived in Adelaide on 3 April, and their herd proved foundational in the establishment of the state's pastoral industry, with cattle numbers increasing threefold within just two years of their arrival.

Hawdon's and Bonney's route was beset with dangers. A fierce electrical storm just a week into the drive saw severalcattle killed. Hawdon hoped to follow the Loddon River to avoid reportedly hostile Aborigines along the Murray River, but was forced to follow the Murray when the Loddon was found to be all but dry. Hawdon's encounters with Aborigines, however, proved to be overwhelmingly positive, with numerous exchanges of gifts including clothing, nets, weapons and food. Bonney played his flute for them, which they enjoyed, and Aboriginal guides in turn gave them directions and advice on where to cross the river. Bonney wrote in his journal that the Aborigines' knowledge was of considerable help to them: 'The paths which they had made in travelling up and down the river afforded us an unfailing guide as to the direction we ought to take'. Even at this early stage of contact, however, Hawdon couldn't help but see evidence of smallpox and other European-born infections.

Edward Curr once described a drover's camp he entered:

> Altogether the scene was picturesque enough, and the overlanders seemed to be enjoying themselves. The campfire, made against the butt of a fallen tree, was on the brink of the river, which ran noiselessly through the towering gum trees . . . Around the fire were the shepherds and bullock drivers seated at their suppers, each expectant sheep dog waiting for his share.

The explorer Edward Eyre overlanded twice to Adelaide; the first time with cattle, departing from the Limestone Plains near present-day Canberra in 1838 around the same time as Bonney and Hawdon but making the mistake of following a route south of the Murray, which caused him to backtrack on a journey that would eventually take him 268 days; and the second journey with 1000 sheep and 600 cattle and a number of oxen and horses. Tracing a line along the Murray, Eyre left us a lovely image of the great river and the landscape through which it passed, of a river that pierced 'a firm, reddish soil . . . covered with scrub', of sandy ridges and open grassy plains, and a river 'timbered with large and lofty gum trees'.

Eyre, too, spoke well of the Aborigines he encountered, describing them as 'exceedingly well behaved', although on occasions they were so fascinated by what Eyre had brought with him, particularly his tomahawks, that they crowded the wagons to touch them until Eyre felt compelled to threaten the Aborigines with firearms.

Fellow explorer Charles Sturt headed the third great drive west, which began in Goulburn in May 1838. Sturt had first journeyed along the Murray on an exploratory trip in 1828, in an attempt to answer the question that was on everyone's mind when it came to our network of inland rivers: where does it flow? His next journey, in late 1829, became the famous 'Murray River Voyage', an expedition complete with bullocks, drays, horses and enough wood to build a whaleboat. Sturt's overlanding of stock in 1838, sometimes referred to as 'Sturt's Forgotten Journey', was his third following the river, but any hopes he had of making a profit from the venture were dashed, and he ended up accepting the post of surveyor-general offered to him by the South Australian governor, George Gawler.

The importance of the overlanding of stock by Hawdon, Bonney, Eyre, Sturt and others to South Australia cannot be underestimated. The risk and reality of occasional famines was not unknown to its colonists, who more than once were forced to survive on kangaroo meat, a last resort to be sure, but not as unheard-of a diet as you'd think. Kangaroos were regularly killed from the very early days of settlement, considered a supplement to colonists' rations and a low-cost alternative to livestock meat. From 1793, kangaroo meat was traded in public markets in Sydney Cove, and constituted part of the rations of every convict sent to Tasmania in the early 1800s.

Cattle that were brought to South Australia in the great overland drives of the 1830s initially were pastured in the well-watered Adelaide Hills, then began to be dispersed over the colony's north, south and east as settlers spread out over new lands. Those who chose to raise cattle faced many of the same problems as the sheep farmer. Next to nothing was known of the nutritional value of their pastures, the toxicity of its plants or the reliability of its water sources. Experience was often gained at the expense of large stock losses.

Squatters on isolated runs had limited access to medical services and diseases that afflicted both human and animal were often left undiagnosed or at best poorly treated. The treatment and prevention of disease was often tackled with everyday items, such as kerosene to reduce the prevalence of lice and fleas and copper filings for distemper. Tobacco was rubbed into snake bites. If cattle suffered from pleuro-pneumonia, bulbs of garlic were inserted into their dewlap.

The idea of quarantining animals that entered the state from overseas and overland from the other colonies was talked about and even attempted, but for many years proved unworkable. An Inspector of Disease was established under the *Scab Act 1840*, but the position only lasted six months, and it wasn't until the late 1850s and early 1860s that bans were imposed on scab-infected sheep from Victoria and New South Wales and bovine pleuro-pneumonia. By 1866, the importation of sheep, cattle, horses and pigs from Great Britain and Europe was prohibited unless accompanied by a certificate stating they were free of disease.

It had been the intention of its founding fathers to transform South Australia into an agricultural paradise, but the colony's sparsely populated extremities meant life was destined to be hard, and lonely. Stations like Angepena in the Flinders Ranges and Wooltana, 650 kilometres north of Adelaide, were separated by great distances. There was no cheap convict labour, and squatter numbers were not significant enough even to 'grow' communities. Rural townships would not develop in South Australia until the advent of mining, and the squattocracy there was also slow to develop. The first pastoral leases didn't begin to be issued until 1842, after which pastoralists were required to pay £10 annually for their runs regardless of their size, in addition to a tax on their stock.

Despite this, the vision of the colony's founding fathers was spectacularly realised. In 1838, the first bale of wool was exported to England. At the same time, a police force was organised, and almost 48,000 acres of land was sold at £1 an acre. (While £1 an acre might not sound like much, in fact it was more than land cost elsewhere in the British Empire, and in Canada and the United States land was selling for a comparatively paltry four to five shillings an acre). By 1839, 443 acres of crops were under cultivation and the South Australian Agricultural Society was established. In 1840, the population was nudging 15,000 and the first council elections were held. In 1841, just five years after its proclamation as a colony, South Australia was home to 200,000 sheep and 15,000 cattle, croppers were harvesting their first substantive crops, 57,000 vine cuttings—the foundation of a future wine industry—arrived from South Africa, and 2000 destitute persons were being supported by the government, a reflection of the colony's religious underpinnings.

Unlike in New South Wales, where cheap convict labour could be relied upon, labour costs for free men in South Australia were high. But despite the establishment of large stations in the northern areas of the state, some of which had a hundred or more employees, their isolation still stood in the way of them transforming into towns. Some tried. Farina Station in the Lake Eyre Basin was settled in 1878 and at its zenith had a population over 600. There were two hotels, and even an underground bakery, two breweries, a school and a brothel. Its owners hoped to grow wheat and barley, but the longed-for rains never came, and the population dwindled. Farina is now a ghost town.

Many such runs failed. Those who prospered did so thanks to good soils and a climate better suited to sheep than wheat. Great fortunes were accumulated exporting wool to England, and by 1842 there were 250,000 sheep spread across the new colony. South Australia's early pastoralists also built great stone homes that would stand for generations, homes such as Hawker at Bungeree, Angas at Collingrove and Duffield at Parra Parra. One of the finest of them all was the homestead at Anlaby Station, the centrepiece of Australia's oldest merino stud.

In 1841, Frederick Dutton purchased Anlaby Station from John Finnis, a whaler and sea captain who had bought the land in 1839, and with the help of Dutton stocked it by overlanding 12,000 sheep from New South Wales. Dutton, a politician and pastoralist who'd arrived in South Australia from New South Wales in 1841, made a fortune from the sheep's back. The homestead began as a simple hut, but was added to over and over until it became the grand colonnaded building still seen today. Anlaby covered 70,000 acres, and to fill it Dutton imported Rambouillet and Saxon sheep from Europe, making the property the colony's first merino stud. In a strange twist, Anlaby Station also has more National Trust–registered heritage trees on its property than any other privately owned home in Australia—620 in all—most of which are within its 10-acre garden. It is also home to the 'Squatter's Dream', a hybrid *gigantea* once considered lost until a specimen was rediscovered decades later growing in the Anlaby garden.

◄○►

There were sincere attempts on the part of the new government to treat the Aborigines with a measure of respect that was denied them elsewhere. The notion of *terra nullius*, that all the lands of these new colonies belonged to no one and were there for the taking, the idea that had underpinned the expansion of the eastern colonies, would not apply here. Or at least, that was the thinking. Captain John Hindmarsh, who had served at the Battle of Trafalgar under Lord Nelson and in 1836 was appointed South Australia's first governor, claimed Aboriginal people should be afforded the same rights and protection as any other of His Majesty's subjects. There were Colonial Office attempts to organise Aboriginal welfare and land rights programs, and the first public service appointment in the new colony was that of Matthew Moorhouse, who would assume the role of Protector of Aboriginal People. His brief was to teach Aborigines 'the arts of civilisation', to pursue their 'civilising and Christianising', and train them in the 'habits of useful industry' such as crop planting and construction.

It became an offence to give an Aborigine alcohol, ration stations were set up across the state to provide them with flour, biscuits and blankets, missionaries began setting up schools to introduce them to Christianity, and attempts were made to increase understanding between Aborigines and settlers. All well-meaning, but already the mechanisms were being put in place that would ultimately undermine Aboriginal society, increase their dependency upon white society, and cut them off from their own beliefs and traditions.

Orders were given that prohibited Aborigines from being given work to avoid the appearance of the colony engaging in slavery. Those settlers who felt obliged to ignore the order and provided them work anyway, did so. John Wrathall Bull, an English-born farmer and author, arrived aboard the *Canton* with his family in 1838 and found work as a land and stock agent. Bull thought it fair, if approached by Aborigines for food or clothing, to give them small jobs in return for what they asked, rather than rewarding begging. But nothing could hide the fact that puritanical Protestant window-dressing was no compensation for the loss of rights over their traditional lands. As Bull noted in his book *Early Experiences of Colonial Life in South Australia*:

> ... if the government had from the first treated them as the natural owners of the land and lords of the soil, to whom an ample provision had to be set apart to enable them to lead an idle and independent life, there would have been some justice if not sense in such a proposition. But as in the progress of settlement of their country by our intrusion their game must either be destroyed or driven back, they would have been without means of subsistence in the absence of an appropriate equivalent. The question is: has justice been done them? I say it has not . . .

The world of the Aborigine in South Australia changed forever within a generation. By the 1840s, land cleared for grazing had dramatically reduced native plants and native animal habitats, and conflicts between settlers and local Aboriginal landowners were becoming commonplace. Lands were offered for sale by the government regardless of whether they were occupied by Aborigines or not, and settlers moving cattle overland poisoned waterholes in the wake of bloody encounters with tribal groups. Aboriginal workers, when they were used, were paid in rations, or promised wages that were never seen. Yet despite smallpox outbreaks that devastated the Aboriginal population in 1789 and 1829 and countless acts of slaughter by white settlers, the colony's naive approach to Aboriginal rights continued to find expression. In 1846, the first white man was hung for murdering an Aboriginal man, and the first mixed race marriage was granted in 1848.

In the end, the proof of the level of inhumanity meted out by settlers to the Indigenous peoples they encountered is revealed in the grim historical record. The population of the Kaurna people, known to colonists as the Adelaide Tribe, whose traditional lands included the Adelaide plains, fell from 650 in 1841 to 150 in 1856. Similar reductions in Indigenous populations can be seen occurring across the colony. South Australia's lofty principles of egalitarianism, opportunity and fairness to all were, in the end, never realised. The remoteness of the colony's pastoral districts, combined with a lack of adequate police resources, led to inevitable settler reprisals for every Aboriginal slight. Aboriginal bodies were burned to cover up massacres, and the so-called 'White Man's Law' ruled here just as it had everywhere else, where 'a little cold lead, well applied, affected a perfectly amicable understanding between the races'.

The pace of the early growth and prosperity of South Australia's far-flung communities could not have been achieved without the hardy, tireless bullock. The backbone of the colony's transport network, bullocks were used for travel between townships, pastoral stations and eventually mining towns such as Kapunda and Burra, at a time when no roads existed. They hauled goods from the holds of supply ships and took produce to the coast for export. It took a bullock team an hour to cover 3 ½ miles within the confines of Adelaide, but north of the city in the scrub and elsewhere the pace was far slower—as little as a single mile every hour. The ground they had to cover was so hard and unforgiving they were shod with two bullock cues instead of one, to protect their cloven hooves.

The Great North Road linking the coast to the mining towns in the north was opened up by teams of bullocks and their human 'bullockies'. It took ten days and often longer for a bullock team to make the journey from the Burra mine east of the Clare Valley to Port Adelaide, and by 1846, over 400 drays were keeping the city and the outback connected. In the first six years of the mine's operation bullocks transported more than 80,000 tons of copper ore to port. Towns such as Hanson, Farrell Flat, Manoora, Saddleworth, Marrabel and Tarlee, to name a few, grew out of nothing at 14-kilometre intervals, the distance a bullock could reasonably be expected to travel in an average nine-hour day.

In time, alternate paths were plied between Porter Lagoon to the south of Burra, and Gawler to the north of Port Adelaide. And as towns grew throughout this increasingly sinewy network so did shanties like the Hanson Inn, the Sod Hut, the Emu Hotel and the Stone Hut to give shelter, food and drink to weary bullockies and fodder for their bullocks. Saddle makers, wheelwrights and blacksmiths arrived and found work servicing their copper wagons.

Would-be pastoralists who arrived too late to take advantage of initial land releases found it difficult to gain a foothold in the industry. Many began by finding work with established pastoralists while building up small flocks in lieu of wages. Two such men were the brothers James and John Chambers. Born in Middlesex, England, they came to South Australia with their wives in 1837, arriving as 'agricultural labourers'. James was so excited by his arrival he leaped overboard from the *Coromandel* when it anchored in Holdfast Bay and swam to shore. James Chambers was the first man in South Australia to design and build a bullock-drawn dray, which he used to carry goods on the twelve-kilometre journey from the bay to Adelaide. He brought horses over from Van Diemen's Land and was very likely the first to open a livery stable in the city. He also imported coaches from England, and was the first to provide them as accompaniment for government expeditions and survey parties.

In 1853, after having amassed a small fortune, James sold his coaches and horses, visited England, and returned with some of the colony's finest horses, sheep and cattle. Together with brother John, he took up large pastoral leases in the northern regions of the colony. John Chambers claimed to be the first to plough land in Adelaide, the first to build a house with a fireplace, and would eventually settle down to raise sheep on

1200 acres at Cherry Gardens, a semi-rural Adelaide suburb. Various other leaseholds would follow over the years, though much of Chambers' landholdings would be sold off in 1863 in anticipation of a crippling drought.

South Australia's largest mountain range, the Flinders Ranges, which has been inhabited by its traditional owners the Adnya-mathanha people for thousands of years (and renamed the Ikara–Flinders Ranges National Park in 2016, *ikara* meaning 'gathering place') is believed to have first been seen by Europeans in 1802, by the crew of Matthew Flinders' HMS *Investigator*. Edward John Eyre traversed the ranges in 1839 and the first settlers began coming here in the 1840s. Throughout the 1840s, many of the leases in the Flinders Ranges were taken up by settlers who'd prospered in the eastern colonies and came to South Australia cashed-up and looking for fresh opportunities. Unlike in the east, however, the establishment of pastoral runs did not morph into the creation of inland towns, with pastoral-ists preferring instead to maintain trade links with the colony's coastal settlements. Profits were strong in good seasons, but when drought came stock losses were measured in the thousands. Yet despite the challenge of isolation and a dry climate, by the end of the 1850s most of the southern Flinders Ranges had been settled.

On 7 June 1851, the colony's first newspaper the *South Australian Register* ran a story on a newly discovered 75-square-kilometre mountain basin found by a bullocky, William Chance, who was led there with the assistance of Aboriginal guides. 'A new pastoral country', the story went, 'has been discovered north of Mount Eyre . . . it is a mountainous country, and the ranges rise to a height of about two thousand feet. There are several streams, some of which are said to run the whole year'. The basin had a single point of entry by way of a swampy, narrow gorge. Once any cattle or sheep were herded within its boundaries, all that would be needed to keep them penned was to block their egress through the gorge. This amphitheatre of rock was called Wilpena Pound.

After being surveyed in 1851, a lease was issued and was immediately taken up by the English-born brothers William and John Browne, and a station was soon established there by their business partner, the 25-year-old pioneering pastoralist Henry Strong Price, who chose to build his homestead near the Wilpena Creek. Price had arrived in the colony aboard the *Fortitude* in April 1842 just a few months shy of his seventeenth birthday. The young adventurer quickly took to life as an overlander, saving enough money to take out an occupation licence on a grazing run the following year at Hill River in the mid-north of the colony. Price met the Browne Brothers at their Booborowie Station, which they'd taken up in 1863, and when the brothers purchased the land at Wilpena they asked Price to manage it on their behalf.

It would become one of the nation's most famous pastoral stations. By 1864 Wilpena Pound had grown beyond the mountainous confines of the Pound to encompass 2000 square kilometres, and was running 33,000 sheep and 4000 cattle. A devastating drought in the mid-1860's ravaged the land, and in the decades that followed the station had a succession of owners. Now one of the state's most significant historical sites, Wilpena Pound ceased to be a working station in 1985. Its buildings, including the homestead, bookkeeper's hut, motor house (garage), stables and harness room have been restored and it now stands as a monument to the determination and grit of South Australia's early pastoralists.

One of the most isolated runs in the northern Flinders Ranges was Agepena, a property so remote that even after its hut-keeper was murdered by Aborigines in 1856 it took months for the government to dispatch four troopers and establish a permanent presence there. One of the northernmost runs in the region, Agepena was used as a staging post for expeditions into the interior. It was not until 1861 that the population became significant enough to warrant the introduction of a postal service.

The impact of the settlers and their stock upon the Flinders' fragile environment proved immense. The diet of the sheep and cattle was the same as the region's native animals: grass. As stock numbers increased, the available grasses, not to mention water, were significantly reduced, and with crop planting also inexorably altering the landscape, the region's resident native animal population began to disappear. The rat kangaroo, the tammar wallaby, the hairy-nosed wombat, the stick-nest rat and the marsupial cat all disappeared from the Flinders Ranges.

By the 1870s, rabbits, first brought to Australia on the First Fleet but only reaching plague proportions after an accidental release in 1859, were eating the vegetation right down to the ground. The rabbits were so numerous they provided ample food for dingoes, which increased *their* numbers too and forced the building of expensive dingo fences, which in turn thwarted native animal migration. John Conrick, one of the state's great pastoralists, wrote:

> The rabbit has come to stay. We can never conquer them. Of course, their skins are now saleable, but they use up country on which valuable stock could be grazed. Anything made out of the rabbit is a mere bagatelle to the damage it does. They can live for years without water in scrub country by burrowing and eating the roots. Poison is too expensive; all you could kill in that way would be like a drop in the ocean. Millions of acres today are breeding grounds for the rabbit and it would not pay to clear them . . . Personally I think it would be a good thing to introduce some disease . . .

In 1876, the owners of Anlaby Station near Kapunda paid exterminators £340 over twelve months to eradicate the rabbits that were overrunning the property. One hundred and forty-six thousand were destroyed. By 1879, the South Australian government had 22 rabbit eradication patrols spread out across the colony, all of them ineffectual. It was akin to holding back the tide, and by 1884 the rabbit scourge had spread from

Naracoorte in the colony's south-east all the way to the Eyre
Peninsula.

Throughout the 1840s, squatters and settlers were roaming
South Australia's horizons in search of land, but were up
against a government determined to influence the pace and the
direction of settlement, with various mechanisms put in place
to make sure the sort of wholesale land-grabbing seen in other
colonies didn't happen here. Surveys of land would always
precede any sales. There would be annual assessments on stock
levels. The government, desperately in need of revenue, had no
stomach for indulging squatters who only had to pay a £5 fee
for an occupation license regardless of the size of their claim.
And when the South Australian government introduced legislation permitting it to reclaim half of a squatter's land providing
they gave the squatter six months' notice, the vexed concept of
'insecurity of tenure' was born.

Insecurity of tenure became a constant irritant to squatters
across the colony, such as to Robert Rowland Leake, formerly
a South Australian Company stock manager and Van Diemen's
Land pastoralist. By 1842, the overweight 28-year-old—who
felt more at home around his sheep than he did 'the ladies of
South Australia' who in his opinion spent far too much time
having picnics and parties—had amassed the colony's fourth
largest flocks of sheep (4000) and lambs (2500). Living in
constant fear his lands would be reclaimed, he moved three
times in 1843, and was so dejected that he wrote in a letter
to his father of his six years of struggle in South Australia,
'enduring every privation that a man could endure and making
nothing by it'. Feeling no better in January 1844 he wrote
again: 'All in all, it is a horrible life, that of a squatter'.

Leake, in the end, would find the paradise he so desperately
sought—in the far south-east of the colony near to the border
with Victoria. Upon hearing a report there was verdant land in

the south-east district, Leake and his overseer John McIntyre gathered his flocks and when they arrived at a hilltop near Rivoli Bay, Leake claimed: 'We have found our paradise!' He went on to establish the shearing station of Glencoe, named after McIntyre's place of birth in Scotland. (The 36-stand Glencoe Woolshed, built in 1863, was never converted over to mechanised shearing and is now belongs to the National Trust. With its arched black beams and cathedral-like appearance it remains one of the nation's finest examples of a colonial-era woolshed.)

The south-east district's palpable sense of isolation for those early settlers did little to deter them from coming, and there was no shortage of enterprising pastoralists and pastoralists-in-waiting intent on subduing it. George Meredith, a wealthy settler from Van Diemen's Land eager to see his son John succeed on his own, purchased a 120-kilometre run near the New South Wales border and put him on the next boat to the mainland. But not before making John promise never to smoke, and to learn to play the flute, which George considered a habit worth cultivating.

Charles Sturt's brother Evelyn also sought to subdue the south-east and established Compton to the east of Mount Gambier in the midst of some of the colony's finest pastures. Sturt raised 6000 sheep and wrote that 'the whole country was so cavernous, and absolute streams and rivers abounded within a few feet of the surface'. Even so, a drought in 1847 devastated his flocks, as it did the young John Meredith, and both men lost labourers to other more forgiving districts.

Others who ventured into the south-east and took up runs too close to the swampy plains that ran along the coast lost countless sheep to a mysterious disease. And the local Aborigines were standing their ground. When 29-year-old English aristocrat Samuel Davenport left the safe confines of Adelaide for Rivoli Bay with his 4000 sheep and tens of thousands more to follow, he quickly marked out his boundaries, turned the property over to others to manage, and returned to the city.

'There is little joy', he later wrote to his father, 'in taking up and opening the way to others in a wild country'. Wild or not, by 1846 the district was running approximately half of the colony's sheep.

Despite the region's initial privations, in time some progress was made. By 1847, a collection of enterprising settlers had established a chain of inns and supply stores that stretched from Mount Gambier to Portland, and a mail route linking Adelaide to Sydney passed through the district. But this did little to alleviate the 'tyranny of distance' all who lived there felt. The nearest doctors were either in Guichen Bay or distant Portland, or in Adelaide, which was 480 kilometres away, and even when you got there was—according to Robert Rowland Leake, who was never short of a miserly phrase—still 'a wretched place to live'. (Though it may not have mattered where in Australia Leake lived, considering he once wrote: 'I doubt that New Holland is a fit place for the Caucasian race'.) Indeed, a dislike of Adelaide seemed a commonly held opinion among settlers in the south-east. Even John Meredith wrote: 'Its chief importations are spirits, beer and tobacco, germans, orphans and harpies', its inhabitants having 'copper throats which enable them to swallow immense amounts of alcohol and convert their mouths into chimneys for the consuming of tobacco'.

In 1851, Robert Rowland Leake finally had his way when it came to the vexed issue of insecurity of tenure, when a squatter majority in the Legislative Council voted to replace occupation licences with fourteen-year leases with yearly payments of just £1 per acre on unlimited acreages. With a requirement to stock each square kilometre of land with a modest sixteen cattle or 100 sheep, squatters rushed to buy as much of the remaining land as they could. By early July 1851, just 83 pastoralists held title over more than 11,900 square kilometres. The irony, of course, is that by keeping their stations large, the south-east district's settlers virtually guaranteed the district would never become a region of towns and communities. Their isolation, once the harbinger of so many ills, became 'isolation by choice'.

According to one farmer, it would be 'a sheep walk forever'.

Among the first settlers to grow grapes in South Australia was John Barton Hack, a British Quaker settler who planted wine-grape vines on an undeveloped block of land in North Adelaide in 1837, at the same time as German settlers were beginning to plant wine-grapes in the Adelaide Hills and the Barossa Valley. Two years later Hack moved to a property at Echunga to the south of the Adelaide Hills, taking some of his North Adelaide vines with him. In the years that followed Hack added more vines to his initial planting at Echunga, built a two-storey farmhouse and, by 1843, had developed a commercially viable vineyard comprising thousands of vines. A financial crisis that same year saw Hack sell his vineyard to a fellow Quaker, Jacob Hagen, who bottled some wine from his newly purchased vines, named it Echunga Hock, and dispatched it to Queen Victoria, along with the claim that he (using Hack's vines) had become the colony's first winemaker.

On 23 April 1838, the first six German winemaking families arrived in Australia, landing in Sydney on the barque *Kinnear*. On 18 and 20 November 1838, two ships, the *Bengalee* and the *Prince George*, arrived in Port Adelaide with 250 German emigrants and the Lutheran minister Pastor August Kavel aboard the *Prince George*. Loading their possessions onto bullock drays they embarked on a four-week journey to land belonging to the English-born businessman George Fife Angas, chairman of the South Australian Company. Angas considered Kavel and his followers to be ideal settlers, and had helped to finance their migration. Settling on George Angas's property after securing a loan of £1200 at an exorbitant interest rate of 15 per cent, they proceeded to build a community—the village of Klemzig. By 1840, almost 270 acres had been fenced into paddocks and planted with wheat, barley and potatoes. There were 34 freestanding houses, and water supplied from the nearby Torrens River. Governor Gawler was so impressed by their industriousness that he claimed he 'wouldn't mind seeing 100,000 of them'. (Sadly, Klemzig would not last. By the 1880s, all its original residents had left, and the majority of its buildings had either collapsed or been demolished).

On 28 December 1838, almost 200 people from Silesia in Prussia arrived aboard the 350-ton three-masted ship *Zebra*, captained by Dirk Meinerts Hahn. Hahn, a Dane who never showed any evidence of being enthralled by the prospect of life in a new land, had nevertheless grown to admire his passengers on the long and difficult voyage, during which a fierce storm east of the Cape of Good Hope left five of the *Zebra*'s sails in tatters, and a dozen passengers had died of typhus. Hahn, despite having fulfilled his contract to bring his passengers safely to South Australia, insisted on staying on to assist the settlers in securing 150 acres of land in the Adelaide Hills, where they established the still-thriving tourist town of Hahndorf, appropriately named after their captain. Hahn returned to his family in Westerland on the North Sea island of Sylt, the island of his birth, and died there on 15 August 1860.

By the mid-1840s, most of the great names in the South Australian wine industry had already gained a foothold in the colony's fertile soils. John Reynell planted his first vines in 1841, Henry John Lindemann in 1843, and Christopher Penfold's Magill vineyard was established in 1844. In 1847, what would become the Barossa Valley's first commercially viable vineyard was planted by the pioneering viticulturalist Johann Gramp, the Bavarian-born farmer who purchased 74 acres of land along Jacob's Creek. German immigrants were foundational in the creation of the South Australian wine industry, with names like Seppelt and Henschke still known and admired today.

German immigrants to South Australia first came to the colony with the South Australian Company in 1836. Of the hundreds that followed most were Lutherans who came from Protestant east and central Germany, emigrating in order to free themselves from religious persecution. They took up rural pursuits first in the Torrens Valley and later in the Adelaide Hills and, as befitted their humble peasant origins, became market gardeners, supplying Adelaide with much if its fresh vegetables, acquiring wealth that enabled them to move, as anyone with money did, into the realm of land speculation, moving into virgin territory that enabled them to lay out and plan their own communities. Homes were built of stone, and later brick, and those who could afford it used corrugated iron for their roofs instead of thatch. By 1845, more than 1200 German immigrants called South Australia home, and wherever you looked there were towns that were unmistakably German in appearance: Hahndorf, Lobethal, Paechtown and Tanunda.

The German immigrants never became dependent upon a single crop. They in large part avoided rushing to the gold fields, unlike many settlers of British origin, preferring instead to stay on the land and, in their words, 'make gold with the plough'. Yet not all were farmers. A third of all German immigrants had a farming background, but there were also artisans, businessmen, pastors, blacksmiths, carpenters, labourers and others, a useful mix of skills that meant when they laid out and settled a new town they could immediately form themselves into genuine, working communities. Lutheran schools were established in the regions in which the Germans settled, there were two German newspapers and even a German hospital. Second-generation farming families established themselves throughout the Barossa Valley and Adelaide Hills, and they were also employed in smelting ore in the Burra mine.

By 1855, Germans made up 8 per cent of South Australia's population and had become as vital a part of the colony's development as any other segment of the population.

◄O►

Sheep scab, the product of the scab mite *Psoroptes ovis*, arrived with the First Fleet and was every pastoralist's worst nightmare. Thriving on a diet of skin debris and the fluids that accumulate in lesions and wounds, the mites caused untold irritation for sheep whose response was to bite and rub themselves, thus causing irreparable damage to their valuable fleeces. Scab spread across the colonies from New South Wales. In South Australia, the *Scab Act 1840* saw the employment of inspectors who could report on all sheep coming into the province and force owners to pay penalties for diseased sheep. It became illegal to purchase sheep from infected flocks, illegal to drove infected flocks, and owners could be fined for any infected sheep left abandoned or found roaming.

In 1843, an editorial in *The Adelaide Examiner* lamented the mite's handiwork:

> We are afraid that some of the fleeces sent home will sell badly on account of the ravages of this disorder. Sheep driven into town for sale at butchers we have remarked to be often very much affected and no doubt farmers will get rid of this description of stock at much less price and more readily than sound ones.

Early treatments were crude yet surprisingly effective when properly managed. One approach was to work a mix of lard and a mercurial ointment into the skin by hand. Occasionally sheep were immersed in limewater to soften the scabs first, and there was even a sulphuric acid mix which benefited from the addition of tobacco, the nicotine combining with the acid to destroy the mites. Sulphur and lime dipping vats were built and the mixture heated to between 37 and 43 degrees Celsius (100 to 110 degrees Fahrenheit). One early treatment 'recipe' went as follows:

> 10 lb (4.5 kg) tobacco boiled in 15 gallons (58 L) of water; add ½ pint (237mL) each of spirits of tar and spirits of turpentine per gallon (3.8 L) of wash before use. This is rubbed into each sheep by hand, using 1-1 ½ pints (474—710 mL) per sheep.

But the problem persisted. Farmers often failed to completely treat their flocks, and an absence of fencing meant the disease could easily spread. No colony was spared, but South Australia was particularly hard hit. As settlers spread out from Adelaide, the disease was taken with them everywhere except, it seemed, to Kangaroo Island, which records indicate may have mercifully been spared. On the mainland shepherds were careless, and dingoes were a constant menace, taking sheep and the mites with them as they roamed. In 1843, estimates to a hastily convened Committee of Inquiry of the number of South Australian sheep infected with the mite varied between 75 and 90 per cent. In its final report the committee concluded that out of a total population of 349,000, 195,000 were infected and 154,000 clean.

A decade of washes and infection control seemed to make little difference. In 1853, a new Scab Act, demanded by the owners of over half a million sheep throughout the colony, was passed. This ground-breaking Act would prove a turning point in the fight against sheep scab. It provided more inspectors and introduced penalties for hindering their work. It permitted the branding of an infected sheep with the letter 'S' and its owner's initials on its rump, and for the slaughter of an entire mob if a single diseased sheep was found in its midst. Inspectors could enter private property and destroy any infected sheep they found, and owners even had the right to stop and examine other people's sheep passing through their runs and, if necessary, kill them.

In 1853, a flock at Evandale on the outskirts of Adelaide was reduced from around 3000 to a mere 1891, with many of the remainder close to worthless. But this would be one of the last significant localised outbreaks as the latest incarnation of the Scab Act began to take effect. The number of infected sheep started to decline in 1854, when a report by John Hamilton, the Chief Inspector of sheep, showed just over 66,000 infected animals out of a population of 1.24 million.

No other disease imprinted itself so indelibly upon the consciousness of the colony, both city-dweller and farmer alike, and its legacy left deep wounds. When a small outbreak occurred in August 1867 in the Wellington district near Lake Alexandrina, an editorial in the *South Australian Chronicle and Weekly Mail* read:

> For even if we are absurd enough to let epidemics to rage unchecked amongst the human species it is no reason why we should allow contagion to spread amongst our flocks and herds. At all events the appearance of scab at Wellington has aroused the whole country. In and out of Parliament it has been a daily topic of conversation. Dispatches have been sent off by every post, telegrams flashed incessantly along the wires and mounted troopers and sheep inspectors sent galloping hither and thither.

By 1869, however, with wire fences now common, the only remaining infected sheep were confined to a few properties adjacent to the Victorian border and no new cases were reported in the state after that year.

Sheep scab significantly strained relations between South Australia and its eastern neighbours, with fines able to be imposed upon the owners of any infected sheep found to have crossed the border. The *Introduction of Stock Act 1861* made it illegal to drive sheep from New South Wales and Victoria into South Australia, with a permit only able to be issued if the sheep had come from a scab-free flock, not been dipped for six months, and not been in a region where scab had been detected for three months.

With so many restrictions, few sheep made it through, and in 1866 the same restrictions were applied to sheep from Queensland, Western Australia, Tasmania and even New Zealand. Inspectors were stationed at crossing points and given orders to shoot sheep found straying onto South Australian territory.

◄O►

'Rain follows the plough' was a naive and deeply flawed nineteenth-century phrase created by the American land speculator Charles Wilber who was desperate to settle the Great Plains. It was an attempt to encourage the belief that if you ventured forth into dry, barren country with a poor history of rainfall, and went ahead and ploughed the land anyway, rains would somehow soon come.

From 1863 to 1866 a severe drought saw farmers increasingly in need of information on growing conditions and climate behaviour, and in 1865 George Goyder, the colony's Liverpool-born surveyor-general, was charged with mapping a boundary between the areas that had good rainfall, and those that were drought-prone. Goyder rode almost 5000 kilometres on horseback, and in December submitted to the government a 'line of drought' that became known as Goyder's Line. South of the line it was safe to plant crops, with areas to the north of it suitable only for pastoral use. But when unseasonal rains fell in late 1865, that advice was ignored and settlers quickly forgot their own experience as they ventured further north than Goyder considered prudent. They were following the notion that rain would continue to 'follow the plough'. It did not. And they paid a heavy price for their ignorance.

Every station in South Australia, like every station across the nation, has its own story to tell and it would be impossible to list them all. One of the most remote of South Australia's sheep stations is Holowiliena in the Flinders Ranges, which exists today as the state's oldest leasehold property that still retains the original family name. When the Warwick family first came to this remote region 400 kilometres north of Adelaide in 1852 the area was described as 'vacant waste land'. William Warwick and his wife Jennett, who arrived in Adelaide from Scotland in 1839 with their ten children, took up the station's pastoral lease in 1853, pastoral lease 318, and set about constructing its first stone buildings. (A chimney from one of those first buildings still stands today.) Within two years they'd even built a school for the Warwick children and the children of their employees. The station has since been operated by five generations of the Warwick family, runs a maximum 7000 sheep, and remains a property built upon the principle of producing good merino stock.

Poltalloch Station on the shores of Lake Alexandrina was established in 1839 by Neill Malcolm of Poltalloch Estate on the windswept coastline of Argyll in Scotland. It was purchased by the Bowman brothers, John and William, in 1873, pioneering pastoralists who had accompanied their father to Hobart from England before sailing to South Australia aboard the *Parsee* in 1838. The brothers, who had taken a flock of 2000 sheep to South Australia in 1839, the same year Malcolm completed Poltalloch, added it to a string of pastoral leases they'd built up throughout the 1850s and 1860s, and by the early 1900s John's own son, Keith, was in charge of a vast 30,000-acre estate that had, at its peak, 40,000 sheep.

The generational division of the property has since reduced it to 5500 acres, including a precious 17-kilometre stretch of Albert Channel and Lake Alexandrina waterfront, as well as hundreds of acres of native bushland. Sheep have long since been replaced by stocks of Black Angus cows, but its impressive array of colonial buildings remains remarkably intact. Poltalloch still has John Bowman's 27-room two-storey 1883 homestead, built at a cost of £4000 from locally quarried sandstone, its unique shearing shed with its double curved corrugated roof that was shaped onsite after being brought down the Murray River on a paddle steamer, an old stone hut once used for itinerant shearers, the shed's storage rooms that once contained over 500 wool bales, and the buggy room with its buggy that was once attached to the back of the family's Model T ford that took the Bowman children on idyllic afternoon rides.

The station's windmills are long gone, but there's still the round brick pumphouse that replaced them to bring water to

the estate from the lake's edge, and you can see the chopping
blocks and iron hooks in the stone meat house that once
contained the carcasses of sheep slaughtered for the dozens of
staff who were employed here. There's even a general store
that still contains countless everyday items including medicine
bottles, matches, Bex tablets, and even coloured glass balls
filled with powder used for target shooting. There are jigs and
old wooden vices in the carpenter's shop and handmade nails
in the blacksmith's barn. The groomsman's room, used by the
groomer of Keith Bowman's stable of thoroughbred horses, still
has original saddles, side-saddles, polo mallets and clippers.

It has always been a working cattle station, and today
remains one of Australia's finest intact collections of pioneer-
era cottages and outbuildings, including the state's oldest stone
house east of the Murray River that has been converted to
accommodation. The Old Station Hands' cottage, the Overseer's Cottage and the Boundary Rider's Cottage have been
'minimally' upgraded from their original appearance and
are situated around a 'village green' where today a series of
well-placed spotlights create an ethereal glow. There are few
pastoral stations left in Australia that can match this degree of
authenticity.

The stocking of stations like Poltalloch was made possible by
the great cattle drives that originated in the eastern colonies
and filled South Australia with cattle. In 1872, three young
men led by John Conrick left Koroit, a small town north-west
of Warrnambool in Victoria, with 1000 head of cattle, and
brought them all the way to Cooper Creek in South Australia—a 1900-kilometre journey that took eleven months to
complete. Conrick went on to become one of South Australia's great pastoralists, establishing his station, Nappa Merrie,
on the banks of Cooper Creek. He then opened up one of
the great stock routes from Queensland to South Australia,

tracing a line down Strelitzki Creek. Conrick's shorthorn cattle became famous across the country, and his deliberately isolationist approach to establishing his stations in places where civilisation wouldn't reach them for generations to come saw him acquire vast tracts of land. Nappa Merrie (which remained in the Conrick family until 1954) is considered something of a 'model' pastoral station, with its 160-kilometre river frontage on Cooper Creek and today the property covers an area of 7275 square kilometres.

South Australia continued to prosper in the 1870s and 1880s. In 1872, the Overland Telegraph was completed and Port Pirie was surveyed. The University of Adelaide was founded in 1874, and five years later the first bridge across the Murray River was opened. In 1881, Adelaide became the first Australian city to construct a water-born sewerage system, and the following year the nation's first cement was commercially produced. Australia's first telephone trunk line opened between Adelaide and Port Adelaide in 1886.

The future of South Australia seemed robust. What would the 1890s bring?

Three boys with a bullock cart on a steep hill, Walhalla,
Victoria, early 20th century.
Museum of Victoria

4

'MORE ENGLISH THAN ENGLAND'

'How shall we sing the Lord's song in a strange land?'
—Robert Knopwood, cleric and diarist
The Diary of the Reverend Robert Knopwood, 1803–1838

The first glimmer of one of the most fundamental ideas about what it means to be Australian can be traced to Van Diemen's Land in 1805. Its significance was missed by all, and was made possible by, of all things, the ending of the monopoly on the ownership of dogs and hounds. Dogs were more valuable than guns in the hunting of kangaroo, emu and other game, and if a convict possessed a dog he was able to live in the bush without restraint, independent of society. By the end of 1805, a succession of convict absconders had already been noted. The colony's first chaplain, Robert Knopwood, wrote of one particular group of five convicts who returned to Hobart after spending three months living apart from others in what he presciently referred to as 'the bush'.

As dog ownership increased in Van Diemen's Land, so too did the accounts of convicts living away from settlements in the wilds of the island colony. (There were no jails on Van Diemen's Land until the early 1820's.) Without dogs to hunt game, the bush was a death sentence. With dogs, its grassy woodlands— the bush—became a haven. And so it happened. In an historical instant the bush, that unlikeliest of places, transfigured from wilderness to sanctuary, a place of freedom and self-realisation, the ideal so beloved of Henry Lawson and Banjo Paterson. No longer to be feared, it became a crucible which would, in the decades to come, become home to the squatter, the shepherd, the jackaroo, the boundary rider, the overlander, the bushranger and the prospector.

In Knopwood's casual observation, the myth of the Australian bush was loosed.

The first non-Indigenous settlement in Van Diemen's land was at Risdon Cove on the Derwent River in 1803, although its poor soils saw those who settled there move to Sullivan's Cove, the site of present-day Hobart, the following year. At Risdon Cove in 1803 there were nine cows and a bull, and their numbers were slow to increase. By far the largest importation of cattle occurred at the northern settlement of Port Dalrymple on the Tamar River, first explored by George Bass and Matthew Flinders in 1798 and established in December 1804, on orders of the governor of New South Wales Philip King to deter any idea the French might have of beginning a rival settlement. In 1805, 632 out of 910 head of cattle ordered by Governor King from India (the balance having perished on the voyage), travelled up the Tamar on a sailing boat. It had been a costly exercise—£15,600 just to land 632 cattle valued at £25 each! But their importance as a lasting resource to the new settlement couldn't be overestimated, and despite the loss of almost a third of the shipment, the remainder were landed in excellent physical condition.

Within six months every cow was in calf, and their numbers soon recovered. Although precise stock numbers in the north in those early years are problematic at best, by 1816 the number of cattle in the northern settlement had increased to 1956. (From 1804 until 1812, the northern settlement was called Cornwall, and was placed under the jurisdiction of the Scottish soldier and explorer Lieutenant-Governor William Paterson. The southern settlement was named Buckinghamshire, and placed under the command of the British administrator Lieutenant-Governor David Collins. The dividing line ran east–west across the centre of the island at the 42nd parallel.) By 1818, total cattle numbers for the entire colony stood at over 12,300, by 1821 around 35,000 and by 1829 more than 100,000.

Cattle numbers increased so markedly that Edward Curr, who had been appointed manager of the farming corporation of Van Diemen's Land Company in 1824, noted that it was 'by no means uncommon to see a calf sucking a young heifer, at the moment the heifer herself is sucking her own mother'. No doubt a ban in those early years on the slaughtering and export of cattle (with the only documented exception being a Christmas dinner with roast beef for officers in 1806) helped boost numbers, but most agreed it was the climate that was the biggest factor, with cooler days producing better grasses that were more nutritious and without the 'scorching' commonly seen in New South Wales. Healthier and more abundant grasses also produced heavier beasts than those bred on mainland paddocks.

We all think we know the Van Diemen's Land story, a colonial dumping ground for four out of ten of all the convicts who were ever sent to Australia—some 75,000 in total. It was a penal colony, a place of deprivation and hopelessness, its prisoners vile and beyond redemption. By the time the last convict ship, the *St Vincent*, arrived in 1853, the name Van Diemen's Land had a stigma all its own. Yet how different it was in reality.

Rather than a society that harboured convicts, here was a *convict society*. Nowhere else in the empire did prisoners, both

imprisoned and freed, and later via their descendants, consti-
tute such a large percentage of a general population. And if
you were a convict, you hardly could have been dispatched to
a more agreeable destination. The English novelist Anthony
Trollope, after visiting the colony in 1872, wrote: 'Van Diemen's
Land had not a great reputation. It had a name that seemed to
carry a taunt in men's ears. But it was prosperous and fat, and
unless when bushrangers were in the ascendancy, the people
were happy.'

Van Diemen's Land was Eden-like. Oysters and mussels
could be plucked from its salmon- and mackerel-filled waters.
In the east and the north, where the bulk of settlement occurred,
it was believed the land possessed a mostly mild climate, with
few predators and native herbivores that were easy prey for
introduced hunting dogs, despite kangaroo meat often being
in short supply, especially after the relocation to Van Diemen's
Land of hundreds of Norfolk Islanders in 1807–08.

Fresh water was everywhere, rainfall was plentiful, and there
were abundant coastal grasslands. It was a bounty that benefited convict and settler alike. (New South Wales, by contrast,
was founded on far less hospitable shores, on a coastal strip
with poor soils and limited game, with the environment around
Port Jackson considered more an obstacle than a blessing.) The
eating was so good, in fact, that the settler William Williamson wrote in a letter home contrasting what he considered 'our
starving countrymen in England' with Van 'Diemonians' who
would 'grumble excessively if they don't have three fresh joint
meals a day'.

Those who shaped and defined Van Diemen's Land were
not criminals. Criminality here was born out of poverty, a
fact reflected in the colony's low crime rate in the decades
to come when, following the end of their sentences, convicts
demonstrated the petty nature of their 'crimes' by integrating
successfully back into society. Of the 7 per cent or so of convicts
actually sent to Port Arthur, for instance, only 10 per cent of
those returned there a second time. By 1835, there was one

policeman for every 88 people, a gross waste of manpower and a statistic that made Van Diemen's Land one of the world's most heavily policed societies. Far from being a drag on the development of the colony, it was the skills and manpower of assigned convicts, sent mainly to farming properties and left under the 'moral guidance' of their employers, that proved so vital to the prosperity of estates like Woolmers and Brickendon.

The climate of this benevolent land, its flora and fauna, seemed made for the pastoralist. Unlike New South Wales, its predator-free plains saw the exporting of meat, wheat, barley and oats within a decade of settlement. Beyond the walls of penal settlements like Port Arthur and Sarah Island, where only one in ten would remain for the term of their natural lives, convicts became servants, gardeners, labourers—and farmers. The Van Diemen's Land story was not primarily one of convicts and incarceration. It never was. It was always a farmer's story.

The first European sighting of Tasmania was made by the Dutch explorer Abel Tasman in 1642. Tasman named it Anthoonij van Diemenslandt, in honour of the governor of the Dutch East Indies, later shortened by the British to Van Diemen's Land. It remained largely ignored by Europeans until 1803, when the third governor of New South Wales, Philip King, sent the 60-ton brig *Lady Nelson* and whaler *Albion,* together with a small military detachment, there to guard against possible French territorial claims, and to establish a settlement. Also sent were a small number of long-haired Bengal sheep, a Tibetan breed from the Himalayas, despite it being illegal to import the breed for private sale as it violated a British East India Company monopoly. (Interestingly in 1793, John Macarthur purchased 30 Bengal sheep, though the word 'Bengal' never made it into any official records.) Imported mostly for consumption, their presence saw queries sent to London about the merits of the colony being used as a wool-growing region. By September that year, only months after the arrival of John Bowen, the man appointed by New South Wales' Governor Philip King to take command of the new colony, the number of sheep in Van Diemen's Land stood at an optimistic 32.

The first generation of Van Diemen's Land sheep farmers, almost without exception, knew little about farming sheep, the majority of them shearing wool only to discard the fleeces as an inconvenience. Nevertheless, the introduction of sheep to Van Diemen's Land was a seismic economic and cultural turning point—and a blight for the island's natural environment. Everywhere they went, sheep gorged themselves upon the island's native grasses. In an era before fences, it wasn't long before settlers began to notice a decrease in the number of wildflowers, while the best grasses in the lush pastures created by the Aborigines seasonal burning of the bush were ravaged.

Van Diemen's Land seemed well suited to sheep breeding. The climate in the east of the island often allowed sheep to lamb early, and there were few if any natural predators, as opposed to the dingo on the mainland. The Tasmanian tiger, or thylacine, now extinct, was quite slow-moving and not considered a threat. In the absence of predators, shepherding was not the priority it was elsewhere. The large land grants that would, in time, become commonplace made possible the grazing of livestock that were left free to roam, and in the process become very, very fat. With the arrival of the *Calcutta* in 1804, the ship that also brought the island's first convicts, sheep numbers rose to 61, and by late 1805 that had increased to over 700, many having been sent from the penal settlement at Norfolk Island. In 1805, sheep were so scarce that purchasing them was a prohibitive exercise for all but the wealthy, and in the years to come their quality varied enormously across the colony. From 1810 to 1817, however, things began to change. According to figures compiled at the annual muster, numbers were growing at an almost exponential rate, with many settlers only hazarding guesses at the numbers of their flocks, and figures routinely being 'rounded off' to the nearest hundred. It's also likely settlers may have inflated their holdings in order to gain a greater share of supplies from the king's stores. Sheep of all ages and sizes were routinely herded together, which accelerated the breeding process, and lambs were allowed to breed when less than seven months old. As numbers increased, land commissioners, appointed by the Governor George Arthur to survey the colony's newly settled districts and ascribe the land a value, were sometimes aghast at the density of the flocks they saw, squeezed into areas that were much too small to support them, as settlers with limited funds purchased minimal parcels of land and grossly overstocked them.

By 1812, the island colony had more sheep than New South Wales, and the numbers grew fast: 127,800 in 1818; 182,000 in 1820; more than 900,000 by 1836. By 1817 it had half the number of cattle as could be found in all of New South Wales and half as much wheat—six times the productivity of its parent colony—and sheep from Van Diemen's Land were exported to South Australia, Victoria and Western Australia to help establish pastoral industries there. Such impressive growth is extraordinary when one thinks how thinly populated the colony was, and that between 1804 and 1823 a mere 1500 people received land grants. Sheep numbers in particular grew so fast that by the 1830s some pastoralists were beginning to think Van Diemen's Land was close to being 'full', and started casting their eyes north across Bass Strait to the almost empty Port Phillip District, and the promise of new, untouched pastures.

Those first sheep—the Bengal, and a smaller number of Cape sheep—were valued primarily for their meat, which was sold both salted and fresh to government stores. The wool of the Bengal sheep was not even close to the finely bred merinos that would come later, but they were good enough to establish an export trade of sorts. In 1818, 1200 sheep, along with a handful of cows, were sent to the Indian Ocean island of Mauritius, and in 1819 the *Hobart Town Gazette* recorded that a single merchant had personally slaughtered 'no less than 120,000 weight of meat for the consumption of Port Jackson'.

Henry Widowson, an early colonial author, talked down the Bengal breed, describing them as having 'a very large head, Roman nose, slouch ears, extremely narrow in the chest, and a coarse hairy fleece', a fact which made them unsuitable for anything but dinner. Which was fine for all those who needed to eat. The Bengal and the Cape were just two of many breeds present in Van Diemen's Land in the early days, none of which were any more prized than any other, although this didn't stop attempts at crossbreeding in vain attempts to achieve improvements.

The quality of shepherding, too, was poor. In Britain and Scotland the shepherd was a highly regarded and skilled worker, and well-versed in the care and husbandry of sheep. In Van Diemen's Land in the 1820s and 1830s they were, by and large, convicts, employed mostly to deter theft and make sure sheep were contained within the settler's unfenced plains. Those fortunate enough to employ Scottish shepherds saw how they took great care to make sure only the best rams were selected for breeding, and some settlers did, over time, manage to improve their flocks.

If the quality of shepherding was poor, that of the shearer was at times appalling. All but ignorant of even the most basic rules governing the craft, those in the 1820s who bothered with wool at all did it mostly for the comfort and health of the sheep. There were barely any professional shearers to be found in the colony, and the vast majority of farmers simply did the shearing themselves, teaching their servants to shear, and occasionally practising on dead sheep and those about to be slaughtered. An early settler in the Shannon region, James Ross, later reminisced that:

> At that time there was no thought of sending wool to England. If it were not necessary to clip the wool from the sheep annually for the sake of the animal's health, sheep owners at that time would never have troubled themselves to shear the fleece.

In the early 1820s very few settlers knew of anyone who made their living from wool, as another settler, Peter Harrison, noted in his journal:

> Wool is in general greasy and badly managed by settlers . . . it will be some years before the quality of the article will be sufficiently improved to make the middle class of settlers interested in producing a fine fleece, or having their wool in good order.

The climate of Van Diemen's Land, initially considered mild and healthy and conducive to the pursuit of sheep farming, was subject to extreme variability and high rainfall depending upon where you were. Some areas were susceptible to footrot (though footrot remained much less of a problem in Van Diemen's Land than it was in New South Wales), with another meddlesome condition being the island's icy winds—they could blow in from anywhere and at any time, especially on the high plateaus, and after shearing could make make ewes so cold they'd lose their milk, starving their lambs. In November 1817, the *Hobart Town Gazette* reported that one settler found 50 dead sheep on his run the very day after they'd been shorn, victims of an overnight storm that had sent temperatures plummeting.

In 1820, the issuing of land grants continued at a slowish pace, but would soon gather a wave-like momentum. Only 63 land grants totalling over 10,000 acres were made that year, the majority of which were small and made to freed convicts and their families in areas already in the process of being settled, in order to limit the temptation to use isolated lands for stock rustling (and also to minimise any threats from Aborigines and bushrangers). The following year saw an almost five-fold increase in land grants—116 in total covering almost 50,000 acres. In 1823, however, came the record—1027 grants totalling over 440,000 acres. That year the island's population exceeded 10,000 for the first time since European settlement, spreading across the entirety of the island's explored lands, following rivers like the Tamar, the Derwent, the Clyde, the Shannon, the Elizabeth, the Macquarie, and the North and South Esk. By 1823, Hobart Town and Launceston may have still functioned as the island's administrative hubs, but they were no longer its only settlements.

Most settlers were content to locate their grants within the boundaries prescribed by the government, but as with Victoria and New South Wales, some squatters didn't wait for the release of land grants and began finding their way into the island's unchartered interior, a land grab made all the easier as it wouldn't be until 1828 that the formal leasing of Crown land would become the law. Van Diemen's Land was a land of lakes, plateaus, hills and mountains, with few regions outside the eastern third of the colony possessing the sort of extensive plains that would benefit the pastoralist, and it was the island's geography that determined where settlement would occur. As the population increased and areas long illegally occupied by squatters came to the notice of newcomers, the squatters began legitimising their runs by purchasing or leasing their land.

Prior to 1830, there was no concerted attempt to catalogue the number of breeds of cattle in the colony. Lieutenant-Governor Collins wrote that the original arrivals on the banks of the Derwent seemed to be of the Bengal variety, and thought improvements might be made by crossing them with South African Cape bulls. The Yorkshire-born chaplain, missionary and farmer Samuel Marsden, who'd gained an enviable repu-tation as a breeder in New South Wales, sent several cattle to Van Diemen's Land in 1818. In the 1820s, Bengal and various English breeds arrived, including a Devonshire heifer. Normandy and Fifeshire breeds followed, as did the first shipment of Black Angus.

On 20 January 1824, eight Black Angus from Fifeshire in Scotland were unloaded off the decks of the *Troton* and onto the docks at Hobart Town. It was a seminal moment in the island's development. The forerunners of the Aberdeen Angus breed that would develop there over the coming six decades, they were walked to the property of Dennistoun, near Bothwell, owned by Captain Patrick Wood, a retired officer of the East India Army. The genes of those eight cattle are still present in the Dennistoun Angus herd today, and Black Angus now comprise more than 75 per cent of Tasmania's beef industry.

The first shipment of Herefords arrived in May of 1826, courtesy of the London-owned Cressy Company, a large agricultural company that owned a significant portion of the fertile Norfolk Plains. Cressy Company staff arrived along with servants, shepherds and stock, including a number of shorthorn and Hereford cattle, Flemish and Cleveland horses, and some Southdown, Leicester and merino sheep. They took a 20,000-acre grant south of Launceston and within a year had erected 15 kilometres of post-and-rail fencing.

Yet cattle lines often stubbornly failed to improve. One of the reasons for this inferiority was that they'd long been left to wander the interior of the colony unsupervised, a practice that led to widespread interbreeding (and a degree of stock loss). Unfenced cattle also meant a poorer diet as artificial feeding wasn't practicable. A lack of fencing also encouraged rustling, which in turn discouraged new settlers from taking up land. The fact that cattle *could* be left unsupervised had proved both a blessing and a curse. On the one hand fewer hours were spent herding and supervising, but because they required so little supervision as few as two shepherds were generally thought enough to keep an eye on literally hundreds of cattle, a dearth of human contact that made the cattle virtually wild.

Van Diemen's Land cattle also, at least in those first decades, proved awful 'milkers'. Edward Curr wrote that he considered them 'more adapted for slaughter than for the dairy', with the result dairy products in all corners of the colony were in short supply. Visitors would always be surprised if a family they called on had any stocks of milk, butter, cream or cheese. Only properly cultivated fields had any hope of producing grasses with the required nutrients for good dairy, and such fields needed buildings with the proper equipment for storing the milk, and the fields sufficient fencing to keep the cattle contained—the capital requirements for such infrastructure were often well beyond the reach of even the most comfortable settlers. (Where fences were required, an ingenious method was used to set out the fence line. At nightfall, fires were lit at either end of the boundary, then two men holding lanterns would begin to walk towards one another, marking out the ground as they went and always keeping the distant fire and the approaching lantern in line.)

By 1820, there was only one specialised dairy farm in the entire colony, and butter and cheese were every bit as rare a commodity as veal, farmers being so keen to build up stock numbers that fattened calves were rarely slaughtered.

In addition to a want of butter, cheese and veal, there was also a surprising absence of disease in the new colony, a fact that benefited sheep, cattle and settler alike. In fact, Van Diemen's Land was one of the healthiest outposts in all of the British Empire, and there were numerous reasons for this. The particularly long voyage to get there meant infections were often eradicated along the way. Prior to 1816, only one convict ship arrived, further reducing the scope for disease, and a successful smallpox vaccination program was also introduced. There were ample supplies of clean water, and plentiful supplies of meat meant a protein-rich diet for all. Aborigines, too, seemed free of disease except for isolated cases of gonorrhoea and a skin disease that didn't appear to be lethal and may have been linked to canine scabies, a result of the introduced dog. Things would of course change for the Aborigines of Tasmania in the years to come, succumbing to disease when put into detention, and in the Black War from the mid-1820s to 1832, when they were hunted almost to extinction.

◄○►

In 1824, the need to supply cheap wool for British factories led to the establishment of a pastoral and agricultural industry in the colony's underdeveloped north-west. The Van Diemen's Land Company, a British-owned company, was to be created 'remote from settlers', and its chief architect would be the surveyor and the region's foremost explorer, Henry Hellyer.

Hellyer, a courageous and talented man though prone to bouts of melancholy, arrived in Hobart Town in October 1826, and that same month a settlement was established at Circular Head (present-day Stanley), where there was a good harbour and plentiful supplies of fresh water. Within months, over a hundred acres of land at Circular Head had been broken up and put under the plough and crops established including turnips, oats, barley, wheat and potatoes, as well as good supplies of hay from the area's abundant native grasses. The first-ever attempt by Europeans to settle the remote and rugged north-west had begun, bolstered by royal assent to select 250,000 acres and spurred on by a vision to build a wool-growing behemoth on the very edge of empire.

The earliest dwellings in the settlement were simple structures of turf and shingles, and a stables and blacksmith's shop were erected. Circular Head made a good base for further exploration, but when Hellyer, fellow surveyors Joseph Fossey and Clement Lorymer and their associates set out to map new tracts of land they were sorely disappointed. Mosquitos, thick, wet myrtle forests and poor terrain studded with spiky patches of bauera shrubs, steep ravines and giddy precipices hampered their progress. Through it all however, Hellyer ably recorded every detail of their ordeal, and in the process painted a vivid picture of Van Diemen's Land before the arrival of Europeans:

> Large tracts of closely matted scrub, with cutting grass, greatly impede our progress. Fern trees and fern occupy the more open spaces, under the dark spreading branches of the large forest trees . . . A great proportion of the soil here is mixed with slate

and rock; but there are many cultivatable tracts of great extent, with a rich loam of considerable depth: creeks and cascades are to be found in every gully, up to the very summits of the mountains.

The exploring party was caught in a snowstorm while traversing a plateau above the Fury River, and roasted wombats and slept in fields of buttongrass—typical of the sort of obstacles that would have halted the progress of less enterprising men. Either Hellyer or one of those travelling with him, possibly Fossey (the record is unclear), became the first white person to climb to the summit of Cradle Mountain.

Eventually the Van Diemen's Land Company's grant would total 100,000 acres at Cape Grim, over 25,000 acres on various offshore islands, 20,000 acres at the settlement of Circular Head, over 150,000 acres at Surrey Hills (an area which Hellyer had initially thought represented good grazing ground, bounded by creeks and with bountiful shrubs in every vale but had become, in his words, 'a graveyard for sheep'), 10,000 acres on the Middlesex Plains, and a series of long runs paralleling various stock roads.

By the early 1830s, however, it was becoming clear that the climate was far less forgiving than had been hoped for, the stock ill-equipped to survive bone-chilling inland winters, far removed from the colony's more temperate coastlines. To make matters worse, the company had become embroiled in a series of legal entanglements with the authorities in Hobart Town, including a series of seemingly intractable disagreements over the placement of boundaries. There were labour disputes, too, and opposition from squatters who railed against the government for allowing a monopoly over such a large area of the colony.

And then there were the inevitable ongoing bloody clashes between workers and Aborigines. In 1827, three Aborigines were murdered in the wake of the spearing of several sheep and the burning of station huts. In 1828, a shepherd was speared after station workers attempted to abduct some

Aboriginal women, and reprisals led to the infamous massacre of 30 Aborigines by four Van Diemen's Land Company shepherds just days later.

In the end, it was the lack of suitable grazing lands that proved the greatest obstacle to progress, despite a topographical map of the interior extending south all the way to Cradle Mountain being completed, with trails established and the course of the Pipers and Duck rivers successfully and very accurately plotted. The map was an achievement of some magnitude, with the terrain and landforms of the region recorded on paper for the very first time. And it isn't to say no progress had been made. Lands were cleared and cultivated, sheep were grazed, and there were attempts to stock the land with cattle and even breed horses. But the vision of the area becoming a major wool producer was never realised, and by the 1840s most of the company's holdings had either been sold or leased off. A distinctly more 'urban' approach to settlement in the region took hold.

Initial assessments of the north-west region were positive, but incomplete. They would discover the area's long, wet and exceedingly cold winters. The native snow grass was severely lacking in nutrients, and the first few winters saw in excess of 5000 sheep perish from malnutrition and cold. Henry Hellyer could already see what was coming. In 1832, with his vision of a north-east wool empire already in tatters, he committed suicide.

Through all of these pitfalls, however, the quest to produce large flocks and fine wool never ceased. Three hundred merinos from John Macarthur's own flock in New South Wales were shipped from Sydney in 1820 to Hobart Town. Ninety-one perished on the voyage (many were lambs placed in cramped quarters in between decks), but the remaining 209 arrived in relatively good condition and when disembarked on 20 September were distributed—at up to seven guineas each—to those buyers it was thought best equipped to nurture them and improve their fleeces. Over £1330 was raised from the sale, and if there is a date that can be looked back on and viewed as the beginning of a concerted effort to establish a viable wool industry in Van Diemen's Land, 20 September 1820 surely must be it.

Whether or not Macarthur's 209 sheep were, in fact, pure merinos was questioned by some at the time, but what is not in dispute is the tracing of subsequent shipments of pure merinos that arrived from Europe. John Leake, an English-born pastoralist, arrived in Hobart Town in May of 1823 and by 1828 had imported a hundred Saxon sheep which he added to his improved flock of more than 1500 on a 2000-acre property along the Macquarie River at Campbell Town. Merinos from Europe were sourced by other settlers at around the same time, and by the end of the 1820s the foundation had been laid for the fine wools that would replace the coarse fleeces which characterised the colony's early, more experimental, years. The increasing quality of fleeces soon made wool the colony's most important commodity; its felting properties were superior to fleeces from almost every other country, and its soft textures made it particularly sought after by cloth manufacturers.

Importing sheep from Europe was a daunting and time-consuming prospect regardless of how experienced or well-connected you might be, but for one Scottish family, who had already endured the loss four of their six children to tuberculosis, it was a hurdle that perhaps seemed easier to clear than for most. John and Eliza Forlonge were born in Glasgow; he was a wine merchant and she the daughter of a respected teacher. For the sake of their two remaining children they were told it would be advisable to move to a warmer climate. They decided to emigrate to Australia, and in April 1828 applied for a land grant. John counted as a friend the former governor of

New South Wales, Sir Thomas Brisbane, so there never was any doubt as to the success of their application. Before they left, however, they thought it prudent to purchase some sheep.

Aware that the best prices for fine merino wool were being achieved in the German kingdom of Saxony, Eliza took her sons William, fourteen, and Andrew, twelve, and travelled first to Rambouillet in France (the finest merino stud in the country) and then to Leipzig in Saxony, spending days there going by foot from one stud to the other buying a ewe here and a ram there, diligently selecting the finest examples of the breed she could find, while her sons were put to work on local farms where they would gain experience in the art of handling sheep, and in the sorting and stapling of their precious wool.

Using tools to help determine the fineness of the wool, a sheep would be selected, and a collar attached bearing the Forlonge seal. Once all the sheep—90 ewes and seven rams— had been selected, the task of herding them north to the port city of Hamburg began, a 480-kilometre trek that took several weeks, driving the sheep 16 to 18 kilometres every day. Once in Hamburg, the sheep were then put on a ship for the short voyage to Hull, where they were again made to walk, this time 200 kilometres overland to Liverpool where they were loaded aboard the *Clansman* for the passage to Australia. Twenty-two sheep would perish on the long voyage, before the *Clansman* arrived in Hobart Town in November of 1829. William accompanied the sheep on the voyage and despite being underage, the importance of arriving in the fledgling colony with pure-bred sheep outweighed any legal obstacles that might stand in the way. He then successfully petitioned Governor George Arthur for 1500 acres of land near Campbell Town and, what's more, received a promise of an additional 1000 acres if he could arrange the importation of more capital.

John didn't share his wife's passion for their upcoming antipodean adventure, and so stayed behind in Glasgow while Eliza made three visits to Saxony over the years. On her final visit, in 1830, she purchased 130 sheep (including 63 Saxon sheep) for her son Andrew, paying with gold sovereigns that had been sewn into her clothing. Together with the sheep, John, Eliza, Andrew and John's recently widowed sister Janet Templeton and her sons, John and James, sailed from Scotland aboard the brig *Czar*. The *Czar* arrived in Hobart Town in January 1831—54 of the sheep had perished on the way. Andrew disembarked to be with his brother William, while John, Eliza and Janet continued on to Sydney. Janet was granted 2560 acres in the Southern Tablelands of New South Wales and built the two-storey stone farmhouse Kelburn, which still stands today on the Mulwaree Plains near Goulburn.

It's often argued that the Saxon merinos brought to Australia by the Forlonges and Janet Templeton were more influential in the evolution of the Australian merino industry than any other imported examples, including those of John Macarthur, the Hentys and Samuel Marsden, providing much of the foundation stock for the great Tasmanian studs that would follow.

Despite the advances made in wool production in the 1820s, there were many older settlers who refused to 'pamper' their sheep and put the effort into breeding merinos, men who longed for the earlier breeds which bred quickly, were hardy and cost little to maintain. With a single shepherd able to watch over as many as a thousand sheep, is it any wonder many of the older farmers preferred the traditional breeds? Even as late as 1828, land commissioners were noting that 'the lower order of settler considers the merinos a curse to the colony, that they are eternally scabby, require much attention, and that they diminish in size'.

The period from 1810 to 1820 saw the creation of many of the colony's finest stations, though few went on to garner more praise than Woolmers. On 1 January 1817, Thomas Archer— the son of a Hertfordshire miller who'd arrived in Sydney as a clerk in 1812 before becoming head clerk of Port Dalrymple in northern Van Diemen's Land, and later coroner of Cornwall County—took up residence on an 800-acre land grant in the Norfolk Plains awarded him by Governor Macquarie. Blessed by its proximity to the Macquarie and South Esk rivers, he named his new property Woolmers. In 1824, his brother William took charge of an adjoining estate and named it Brickendon, which remains to this day one of the finest examples of an intact colonial farm. Sharing their 100 assigned convicts between them, the Archer brothers were quick to prosper thanks in no small part to their convict labourers and the 'Englishness' of the soil, which was ideally suited to the farming practices they'd brought with them.

In a collection of letters titled *The Journal of a Voyage from Calcutta to Van Diemen's Land*, Augustus Prinsep, an English-born artist and writer, describes entering the estate as being akin to 'driving through a park', bordered by 'hills whose sloping sides were studded with trees' and nurseries filled with 'oaks, ashes, acacias, elms and firs'. The soil was so rich that wattles, which grew to the size of shrubs elsewhere, were the size of trees. The estate's size seemed paltry for all it contained. Flocks of sheep numbered in the thousands, and the view from the main house was a panorama of frolicking mares and colts, wooded hills and sweeping valleys cut by the picturesque Macquarie River.

Thomas lost no time in establishing himself as the region's most influential settler. The construction of Woolmers House was begun in 1819 and was close to being completed when Governor Macquarie paid Thomas a visit in 1821. By 1825, the Archer holdings had increased to almost 8000 acres, swallowing up the neighbouring properties of Cheshunt and Fairfield. One of the features of Woolmers is its fabulous walled garden, a circular formal retreat built for privacy away from the estate's convict workforce, with haphazardly fashioned pathways through a typically English-style cottage garden. The croquet lawn, heritage-listed mulberry tree, even a rare twin 'thunder box' built into the wall are all still there today. The woolshed at Woolmers dates to 1820, making it one of the earliest woolsheds in Australia, alongside Brickendon (mid-1820s) and nearby Panshanger (1821).

Another great estate, Mona Vale, was the dream of pastoralist William Kermode. Kermode arrived in Van Diemen's Land in 1823 and was elected director of the Sydney and Van Diemen's Land Packet Company. By 1825, he owned 5000 acres on the Salt Pan Plains near the present-day town of Ross. One of the most progressive settlers of his time, Kermode continually improved and cultivated his flock of Saxon sheep, establishing his own stud in 1829, and even becoming something of a pioneer in water conservation when he dammed two poor-flowing streams on the Salt Pan Plains and devised a system of irrigation that turned once useless land into green pastures.

Kermode, Archer and others like them, mostly emigrants of modest means, would go on to become part of the 'Midlands Gentry'—families who acquired land grants prior to 1831 when there were still sizeable amounts of land to be had. The fortunes of these retired officers, merchants, yeoman and a smattering of former convicts rose or fell depending on all of the usual vagaries of life: a penchant or otherwise for alcohol or hard work, starting a family, the ability to properly handle finances, or simply good luck. Some families failed to prosper and disappeared into history, their hopes dashed by common misconceptions about breeding, such as the idea that good meat and fine wool can come from the same beast, an idea that would be discarded in time. Other more enlightened breeders concentrated only on the fleece, and built dynasties.

In 1828, George Hobler, a farmer from Hertfordshire who arrived in Van Diemen's Land in 1826 with just two stud merinos (another eight died en route) amassed a flock of almost 300 ewes in just two years. Hobler, however, took a different path to many other Van Diemen's Land pastoralists, deciding better opportunities awaited him in New South Wales than the Port Phillip District. In 1836, he leased and later purchased a 1450-acre property near Maitland for £5000, which included a small but comfortable cottage. In 1838, now openly acknowl-edged as the colony's finest breeder of Hereford cattle, Hobler began construction of a grand sandstone mansion, a house that would, in time, become one of the colony's finest examples of Greek Revival architecture. Sadly, drought and depression ravaged his finances. Declared a bankrupt in 1843, the house passed into the care of a trust company until purchased in 1853 by William Nicholson, a local innkeeper and businessman. The house, Aberglasslyn, was finally completed in 1858, and today remains in private hands.

Insolvency, however, wouldn't be enough to stop the indom-itable George Hobler. In 1844, he became a squatter, and moved ever-further westward in search of land. He moved first to Goulburn and then to the Murrumbidgee district and, with help from a financial acquaintance, took possession of an unl-icensed run west of the Murrumbidgee River near its junction with the Lachlan. The station, which Hobler named Paika, was well outside the prescribed squatting districts, and when the land Paika was on was gazetted in 1847 as the Lower Darling district, he was outbid for the property and was again landless. Hobler sailed for California in 1851, made a living out of pro-specting and trapping, and died in 1882.

Rural Van Diemen's Land was a male-dominated world. Ninety-six per cent of those granted leases were male, a lop-sided approach explained by two overriding, and erroneous, principles: the common law opinion that any property a woman might have would pass to her husband upon marriage, and because it was thought women were incapable of cultivat-ing the land and thus would not be in a position to add to the wealth and resources of the colony. And so the situation may well have remained, were it not for the indomitable efforts of Eliza Walsh, who argued no law forbade women from 'making use of their money for the benefit of the colony'. In 1827 the government agreed, saying women could no longer be denied land grants providing they met the same requirements as men.

Success as a pastoralist in Van Diemen's Land seems to have hinged on whether or not one had a prior tenure as a public servant. Governor Macquarie thought civil officers were poorly paid, and thus considered it reasonable that they be rewarded in other ways, a favourable nod that saw civil officers—magistrates, surgeons, constables, former military men and so on—to go on to become some of the largest landowners in the colony, albeit with little experience in making a living off the land. Of the 1500 settlers granted land up until 1823, just 21 were recorded as having any prior experience on the land. And farming experience in England was no guarantee of success. Often areas were selected injudiciously in low-lying marshy areas that were poorly drained and with unprofitable soils.

And yet there was a certain 'Englishness' about the land. Certainly the weather was bleaker, wetter, more akin to Britain than to New South Wales, with some describing the landscape, too, as not unlike an English gentleman's estate, with rolling hills sprinkled with green pockets of tall, healthy trees. When the colonists began to build their towns they even gave them English names—Oatlands, Richmond, Launceston and Cambridge. The rivers, too, were named after meandering waterways back home such as the Derwent and the Tamar. Settlers farmed using British methods, and organised cricket matches. In Van Diemen's Land, and indeed on the mainland, associations known as 'acclimatisation societies' were being formed to do what they could to transplant England in the Antipodes.

Throughout the nineteenth century, these collectives of essentially homesick Britons flourished across Australia. Members did all they could to anglicise the landscape including introducing deer, pheasants, partridges, skylarks and bullfinches. By the time the English author Anthony Trollope visited in 1872 it was hard to tell motherland from colony. 'Everything in Tasmania', he wrote, 'is more English than England'.

◄O►

In Van Diemen's land, as across the country, the most active time on any sheep station was shearing time, when the squatter could at last gauge the success or otherwise of a year's work. Timing was crucial, and varied due to a number of factors such as lambing and the dropping of grass seeds in spring. As a result, shearers moved around from region to region as weather and lambing seasons dictated.

In the early days, shearing wasn't the specialised skill it would later become—every station hand, even itinerant labourers, was expected to shear. Fleeces were simply laid over drays for transport to town or, if one could afford it, tied into bales. A full bale could contain anywhere from 80 to 100 fleeces.

But when shearing achieved the status of 'specialised skill', two distinct schools emerged: the Sydneys and the Derwenters. The Derwenters crossed Bass Strait to the mainland every season, wore tall hats and carried kangaroo-skin knapsacks. They sheared between 60 and 80 sheep a day compared to the Sydneys' 100-plus, but were bound by a sense of brotherhood that would see all of them down their tools should even one member of either school be treated unfairly. Looked down upon by squatters for their drunkenness and foul language, what their employers feared most of all was their solidarity, and the chance that they could, at any time, put down their shears over some perceived slight and bring the industry to a screeching halt.

The importance the British government traditionally placed on agriculture and the raising of crops never really worked in a land where the grasslands offered so much. Few settlers spent any time growing crops beyond those to feed their own families, and agriculturalists were generally seen as poor cousins to the 'shepherd princes'. Which is not to say the colony was bereft of foodstuffs. As one settler told the *Sydney Gazette* in 1819: 'The want of maize . . . is made amends for in the luxuriant growth of the potato and the pea and bean . . . apples and pears attain a fine size and flavour, a variety of plums come forward to the desert, the grapes are beautiful and delicious, the walnut flourishes . . .' In fact every crop that was known to grow well in Britain proved successful in the Van Diemen's Land soils. Most vegetables and fruit grown, however, were for private consumption.

The exception was wheat. Van Diemen's Land was self-sufficient in wheat early on, a not inconsiderable feat. Its soils were so forgiving they produced up to 2.35 tonnes per acre even in the absence of manuring, crop rotation and land clearing. Agriculturalists seemed to make few if any improvements to the lands they owned, and farms were rarely if ever enclosed or subdivided, facts not lost on Edward Curr who lamented, 'The beautiful appearance of a hedge is unknown in Van Diemen's Land'. Even so, the colony continued year after year to grow more wheat than its inhabitants could consume.

By 1840, Hobart Town, which, like Sydney, began as a garrison, had become a thriving centre of trade and commerce. Ships were crowding its harbour, filled with goods from across the empire. And not just the empire, but from mainland Austra-lia as well. Squatters from New South Wales and Victoria had been moving into western Victoria's Gippsland squatting district, keen to take advantage of an emerging beef trade with the island colony. Pastoralists in the Port Phillip and Portland districts had been dissuaded from exporting meat to Van Diemen's Land after disputes with the Legislative Council over supposed meat quality. At the same time the convict popula-tion of Van Diemen's Land was steadily increasing, thanks to a decision to cease transferring convicts from Van Diemen's Land to New South Wales.

The convict population was going up. By 1840, there were 17,700 in Van Diemen's Land, representing 35 per cent of the island's population. By 1847, that number had increased to almost 25,000. Not only did they need to be accommodated, they also needed to be fed. Normally this would not be such a problem, as convicts were largely assigned to settlers who would in turn feed them. But an economic downturn in the early 1840s meant settlers had little need for convicts, and so it was increasingly becoming the government's responsibility to provide for them. A new market suddenly emerged, and across the waters of Bass Strait in the Port Phillip District, opportunistic squatters began to smell a profit.

Squatters in the fertile grasslands of Gippsland saw an opportunity to export meat to Van Diemen's Land and grabbed it with both hands, and by the 1840s the export trade south across the strait was again becoming well established. One of Gippsland's earliest squatters, Patrick Buckley, kept a journal detailing his transactions with the island colony. Buckley had arrived in New South Wales in 1818 and by 1831 was managing the 12,000-acre Wullwye Station on the Snowy River (now sadly abandoned and in a derelict state). In 1842, Buckley visited the region known then as 'Gipps Land' and began to search out land for a cattle station of his own. He found land on Merriman's Creek close to the present-day town of Seaspray, and established two substantial runs: Coady Vale (53,760 acres) in 1843, and Tarra Creek (23,020 acres) in 1844. Buckley took his first cattle to Hobart Town in May of 1844.

This era of trade with Van Diemen's Land is an oft-neglected part of the history of the two colonies, and yet the demand for meat by the island colony, it can be argued, was a primary impetus behind the settling of the Gippsland region. The first two shipments of cattle from Gippsland were made on the schooner *Water Witch* in June and August of 1842. The cargo landed in an economy a long way from self-sufficiency, a fact acknowledged by the Van Diemen's Land government which had long been running advertisements for tenders covering a vast array of private sector goods.

◄O►

In the late 1840s, pastoralists in Van Diemen's Land could apply for ten-year leases on parcels of land from 500 to 5000 acres, renewed annually, with no limits on the number of leases. But a pastoral lease issued to a squatter did not convey any right to ownership, nor really even of possession, which is what leases normally guarantee. All a pastoral lease permitted, here and on the mainland, was to allow one the right to pasture livestock. A lease was little more than a temporary right to *occupation*, a right that could be taken away without notice if the government decided the land was suddenly required for other purposes. It was a precarious position, and no one knew this more acutely than the squatter himself. But with large returns from wool being made with only minimal expenditure, it was an insecurity worth living with.

The concept of ten-year leases, however, lacked vision, favouring existing pastoralists at the expense of new, landless applicants who had to provide character references to the surveyor-general just to be considered. By 1848, the average estate size of an established pastoralist was over 3000 acres, and by 1856 most of the best land was already in the hands of a new Tasmanian gentry who in many cases occupied the land unlawfully while still managing to achieve the status of 'respectable citizen' after rising above their own humble beginnings, living in simple huts and surviving on whatever they could hunt or trap.

From 1857 to 1875, while the rest of Australia thrived, Tasmania endured a prolonged economic depression as the colony transitioned from a penal colony to a self-governing, free-market economy. The causes of the depression were argued about constantly in town halls and hotel bars. Some blamed a fall in wool prices after the worldwide financial crisis of 1857, others a loss of labour to the gold fields of Victoria and a general decline in the population. Yet others blamed the poor quality of education for the colony's rural young people. Some blamed merchants for leaving the island to chase profits in Marvellous Melbourne, while others viewed an increase in duties for exported goods a decade earlier, introduced by the government in the 1840s to counteract a fall in revenue, as the start of the rot. Whatever the reason, signs of an economic recovery weren't felt until 1872, with an upturn in production, wages and demand likely triggered by the arrival of steamships, the expansion of the rail network and the electrification of the telegraph.

And how did the pastoral industry fare in all this? Not too well. Sheep numbers declined from about 180,000 in 1850 to around 130,000 in 1871. Scab also intervened in the 1860s to keep sheep numbers low, and part of the eventual recovery in flocks was as much a result of mandatory sheep dipping and the controlling of sheep movements which limited the spread of the disease as it was from a gradual but sustained rise in the price of wool. The 1870s heralded a dramatic increase in the quantity and quality of exported wool, and the value of breeding stock for the mainland colonies also rose. Pastoralists aside, the island's economy began diversifying as old industries made way for a raft of new entrepreneurs who were growing fruit and making jams, and also planting potatoes and hops.

In 1858, the Waste Lands Act was the first in a series of Acts spanning twenty years designed to stimulate the economy by allowing farmers to buy land on credit. Unlike Victoria and New South Wales, in Tasmania every European born there had a *right* to land regardless of class or background. On 8 June 1857, the *Mercury* newspaper editorialised the 'equality of right in all to cultivate land for their own advantage', and that 'the lands belong to the people'. No system of allocating land, it said, would be legitimate unless it met the reasonable expectations of the working class. With land becoming scarce, the *Waste Lands Act 1870* marked the first attempt to contain the practice of squatting by introducing penalties of up to £50 for the illegal running of cattle or sheep on Crown land. Bailiffs were employed to prevent 'intrusion, encroachment and trespass' and to recover lands, and impose or recover rent or licence fees. The wealthy elite were still holding sway in a colony that was set up to coddle their interests from the very beginning when, in 1820, government policies were deliberately crafted to uphold and further a privileged gentry.

By the close of the 1870s, more than ninety of Tasmania's 100 wealthiest rural estates were still owned by families that purchased their land prior to 1832, and the island's pastoralists so effectively controlled the colony's non-wilderness areas that prospective squatters had little choice other than to cross the waters of Bass Strait and try their luck in Victoria. The colony's rural elite also had an unfortunate degree of influence when it came to the island's precious endemic fauna, in particular the now-extinct thylacine, the Tasmanian tiger.

In the 1880s, in an effort to increase their already considerable influence, a group of wealthy Crown land settlers decided, without any evidence to support their claim, that if it weren't for the presence of the thylacine the colony would have 700,000 more sheep than it did, and a petition was sent to the Tasmanian government demanding a levy be placed on the lands within their boundaries to provide funds to eradicate the animal. The petition failed, but the move to kill off the thylacine continued, and in 1887 an annual sum of £500 was legislated to provide a bounty of £1 for every (deceased) adult thylacine, and ten shillings for every pup. The bounty continued until it was suspended in 1909, and although the thylacine survived until 1936, twenty years of culling made its extinction all but inevitable.

The days of the thylacine may have been numbered, but better times were coming for this soon-to-be diversified island colony, thanks to a renewed and invigorated prosperity that had nothing to do with either the soft touch of fleece or the meat of cattle, but of the bright, shining glare of tin.

Two men outside slab huts surrounded by forest, Victoria, 1909.
Frank Ernest Allen, State Library Victoria

5

'THE FINEST PARK LAND I EVER SAW . . .'

'I stuck a plough into the ground, struck a she-oak root, and broke the point; cleaned my gun, shot a kangaroo, mended the bellows, blew the forge fire, straightened the plough . . . and turned the first sod in Victoria.'

—Edward Henty, pioneer and pastoralist

In 1834, Edward Henty and his brother Stephen became the first Europeans to settle, illegally, the virtually unknown area around Portland Bay in what was then called the Port Phillip District. They had arrived in Western Australia two years earlier with their father Thomas but after constant disasters they had abandoned their 84,000-acre Swan River property and sailed to Van Diemen's Land, only to arrive there too late to take advantage of its productive, freehold lands, all of which had already been sold. Packing up again they boarded their family-owned brigantine schooner the *Thistle* and arrived in Portland Bay in 1834, complete with bullocks, cows, pigs and baskets of flour and tobacco. If settlers were getting away with squatting beyond the reach of the law in the heavily settled colony of New South Wales, imagine what could be gained for yourself in far away Portland Bay!

The Henty family were in the Portland Bay area for six years before they came to the notice of the New South Wales surveyor-general in 1840, after the soon-to-be colony of Victoria began being subdivided into districts, and commissioners were appointed to legitimise their graziers by issuing licences. Their presence there had not been wholly unknown, however. In September 1834, a grazier near Campbell Town in central Van Diemen's Land wrote to Governor Arthur Phillip in Hobart: 'It has become known to me that a party has it in contemplation to take possession of a tract of country at Portland Bay, independent of His Majesty's Government, by virtue of a treaty with the natives'. Although the dating of this letter seems odd considering Edward Henty's own diary doesn't reference first negotiating with Aborigines until two months later in December, there seems little doubt that in the absence of government support, the invincible Henty family had decided to create a treaty of their own.

The Hentys have long been considered Victoria's first squatters. They established their farm and a little more than two years later began a whaling station at Portland Bay. When the surveyor and explorer Thomas Mitchell, to his utter surprise, encountered the family on 29 August 1836 while on his exploration of western Victoria, he suggested they move their station north to the fertile, lush pastures he'd seen around the Wannon River, a region he called *Australia Felix*, Latin for 'fortunate Australia'. The Hentys heeded his advice, and after gathering their flocks and herds set out towards Merino Downs, which they reached on 3 August 1837.

The family prospered from Mitchell's advice, increasing their stock to 30,000 sheep and 500 head of cattle in just three years. (The ruts made by Thomas Mitchell's drays in the soft untrammelled soils of western Victoria remained visible long after he was gone, and became known as the 'Major's Line', there to guide future overlanders into one of the finest pastoral regions in the country.) The homestead they built at Merino Downs has long since been demolished but many of its build-ings have survived, including the woolshed with its roof of split timber shingles, the brick coach house, stables and blacksmith's shop, plus a substantial portion of the original garden.

The Henty brothers were also instrumental in opening up a new road from the plains to Portland. Described in a report by the *Portland Guardian and Normanby General Advertiser* on 31 December 1842 as 'new and good', it cut the number of days it took a dray to make the journey from Portland to the plains or vice versa from six to just three. It was 'a thousand percent better than the old road', the report said. At the end of one particular journey 'the ropes that secured the bales of wool were as tight as if just fastened, and the loads on the three drays discovered as smooth and unruffled an appearance as though they were commencing the journey and not finishing it'.

The *Portland Guardian* not only gave considerable edito-rial space to the new road, but was also determined for the Portland District colony to know who was responsible for it, a road which, the paper rightly claimed, was due solely to 'the intelligence, time, labour, and hazard of person and property of the Messrs. Henty have laid open to their enterprising fellow colonists'. The Reverend J.Y. Wilson, the Anglican chaplain of Melbourne who frequently visited families on the Plains, also thought the road far superior to anything that had come before, but had a word of warning. 'The inhabitants', he said, 'must be prompt in widening it otherwise it will soon become, by constant traffic, nearly as bad as the old one'.

The Hentys were the vanguard of an initial wave of pioneers who began filtering into the unknown Port Phillip District. This pastoral incursion was rapid—and violent. Within fifteen years of those first arrivals, 80 per cent of Victoria's Aboriginal population had been killed, either by disease or with a bullet. The elimination of Tasmania's original inhabitants has often been spoken of as an act of genocide, yet somehow that same language is rarely applied to the other colonies.

Victoria was settled by pastoralists who were more than adept in the act of colonising. They were better resourced, came in greater numbers—primarily from the colonies of New South Wales and Tasmania—and were more experienced at dealing with Aboriginal resistance. Thousands of killings are recorded to have occurred in western Victoria and in the Gippsland region between 1836 and 1853, and countless thousands more beyond the reach of prying eyes.

The Port Phillip District, like South Australia, prided itself on the fact it was not a penal colony. Unlike New South Wales and Van Diemen's Land, it never wanted or felt it needed the labours of the convict 'stain'. Opened up in the 1830s when emigration schemes were in full swing, it was thought there was much to be gained by distancing itself from the crime and corruption that were the mark of the convict colonies. This is not to say, however, that there were not convicts present. As private pastoralists and other agricultural interests moved to Melbourne from New South Wales and Van Diemen's Land they brought with them their 'assigned servants', a polite term for convict that was often used by emancipists and others who were keen to distance themselves from all of the connotations that came with the word in pursuit of the more agreeable notion of 'master and servant'. There were also convicts with their ticket of leave, and convicts sent down from Sydney to work on road gangs and various construction sites.

The birth of Melbourne predated the town's official founding by Governor Richard Bourke, which took place on 19 May 1837. Surveyor Charles Grimes, part of an expedition dispatched by Governor King to explore and map Port Phillip, first set foot on the site of the future Victorian capital on 4 February 1803, with the expedition's gardener, James Flemming, noting it as a 'most eligible place for a settlement because of the availability of fresh water'. Despite this early interest it wasn't until until 6 June 1835 that John Batman, one of a number of Van Diemen's Land businessmen and pastoralists who came in search of good grazing lands, sat down with eight elders of the Wurundjeri clan, and purchased the 600,000 acres that today comprises much of suburban Melbourne. (Though often portrayed as a humanitarian in regards to Aborigines, Batman's pivotal role in the establishment of the infamous 'roving party' in Tasmania in 1829 led to the formation of hunting parties and the deaths of countless Indigenous peoples.) It's not clear precisely on what river Batman described as a 'lovely stream' the signing took place, but we do know from his diary entry that two days later he travelled 'six miles up river' and then declared, upon reaching a point where he considered the water deep enough: 'This will be the place for a village'. And Melbourne was born.

A report Batman wrote upon his return to Launceston fuelled growing curiosity in Victoria's seldom-visited coastline, a curiosity which eventually resulted in John Pascoe Fawkner's determination to establish a settlement there. Fawkner was an interesting character: a publican, builder, timber-merchant, auctioneer and newspaper-owner. Fawkner came to Australia in 1803 as a ten-year-old with his convict father, his mother and sister Elizabeth, settling first in the ill-fated colony at Sullivan Bay, and then Hobart. His father, through hard work and dedication, lived the life of a typical settler, and by 1806 the family was working a 50-acre plot just 11 kilometres from the centre of Hobart Town, running cows and sheep and even growing wheat, reaping just over 4000 tonnes within two years of planting. With new business opportunities often taking his father to Hobart, John, now a teenager, would work the farm, tilling the soil without horses, with barely any money, and almost no implements save for a hoe and spade. In his father's absence, John was also tasked with shepherding their livestock and for weeks on end would live alone in a sod hut. Nevertheless, their livestock increased in number, and when Governor Lachlan Macquarie visited the colony in 1811 the young John was granted his own 50-acre plot, which ran alongside his father's farm.

In 1814, he took charge of a Hobart bakery his father had built up, but in 1819 moved north to Launceston where he established his own. In 1826, he received a licence to operate the two-storied, 23-room Cornwall Hotel, which he built himself two years earlier. The young John Fawkner was now in his early thirties. He was not only adept at raising livestock and growing wheat, but good at growing businesses too. In 1828 he established the *Launceston Advertiser* and was its editor for two years. He was now a self-made man.

Intrigued by the accounts John Batman had brought back with him from Victoria, Fawkner purchased the schooner *Enterprize* in April 1835, eager to set sail on his own voyage of discovery. But a combination of debts and poor weather combined to delay his departure, and the *Enterprize* set sail without him, arriving in Port Phillip Bay on 16 August 1835.

This initial sailing of the *Enterprize* was significant despite Fawkner's absence. After searching for a site in present-day Western Port Bay (Western Port was the term then used in Sydney to describe pretty much all of what is now Victoria) as well as along the eastern shoreline of Port Phillip, the ship's captain, John Lancey, sailed the *Enterprize* up the Yarra River to the Yarra Falls, not far from presentday Queens Bridge, a deformation that effectively held back the tide and was able to provide access to fresh drinking water. On 30 August, he moored his schooner close to the foot of the hill where the Customs House is today. He discharged his cargo, constructed a storehouse to keep it in, and began clearing a 5-acre parcel of land for the planting of wheat and vegetables. A week later Lancey set sail back to Van Diemen's Land, leaving behind a party of five to tend the soils he'd planted.

In mid-October, John Fawkner finally arrived on the *Enterprize*'s second sailing, bringing flour, bricks, timber palings, nails, books, pottery, furniture including chairs, tables and cupboards, clothing, butter, meat, tea, horses, cows and alcohol.

He lost no time in transforming a two-room sod hut at the corner of what would one day be William Street and Flinders Lane: with a new roof, it opened on 7 November 1835 as the settlement's first hotel. The expansion of Melbourne had begun.

By January 1836, more than a hundred Van Diemen's Land settlers followed in Batman's and Fawkner's footsteps, bringing with them 1750 sheep and more than 50 cattle. In spite of Governor Bourke's proclamation on 26 August 1835 that all who arrived at this new settlement would be considered trespassers, by 1 June 1836 there were almost 180 residents— and 26,500 sheep! Although they mostly occupied land along the banks of the Maribyrnong River, an initial settlement at Melbourne, called Bearbrass, was well and truly established, even if it did only comprise three weatherboard buildings with a dozen or so slab and turf huts.

Together, John Batman and John Fawkner kick-started the settlement of Melbourne and the settling of Aboriginal lands that would flow from it. They laid the foundations for the flood of people that came across Bass Strait from Van Diemen's Land, where good arable land was in short supply, to try their luck in a new settlement.

John Batman settled on 'Batman Hill' at the western end of present-day Collins Street, in a mud hut 6 metres by 3.6 metres, its chimneys made with Van Diemen's Land bricks, and large enough to accommodate more than a dozen people. He never lived long enough, though, to witness the growth of the city, dying in 1839.

Fawkner, at least, lived long enough to see the potential of that initial site on the banks of the Yarra River begin to be realised. He went on to become a town counsellor, was elected to the Victorian Legislative Council in 1851, and was elected to the first parliament of a self-governing colony of Victoria in 1856.

From 1839 to 1841, 1100 British settlers arrived in the district, and an acre of land within 8 kilometres of the town centre was already costing in excess of £10. People who couldn't afford such prices began to look elsewhere, and beyond the limits of the burgeoning city, life was hard. Squatters who had left town life behind between 1839 and 1841 and moved out into rural areas were hit by the downturn in wool prices in 1840 and incurred heavy losses, forced to live on credit at exorbitant interest rates. Land sales nearly ceased, and that revenue disappeared. Immigration to the colony ceased in 1842 when the government withdrew its land subsidy, which hit speculators and quashed their subdivisions. Between 1842 and 1845, almost a third of the colony's businesses became insolvent. One dispossessed squatter, George Russell, who'd arrived from Van Diemen's Land in 1836 with 3000 head of sheep, wrote in 1843: 'There is no money, no credit, no trade; nothing but failures . . . land is worthless and cattle and sheep little better'. In time, conditions improved and the pastoral industry recovered. Immigration from Britain may have ceased, but thousands came from Van Diemen's Land and New South Wales. By 1848, 50,000 people were living in the new colony.

Squatters first began to move into the Wimmera district in 1844. Bounded by the Grampians to the south and the Murray River in the north, they were buoyed by the overly optimistic assessment of the area written by Thomas Mitchell, who had passed through it eight years earlier in the wake of unseasonal rains which had filled its rivers, greened its pastures, and given the false impression it was a fertile land. It would indeed become part of the great Australian wheat belt, but a lot of sweat and toil would be expended upon its scrubby, fickle plains before those days would come.

Within just a few years of settlement, the Wimmera had 69 sheep runs, but the squatters there not only had to deal with greater uncertainty in terms of water supply and grass than elsewhere in the colony, the local Aborigines proved particularly troublesome too, rounding up sheep and driving them into their camps where they'd break their legs and keep them for food. By 1845, squatters were forced to hire additional boundary riders to protect their flocks, and requests were made to Governor La Trobe for troops, which were dutifully sent. Inevitably, there was violence. Small-scale clashes resulted in the killing of Aborigines, and one of their leaders, Yanem Goona, was captured, tried in Melbourne—where he was found to be 'without education, intelligence, or knowledge of society'—and put on a transport to Van Diemen's Land. Over the years many of the original Wimmera runs were either sold off or subdivided. By the early 1880s only 23 remained. Droughts, dust-storms, rabbit plagues—all had taken their toll.

In the late 1830s and early 1840s, pastoral squatters from Van Diemen's Land and beyond were plying the waters of Bass Strait in increasing numbers to 'clandestinely' settle the Port Phillip District of New South Wales. Among them were two of Australia's truly great pioneers—Anne Drysdale and Caroline Newcomb, the so-called Lady Squatters.

Caroline was born in London in 1812, the daughter of Samuel Newcomb, Britain's commissioner to Spain, and migrated to Van Diemen's Land in 1833 after the death of her father and on the advice of doctors. As governess to John Batman's children, she travelled with the family to Port Phillip in 1836. The following year she moved to Geelong and became acquainted with Dr Alexander Thompson, who came to Australia from Scotland as a surgeon on a convict transport more than once, finally settling in the Geelong district in 1836, becoming one of the region's early pastoral leaders. It is said he was the first man to drive a team of bullocks from Geelong to Melbourne. He was also the first in Geelong to establish regular Presbyterian church services, and vehemently opposed the use of convict labour.

Anne Drysdale was born in 1792 in Fife, Scotland, the daughter of a town clerk. After working in Scotland for much of her life on a farm she leased herself, she left for Port Phillip—again, like Caroline, on the advice of her doctor—arriving there in March 1840. One of just four people in cabin class, she disembarked with a single-minded determination to become a sheep farmer. Well-educated, cultured, strong-willed and financially independent, Anne travelled to the Geelong district where she held a licence on 10,000 acres in between the Barwon River and Point Henry. She constructed a modest house at Boronggoop, and it wasn't long after that she and the much younger Caroline first met. Anne liked Caroline so much she invited her to move in to her house at Boronggoop, an offer which Caroline gratefully accepted.

An unlikely partnership was forged. Whether or not the two were also intimate, which has long been suggested, can never be proven. No outward displays of affection were ever witnessed, and even though they admitted to sharing a bed this was not of itself unusual due to the often cramped conditions many were forced by circumstance to live in at the time. What cannot be denied is the respect and enduring friendship the two shared, as is seen in the following extract from Anne's own diary:

> Miss Newcomb, who is my partner, I hope, for life, is the best and most clever person I have ever met with. There seems to be magic in her touch, everything she does is done so well and so quickly.

Anne and Caroline did not fit the usual images and stereotypes of colonial women. The pastoral empire the two women built up was done by appropriating unproductive land and making it productive. On a personal level, both 'dared' to live independently of men. In 1849, they moved out of their cramped timber cottage and into Coriyule, a grand Gothic-style stone mansion on the Bellarine Peninsula that reflected Anne's own cultural beginnings and also was reflective of their success, with six bedrooms, two parlours (one of which had a piano) and a waiting area. By this time they had amassed over 1000 acres, all of which Anne owned and managed. Their time there together, though, was cut short when Anne died of a stroke in 1853. Caroline, though beset with grief, continued to maintain the lovely garden they had created at Coriyule, opening it in the summers for events and exhibitions, and also ran the business and was involved in various local, political and religious affairs. Defying convention and to the surprise of many, Caroline would later marry a younger man, the Reverend James Davy Dodgson, travelling with him throughout the colony of Victoria until her own death in 1873.

For many emigrants, the Port Phillip District was everything they'd hoped for, and more. Thirty-five year old Niel Black was a tenant farmer in Argyllshire, Scotland, who set sail from the Clyde in April 1839, tasked with purchasing pastoral properties for a business consortium. After cooling his heels in Melbourne, attending to various personal matters, he purchased a horse (an exceptional horse, by all accounts, as he was a large man and needed a horse of similar stature), turned the reins to head westward, and galloped off towards his destiny with nothing else but a compass, a tether, some matches, a spare shirt, two pistols and a pair of stockings.

Black was a striking figure who wore a black top hat and black-tailed coat and must have struck those who saw him as the epitome of the gentleman citizen. He looked nothing like the typical squatter, described by Edward Curr as dressed in 'blue serge suits with cabbage tree hats', and 'belts supporting leather tobacco pouches'. As he headed into the unknown, the anxieties Black felt in those final frustrating days in Melbourne gave way to elation. He was overwhelmed by the broad horizons that seemed to swallow him. 'I traversed plains thousands of acres in extent', he wrote, 'and as level as a billiard table without almost a tree. If distance lends enchantment to view, I had it in perfection'. He rode out to the Barwon River and observed 'miserable huts' lived in by young graziers who 'eat damper and drink tea three times a day', and neat cottages with shingled roofs, timber floors and healthy gardens.

Black returned to Melbourne for a short time, and while there became dismayed at what he considered its descent into moral decay. His accounts of daily commercial life were peppered with observations that otherwise good people were prepared to cut corners to further their own schemes and enterprises. No longer could anybody, he wrote, be believed when it came to money. False bidding at livestock auctions tricked buyers into paying inflated prices for stock. Settler competed with settler to be the greater cheat. There was, he concluded, 'no such thing as a market price for anything'.

On 17 December 1839, Black set off again, this time riding further west into the Portland Bay District. He had studied up on sheep runs, and learned what he could about diseases, risk and the carrying capacity of land. And this time he didn't ride alone. Accompanying him was a young Scottish grazier, John Riddell, who in later years would buy his own stock and depasturing licence at Mount Macedon and in 1860 became a member of the state's Legislative Assembly. As they rode westward they passed over grass so luxuriant, Black noted it seemed to 'drag back the horses hooves like snow'.

When the two men arrived at the property of Strathdownie, at Mount Emu Creek near Terang, they were enraptured by what they saw. 'More beautiful than the finest park land I ever saw at home', Black wrote, with grass so high it reached the saddle of his horse. Although the condition of the stock he found there was far poorer than he was led to believe, Black nevertheless purchased the stock and rights to Strathdownie, and renamed it Glenormiston. The lands the station encompassed were enormous—43,520 acres—and after returning to Melbourne, Black negotiated a price with its owners of 23 shillings per sheep (including unborn lambs).

After stocking the property with his own labourers, Black joined in the harvesting of its food and tobacco and took a leading role in fighting scrub and bushfires and generally boosting the morale of his men. Movable hurdles were built to create yards that could be shifted each night to allow the sheep fresh grass to lay on. At sunrise his shepherds would take breakfast, boil up some tea, grab some damper and beef slices and spend the rest of the day following their flocks. In December 1840, Black noted in his journal that the condition of his ewes had vastly improved, and numbers were increasing. Twenty-seven sheep had been taken by Aborigines, 133 had been slaughtered to provide food, while 81 had perished either from disease or from the methods used to treat it. Sheep were being washed in a soaking pen by a stream that flowed into Lake Terang.

Black proved to be a skilled squatter and pastoralist, surviving droughts and disease and going on to become possibly the Port Phillip District's most successful stock breeder in the second half of the nineteenth century. He established numerous properties over the years, and founded a shorthorn stud and pedigreed Cotswold and merino flocks. Even his contemporaries would freely admit without hyperbole that his cattle were the finest in the southern hemisphere. Black made a fortune from his fine merino wool and garnered such an enviable reputation that when Prince Alfred, Duke of Edinburgh, the second son of Queen Victoria and Prince Albert, became the first British royal to visit Australia in 1867–68, he stayed at Glenormiston. In preparation for the visit, Black covered in his front verandah, and organised a corroboree for his royal guest.

Black also left us one of the earliest written accounts of the darker side of settlement, with a candid acknowledgement in his daily journal, dated 9 December 1839, of the inevitability of violent conflict between the settler and the land's traditional owners:

> The best way to procure a run is to go outside and take up a new run, provided the conscience of the party is sufficiently seared to enable him without remorse to slaughter natives right and left. It is universally and distinctly understood that the chances are very small indeed of a person taking up a new run being able

to maintain possession of his place and property without having recourse to such means . . . I believe, however, that great numbers of the poor creatures have wantonly fallen victims to settlers scarcely less savage though more enlightened than themselves, and that two thirds of them does not care a single straw about taking the life of a native.

The quintessential picture of the canny, hardworking Scot, Niel Black died at his home in Mount Noorat on 15 May 1880. Today many of the dynastic families that once called the Western Districts home have sold their properties and moved away to the city or the coast. Richard Zachariah, author of *The Vanished Land*—an account of the demise of the Western District's great pastoral traditions—calls the region today an 'abandoned land'. He laments the loss of its great families and describes their departure as a 'melancholy exodus'. Mansions that once were symbols of lavish lifestyles in what was a Belle Époque few of us could imagine now sit at the end of lonely driveways, hidden from view in the folds of hills. The settling of returned soldiers after World War II saw the carving up of once-great estates. Yet the region has transformed itself. The Western Districts is still as fertile as it always was, and though the presence of foreign interests and a new generation of breeders mean its 'face' has changed, it remains Victoria's premier sheep and cattle region.

In the 1830s and 1840s, in the Port Phillip region and throughout New South Wales, crops needed planting to provide an increasing population food to eat. And as the numbers of squatters grew, the lands that came under cultivation expanded along with them. By the mid-1830s more than 500 acres of land had been planted in the New South Wales Hunter region by the Australian Agricultural Company, which ran 60,000 sheep there. Few stations existed that did not have their own 'cultivation paddocks', though leased land for cultivation was in general prohibited unless for 'supply of family'. In the cities and coastal regions large proprietors held most of the fertile land, but only a miserly 1 per cent of that land was put under the plough. With farmers making up a large percentage of new arrivals (in New South Wales alone, between 1830 and 1850, 11,500 men listed their occupation as 'farmer'), and with the population increasing so quickly, the balance between pastoral stations and crop farming inevitably began to change. In New South Wales in 1846, 125,000 acres were under cultivation.

Where crop-growers had established themselves with free land grants, their production methods were deemed primitive and their financial situations weak. While pastoralists with sheep and cattle fared better, most croppers with limited means generally tilled only small portions of their lands and often had to put up with poor returns—they would wander the colony looking for work until harvest time. Even as late as the 1850s, few could have imagined that within a generation the southern colonies would surpass England herself in crop production and become one of the world's leading producers of grain. How did this happen?

In Victoria, the pioneering Henty family were the first to trial European-style agricultural methods using a plough, a pair of harrows and the six bullocks they'd brought with them on the *Thistle*. Paddocks were prepared for wheat in August 1835, and eight months later came the first harvest. By 1839, they were growing potatoes, vegetables and cereals. Although transporting food from Van Diemen's Land to the Port Phillip District and beyond was a relatively straightforward exercise, many newcomers began planting their own crops along the banks of the Yarra River. Of the 43 households along the Yarra recorded in the 1836 census, 27 practised arable agriculture. Some of the wealthier settlers, such as John Batman and Charles Wedge, had lots as large as 20 acres. But the scale of cropping was still small, a hobbyist's approach that failed to keep pace with the growth of the colony and led to a dependence on imported grains from Van Diemen's Land that would continue for years to come.

Squatters came from diverse backgrounds, and while the bulk of the colony's progress was determined by a wealthy gentry with the finances to establish themselves quickly, others achieved their success by degrees, advancing themselves through sheer hard work. One such man was Scottish-born James Ritchie.

One of the Western District's great pastoralists, Ritchie arrived in Australia in 1841 and found employment as an overseer, eventually saving enough money to purchase 70 cattle, which he fattened and sold. He and his brother then began to search for a run, travelling from Port Fairy to Portland before walking onto *Blackwood*, a sheep station on Deep Creek with 1600 sheep, the majority of which were in extremely poor condition. Within two years the flock had increased to 2700. In 1846, in excess of 3000 sheep were sheared, and in 1855 Ritchie had 40,000 sheep and turned a profit of £8000.

In the 1840s, squatters were continuing their spread across the colony, and by 1845 had established 33 runs across the isolated Murray Pastoral District in the far north-east, with 24 stations listing 400 acres under cultivation. A year later the number of stations had grown to 35, and the acreage to 530. In the east the Gippsland region was also opened up, and no one man did more to achieve this than the controversial explorer and pioneer pastoralist, Angus McMillan.

McMillan was born on the Isle of Skye in Scotland and came to New South Wales in 1838. Employed to explore the Gippsland Plains on behalf of wealthy New South Wales landowners, he led the first of several expeditions into the region in May 1839, named the Nicholson, Mitchell, Avon and Macalister rivers, and arranged with colonial officials in Sydney to register claims for himself and his employers. He was also instrumental in opening up a north–south land route from the plains to Omeo, a route that saw an influx of Scottish immigrants who had been dispossessed of their lands in Scotland during the Highland Clearances of the late eighteenth and early nineteenth centuries. Sadly these settlers, who knew exactly how it felt to have their ancestral homes taken away, were no more merciful to the Indigenous peoples whose lands they now coveted.

Gippsland became infamous for its brutal encounters between these Gaelic-speaking Highland Scots and the local Gunaikurnai people, with estimates of Aboriginal deaths put by some historians as high as 1000. Angus McMillan played a pivotal role in this, as the leader of a twenty-strong posse of stockmen and cattle owners called the Highland Brigade, who carried out a series of massacres of the Gunaikurnai people at Nuntin, Boney Point, Butchers Creek, Slaughterhouse Creek, Maffra, Bruthen Creek, Skull Creek and Warrigal Creek. The Warrigal Creek massacre saw as many as 300 Aborigines killed in an orgy of revenge for the killing of a prominent Scottish settler, Ronald Macalister, and was one of the worst massacres of Aborigines in Australia's history. It is estimated between 2000 and 3000 Gunaikurnai lived in Gippsland in 1840. By 1857, there were just 96.

The Gippsland squatting district was the last region of the colony to be settled, yet within ten years it had more than 90 runs and an established road to Melbourne. The district was fully occupied by the end of 1844. As mentioned in Chapter 4, it lost little time in securing a lucrative beef trade with the island colony. But the stain of what had been done to the Gunaikurnai people could not be erased by mere economic activity. In April 1846, the Gippsland squatter Henry Meyrick, who emigrated in 1840 only to die at the age of 25, referred to the Gippsland massacres up to that time in a letter to his relatives in England:

The blacks are very quiet here now, poor wretches. No wild beast of the forest was ever hunted down with such unsparing perseverance as they are. Men, women and children are shot whenever they can be met with . . . I have protested against it at every station I have been in Gippsland, in the strongest language, but these things are kept very secret as the penalty would certainly be hanging. It is impossible to say how many have been shot, but I am convinced of not less than 450 have been murdered altogether. They will very shortly be extinct.

Meyrick wrote that he was disgusted at the thought of riding into an Aboriginal camp and indiscriminately killing men, women and children. But he was more a product of his time than he realised. When asked what he might do if he were to catch an Aborigine killing his sheep, he replied that he would shoot him 'with as little remorse as I would a wild dog'.

As squatters spread out across Victoria, they wrote lyrical phrases about the beauty of its landscapes. One of the most valuable historical and botanical insights we have into the Port Phillip District of the 1840s is the sketches of the squatter Duncan Cooper. Considered by all who knew him as hard working and self-effacing, Cooper, the son of an officer in the Bengal Army, came to Australia from London in the 572-ton barque *Diamond*, arriving in Port Phillip on 4 November 1841. Within eight months of his arrival he took up the Challicum pastoral run in Victoria's Western Districts, together with two business partners, the brothers George and Harry Thompson. The three men built up an enviable run, their pure merinos—the Challicum fleeces—known far and wide for their quality. Cooper's personal charm was also well known. Women particularly thought him a prince, with more than one describing him as having an uncommon breadth of knowledge, although lacking in self-esteem.

Fortunately, Cooper channelled this lack of confidence into his one abiding love: painting. Acquired by the National Library of

Australia in 1960, his Challicum Sketch Book with its 34 water-colour paintings documents 1840s pastoral life in all its nascent detail, from the flora and fauna of the landscape to how people lived their everyday lives, from their dwellings and the clothes they wore to how they farmed. Cooper was adept at capturing how the light fell on the hills and valleys, a light so subtly portrayed you could almost guess the time of day. His small but highly detailed drawings possessed the clarity of a photograph in works such as *First Settlement at Challicum, Victoria, 1 January 1842; Challicum Third Hut, Side View, Victoria 1845;* and *View from Window of Hut, Challicum, Victoria, 1850.* Nothing escaped his keen eye—poultry houses, wheat fields, she-oak trees, campfires and quail hunts. He even left us a 'cyclorama'—a series of nine watercolours which, when placed end to end, form a 360-degree view of the landscape surrounding Challicum.

Cooper also worked in sepia wash and monotones, but it is his watercolours that secure him a place as one of colonial Australia's most gifted artists, the creator of a treasured visual memoir. Dr Bernard Smith, emeritus professor of contemporary art at Sydney University, in 1960 referred to the collection as 'the work of an amateur of some accomplishment' who made indelible a world of huts and homesteads, pleasant plains and lightly timbered hills.

In spite of the increased settlement in the emerging districts of Victoria from the 1830s, relatively few people worked in the pastoral and agricultural industries for decades, with the 1857 census recording just 37,000 people—16 per cent of the state's workforce. Squatters were becoming even harder to find. In the east of the colony, in the lower Goulburn region, those who described themselves as working in the pastoral industry numbered some 400, but of those a mere twenty were squatters.

On 1 July 1851, the Wimmera, Murray, Gippsland and all the districts to the south of the Murray River separated from

New South Wales and became the Colony of Victoria. The population of the new colony was 77,000, though only 23,000 lived in Melbourne. By the end of 1851, a booming urban population and the discovery of gold saw the new colony's population increase from 97,500 to almost 540,000 in just ten years, which fuelled a demand for agricultural products and raised the spirits of the colony's croppers. On the eve of the gold rush more than 3000 of the colony's residents were involved in cropping and the number of acres under cultivation totalled some 57,000. New arrivals, encouraged to participate in what was suddenly a growth industry, adjusted quickly to the demands of our strange soils and climate.

The gold rush initially proved challenging for Victoria's croppers due to the bleeding of farmhands to the gold fields. And croppers weren't the only ones made nervous by the lure of instant wealth; colonial authorities were also worried about the sudden arbitrary accumulation of wealth in a land that wasn't yet mature enough to cope with the emergence of a formerly disenfranchised, nouveau-riche underclass. Isolated discoveries in the 1840s were kept secret by authorities in an effort to prevent much-feared social dislocation. Farmers who had uncovered their own nuggets were told to keep their finds to themselves. The likely presence of gold *somewhere* on the continent had always been both a fear and a whisper for the colonial governments. The prosperity of the colonies had been built on the sheep's back, on the vaunted 'golden fleece'. How could such prosperity continue, it was thought, if everyone went off to dig for buried treasure among the rolling hills?

They needn't have worried. Total acreage under cultivation multiplied seven-fold over the 1850s, after an initial decline. By the late 1860s the colony comprised around 30,000 small to middle-scale cultivators, on allotments ranging from 30 to 350 acres, four times as many people as there were stock farmers. When miners began to realise that for every 0.64 kilograms of gold dust they could purchase an 80-acre freehold run in South Australia, for instance, the gold rush, to the surprise of many, resulted in an expansion of agriculture that saw Victoria all but self-sufficient in regards to food.

It isn't known for sure what percentage of this burgeoning new generation of post-gold rush agriculturalists were former gold miners, but by March 1853, after two years of scouring Victoria's gold fields, the total amount of all deposits in the colony's four major banks added up to some £5 million. It was assumed that the majority of this money belonged to small depositors, mostly successful miners, with the average sum of each deposit ranging between £500 and £1000. Enough to begin a career in the resurgent industry of crop farming.

As shepherds left sheep runs to find their fortune on the gold fields, the exodus made squatters realise that sheep were perfectly capable of looking after themselves with the advent of wire fencing. The first-ever recorded use of wire for fencing in colonial Australia was on Phillip Island, not far from Melbourne, in 1842, though this was an isolated example. It would be another ten years before a written document attests to its use anywhere else in the eastern colonies.

No longer restricted to expensive and time-consuming timber fences, wire was cheap and quick to install, and breaks could be easily repaired. By the 1870s, more than 32,000 kilometres of fencing had been erected across New South Wales, though despite this surge in demand all wire was imported and Australia didn't have its first wire mill until 1911. When wire fencing reached into the Queensland outback it lessened the need for shepherds so much that the workforce there fell by 80 per cent. As observed by Anthony Trollope, the English novelist who travelled to Australia in the early 1870s:

> Nothing, I think, gives a surer proof of the wealth of the Australian colonies generally, than the immense amount of fencing that has

been put up in the last ten years. A run of 20 miles square, equal to 256,000 acres, is by no means excessive.

Indeed, fencing was often the first substantial improvement the squatter or settler would make in the 1870s, despite its considerable expense at around £40 per mile. Fences allowed squatters to increase their sheep flocks, too, though such fencing was of little use to those who ran cattle, just another reason why sheep numbers rose so dramatically between the 1860s and 1890s. Cattle numbers remained static. However, squatters had tried stud breeding since the 1830s, but had been hindered by having to keep their cattle together. By the 1880s a new kind of wire—barbed wire—allowed squatters and cattle farmers to pen their cattle, an advance that led to a new era of stud breeding, allowing breeders to keep their best cattle apart from the rest of their herd.

In 1862 and 1865, a series of land acts in Victoria aimed to provide affordable agricultural lands for small farmers. Sheep farming was rampant, but people cannot eat wool and there was a pressing need to diversify. This process of 'selection' allowed the government to reclaim lands that were a part of squatters' leaseholds, and sell them to people of lesser means. The terms were £1 per acre for the first half of the allotment and rent on the other half over a seven-year period, at the end of which they would pay the balance of the purchase price.

As had already been the case in New South Wales, the process of selection was deeply flawed, with squatters using sleight of hand and covert 'dummying' to maintain their ownership of the lands. And when covert means failed, overt would do. Squatters weren't averse to turning to blatant harassment to discourage selectors, such as tearing down fences and grazing their stock on selectors' crops. Squatters would tell selectors that any improvements they made to their land would ultimately be theirs. Only a fraction of the land made available to selectors was ultimately taken up, but the squatters, although their role in maintaining tenure was highly visible, were not the only factor.

Barely a governmental thought was given to creating in selection settlements the sort of infrastructure necessary for the growth and prosperity of an agricultural community. With the exception of railways, no money from land sales was allocated for road construction, which was the responsibility of shire councils. Apart from those very few inter-colonial roads linking the colonies, most of what passed for local roads remained little more than stock routes unsuited for the transportation of grain crops. In addition, improvement clauses in the selection acts proved a heavy impost upon selectors, requiring them to build fences, clear allotments, build a home, purchase equipment, and prepare and seed a minimum of 10 per cent of their selection.

When bad times came, selectors were ruined and walked off the land. Most began with little or no capital, and when fires destroyed produce or buildings, rents quickly fell into arrears. Selectors found it difficult to secure bank loans and some turned to unscrupulous merchants who loaned money at exorbitant rates. Defaults meant foreclosure. Even if a selector managed to avoid adversity and grow crops, limited regional markets meant the occupation provided anything but a secure, remunerative future. Transport costs in outlying areas such as the north-east were prohibitive, and there was increasing competition from squatters who began investing more time and money into growing their own crops in increasing volumes.

Outbreaks of disease such as rust, a fungal plant pathogen, drove many selectors to despair. One selector in the Ovens Valley wrote:

Here also the rust tinged every field, and consumed the bulk of the grain: the farmers complain of this evil and the poverty of the soil, and some think of throwing aside the pruning hook and ploughshare and resuming the pick and shovel, preferring the chance of picking up a portion of the gold dust to the chances of a harvest home. Drought and disease would have been problems enough for landholders who were actually farmers, but the truth was many selectors wrote 'farmer' on their land applications when many were in fact novices. Wheat was planted with no regard for soil type, frost or rainfall, and the principles of water run-off barely understood.

The most visible legacy of the wealth accumulated by those squatters and settlers who went on to amass great fortunes are the homesteads they left behind. In Victoria, the 1870s saw the emergence of some of the finest homes in the colony, homes that would have stood shoulder to shoulder with some of the great manor houses in England and were about as far removed from the image of the squatter as one could get. And one of the finest of them all was Rupertswood.

The home began in the 1840s with the construction of a simple two-room cottage on a tract of land north of Melbourne in present-day Sunbury, built by the English pastoralist and soon-to-be voracious landowner William Clarke Snr. Clarke arrived in Hobart Town with his wife in December 1829 and immediately set about building up an 80,000-acre empire in Van Diemen's Land, before moving his business interests across the Bass Strait to the Port Phillip District. (Clarke, however, continued to live in Van Diemen's Land until 1850). By the end of the 1840s, his Victorian interests had accumulated 100,000 sheep spread across tens of thousands of acres, much of it bought at a pittance and in the process throwing nine squatters off their land. Known as 'Big Clarke' and 'Monied Clarke', he achieved fame and notoriety across Victoria for his unquenchable thirst for land. Relentlessly ambitious, he focused single-mindedly on the raising of sheep, buying them at the lowest prices he could and later benefiting from the rise in wool prices, and was the first to import Leicester sheep into Australia.

William Clarke owned a single property that stretched all the way from the rural township of Sunbury to Sydney Road north of Melbourne. Yet despite his ballooning wealth, he remained a miserly character, not only towards his business associates but his family as well. Tough and uncompromising, he dressed in stained moleskin trousers and wore thick twill shirts when he worked, which made him almost indistinguishable from his convict workers. He could shear a sheep, cut up a carcass, brand cattle, shoe a horse and drive a bullock team. When he died in 1874, he left a veritable fortune to his son, William Clarke Jnr (in the vicinity of £4 million pounds), and not long after his father's death his son began the construction of Rupertswood.

Named after his oldest son Rupert, Rupertswood would eventually cost £25,000, and when it was finished it was one of the most modern homes in the colony. There were speaking tubes to every room and hot and cold running water to every bedroom, an unheard-of luxury at the time. A gas-powered plant produced power to light its many chandeliers, and its extensive gardens—including a lake in the shape of Australia— were designed by the noted landscape designer William Sangster, many elements of which remain to this day.

Prosperity, however, was not uniform, and many parts of rural Victoria in the 1870s and 1880s faced real hardships, which can be gleaned not only from written records, but also in the images left to us by the period's artists, men like Samuel Calvert. Calvert was born in London in 1828 and left his job as a clerk for the East India Company to emigrate to Adelaide on the *Symmetry* in 1848. Calvert had been taught painting, etching and engraving by his father, and after moving to Melbourne in 1852 and securing a job in a printing shop, his drawings and engravings appeared in many of Melbourne's illustrated newspapers. Works like *Deserted*, a wood engraving, depicted a derelict squatters' hut in 1887 Gippsland, its roof decayed and falling in, the surrounding bush gradually reclaiming it.

In the 1870s and 1880s, mining towns were quick to decline in the wake of the gold rush. Populations that once numbered in the tens of thousands dwindling away, turning once-thriving communities into ghost towns. But mining towns were not the first to experience falling populations. The coastal town of Portland, which was founded with so much promise in the 1830s, began to decline in influence and population by the late 1840s. On the east coast, Port Albert, which had only recently been surveyed, was abandoned by 1853.

A collapse in the railway boom saw inland towns empty as people moved to Melbourne in the hope of better and more regular employment. In 1861, 26 per cent of Victorians lived in Melbourne; by 1890 this had risen to 43 per cent. The idea that rural life, and the glories of the old pioneering days, were in danger of being forgotten spurred ageing pastoralists to write down their recollections of the 'old days' so that they would not be forgotten.

By the 1880s, Victoria had become overwhelmingly urban. It was the era of 'Marvellous Melbourne', a city larger than many European capitals, its population doubling in a decade. Twelve-storey office buildings were the equivalent of anything in New York and London, and its well-dressed citizens strutted the streets in a city punctuated by domes, towers, turrets and spires. Melbourne possessed more decorative cast iron than any city in the world, keeping 40 local foundries busy supplying over 150 registered designs that would grace the skyline with a kaleidoscope of decorative balconies, its beautiful 'iron petticoats'.

The 1890s must have beckoned as a decade in which anything was possible. How could anyone have foreseen that in just a few years, the era of Marvellous Melbourne would be over, and the city would suffer the ravages of a worldwide depression.

Fletcher and Dean families outside a slab hut, Queensland.
State Library of Queensland

6

SHEPHERD KINGS OF
THE DARLING DOWNS

'The Darling Downs will never grow a cabbage.'

—John Watts, pastoralist, 1860

In February 1606, a small, lightly armed Dutch barque called the *Duyfken* (Little Dove) entered the waters of the Torres Strait between Queensland and New Guinea, two months before those northern waters would be sailed and named by the Spanish explorer Luís Vaez de Torres. The crew of the *Duyfken* are believed to be the first Europeans to ever lay eyes on the Australian continent. Its commander, Willem Janszoon, an officer with the Dutch East India Company, took his ship south to the Pennefather River on the western shoreline of Cape York, and it was there that he and his crew made first contact with the local Keerweer people. The Keerweer allowed the newcomers to sink a well, and put up a small hut. The white people gave the Keerweer tobacco, which they kept, and flour, which they threw away.

The encounter, insofar as the continent's eventual settlement more than a century and a half later is concerned, was inconsequential. But as a symbol it is hugely significant. This was the moment the traditional owners of our continent can look back to as the beginning of the end of their ownership of their land, and of their way of life. And it happened not in the early colonies of New South Wales or Van Diemen's Land. It happened in Queensland.

Queensland's European settlement began with the establishment of the Moreton Bay Penal Colony in 1824. The penal colony housed almost 2400 men and 145 women in hiring depots—distribution points that could be guest houses or warehouses from which female convicts were assigned and then sent out to work—that stretched all the way from Stradbroke Island to present-day Ipswich. Built for hardened criminals and recidivist convicts, it quickly garnered a reputation for extreme violence, death and disease. The penal colony was closed in 1842 when Moreton Bay was opened to free settlement and the area renamed the Moreton Bay Pastoral District.

The English-born botanist and explorer Allan Cunningham explored the lands to the west of Moreton Bay in early 1827. He crossed the Great Dividing Range in the Hunter Region, reaching the Gwydir River on 21 May, and continuing north where he would eventually reach the area west of present-day Warwick on 6 June, and see for the first time the boundless pastures he called the Darling Downs, named after the governor of New South Wales Sir Ralph Darling. Cunningham was overwhelmed by the richness of the land. He also discovered and named Cunningham's Gap, the pass between the Downs and Fassifern Valley that would in time become the major route over the Great Dividing Range.

In 1840, thirteen years after Allan Cunningham first saw the Darling Downs' fertile grasslands, settlers began arriving and established sheep runs to provide raw wool for British mills. They were privileged from the start; the sons of English and

Scottish gentry and commercial bankers who were obsessed with stock bloodlines, they became so successful they were given disparaging titles such as 'Grass Dukes' and 'Shepherd Kings'. They formed close-knit communities, helped along by inbreeding, and their rising political influence began to result in calls for separation from the northern districts of New South Wales. In 1843, the Darling Downs Pastoral District was gazetted, giving pastoralists the right to obtain a lease rather than a licence, which also gave the lessee the right to purchase additional land around their head station. The floodgates to settling the Darling Downs had opened.

Six out of ten settlers who first populated the Darling Downs were of Scottish ancestry, and one of the first to arrive was Patrick Leslie. The second son of William and Jane Leslie of Aberdeenshire in Scotland, William was the tenth Laird of Warthill, and gave Patrick, and his other sons, George and Walter, a brief to travel to Australia and 'create another Warthill'. This sense of elevation felt by those who settled the Darling Downs is seen in an early letter written by Walter Leslie to his mother, dated 20 June 1841:

> It is now the case that any new district is much more respectably peopled than the older parts of the colony, from the influence of that rare commodity in the younger days of the colony—Gentlemen.

Patrick Leslie had departed Scotland ahead of his brothers, and arrived in Sydney in 1835, where he became the superintendent of his uncle's New South Wales property Collaroi. Eventually he became bored with bookkeeping and, in 1839, after the arrival of his brothers, led a daring expedition 965 kilometres north via steamer to Brisbane and then overland to the Downs. In early 1840, the brothers established Toolburra Station, the first station on the Condamine River, and then Canning Downs, where they ran 6000 sheep and two bullock teams and employed 22 convicts. And in keeping with their ever-developing sense of being a pioneering 'elite', Patrick couldn't help but note that Canning Downs was 'surrounded by good neighbours, all Gentlemen and mostly countrymen of our own'.

It was Patrick who laid out the town of Warwick in 1847–48, and he was the first to buy land there. Goomburra Station was purchased in 1846 and Gladfield Station in 1851. The Leslie brothers were typical of the approach taken by wealthy families back home, who turned their sons into pioneering squatters, sent around the world as 'birds of passage' to gain wealth quickly and return home. Although the Leslies have captured much of the historical limelight, they were in fact in the region for a relatively short time. While early historians hailed Patrick as the archetype of the gallant squatter, 'fearless', a 'rough jewel' and the 'prince of bushmen', later writers have been less fulsome, not so ready to buy in to the romantic myths of his earlier biographers.

The second station on the Downs after Patrick Leslie's Toolburra was Eton Vale Station. Originally selected as a grazing property it switched to growing wheat in 1846 and became a sheep station in 1850. Its owner, the Hertfordshire-born, Eton-educated former Royal Navy midshipman Arthur Hodgson, arrived in Sydney in 1839 but moved to the Moreton Bay district the following year. His upward path through the nascent aristocracy of the Downs was hastened when he married Eliza Dowling, the second daughter of James Dowling, the chief justice of New South Wales, in 1842.

Ernest Dalrymple, a Scottish pioneer from Aberdeenshire and an admirer of the journeys made by Allan Cunningham, settled on the Downs in July 1840, and other stations soon followed: Glengallen, Talgai and Rosenthal. By 1844 there were more than 150,000 sheep on the Downs, spread over 26 properties.

One of the great pastoral stations of the Darling Downs was Yandilla. Built by the Gore family who settled in the area after arriving from England in 1841, the homestead stood on the banks of Grass Tree Creek not far from its junction with the west branch of the Condamine River. There were quarters for the station hands and their families, a garden with fruit trees and grape vines, a schoolhouse, a chapel, and a palpable air of order and comfort. The scale of Yandilla was impressive—over 1784 square kilometres, so large it was the size of a town and even had its own telegraph station.

In Queensland, the squatter was king, and the so-called 'pure merinos' of the Darling Downs became well known for their disdain of using their land for such a mundane pursuit as agriculture. Arthur Hodgson, who had been persuaded to move north in 1840 by Patrick Leslie and spent ten years trying to make ends meet before transforming Eton Vale into the centre of Darling Downs society, wrote in 1855:

> Take that immense tract of country known as the Darling Downs, which feeds nearly one million sheep, exclusive of cattle and horses—who would be mad enough to attempt cultivation there? If it were practicable, do you not think we would not, one and all, grow wheat for our own consumption?

In the 1850s, prior to tendering for runs, applicants were required to provide a clear description of their run's boundaries, descriptions that relied heavily upon topographical features such as rivers, creeks and hills in the area, as well as nods to any surveyed trees or lines marked by the applicant on an adjoining lease. The government wanted to have each boundary surveyed so that precise descriptions could then be inserted into the lease rather than simply relying upon a description given to them by the applicant. During the 1850s demand for leases was so high, and the number of surveyors so few, that the government had no alternative but to advise pastoralists to hire a private surveyor at their own expense. The majority of squatters, however, could ill afford such an 'extravagance' and were content to rely on the government's promise of a lease. (Interestingly, in 1845 the area of a run had been fixed at 65 square kilometres, the very same area given over to a parish. A reason, perhaps, why many parishes took their names and locations from these early squatter runs.)

In the 1850s, the cries of 'separation' from New South Wales grew ever louder. According to historian Manning Clark 'the pastoralists of the Darling Downs and out on the Maranoa and the planters in the tropical north wanted to escape from domination by the noisy democrats and ruffians in Sydney'. The first murmurings of separation could be heard as early as the mid-1840s, but weren't given impetus until the arrival of two boat loads of separatist-minded immigrants, the first in 1848 aboard the *Artemisia*, and the second in 1849 on the *Fortitude*. In 1850, a meeting at Drayton formed a Darling Downs Committee, which in turn led to the creation in Ipswich of the Northern Districts Separation Association in 1851. George Leslie, who like his brothers had become vocal supporters of the push for separation, along with many other Northern Districts squatters, continually argued the cause, including making several representations to London.

On 21 July 1856, the Colonial Office finally gave its assent, but it wasn't until 10 December 1859 that George Bowen arrived in Brisbane to become the new colony's first governor. On a tour of the colony not long after taking office, Bowen wrote of his impressions of the independent-minded Queensland squatter:

> These gentlemen live in a patriarchal style among their immense flocks and herds, amusing themselves with hunting, shooting, fishing, and the exercise of plentiful hospitality. I have often thought that the Queensland gentlemen-squatters bear a similar relation to the other Australians that the Virginian planters of a hundred years back bore to the Americans.

In 1860, Rockhampton and Ipswich were declared towns, and the following year Maryborough and Warwick. Queensland Parliament opened for its first sitting in May 1860, and lost no time in devising a land order system that would attract new settlers, legislation which brought in 25,000 people over the next three years. By the middle of 1861, farmers in Queensland owned 3000 acres while squatters held sway over a vast 25 million acres, an expansion driven by disillusioned Victorians who came north after having had enough of what they saw as restrictive land reforms—primarily the process of 'selection'—in that colony. In 1860, Niel Black, the pioneering Western Districts squatter, even claimed the era of squatting in Victoria was 'over, never to return'. 'Queensland', he said, 'is the land for the herdsman nowadays'. And why wouldn't it be when selling a 20-square-mile station in Victoria meant you could buy a 600,000 square mile station in Queensland (though admittedly considerably more arid). By the 1880s, the saying that the Melbourne suburb of Toorak 'was keeping half of Queensland', was no exaggeration.

New South Wales may have been filling with people, but in the Darling Downs, even as late as the 1860s, the horizons were still broad, and often empty. Katie Hume, the wife of Walter Hume, an official in Queensland's Department of Public Lands, described returning home one day after visiting a neighbouring property:

> We rode a few miles into the bush and halted in the middle of the day at a spot where the grass seemed good for the horses, which were soon unsaddled, hobbled, and turned adrift while we sat down under the shade of a gum tree and 'recreated' on sandwiches and sherry provided by our hosts. The solitude here is so striking to one not accustomed to it. In the course of a 20 mile's ride on the high road you may meet one dray and team, two flocks of sheep, one cart, one horseman!

The pastoralists of the Darling Downs and the Logan and Brisbane valleys would go on to hold far greater sway over

Brisbane than their southern namesakes did over Sydney. They built plantation-style mansions using locally quarried basalt that were the equal to anything in the dominions of the British Empire. They hunted imported quail, had sumptuous picnics, excavated wine cellars and filled them with the finest clarets, and formed their own exclusive associations—all the trappings of a powerful aristocracy. They even had the newspapers on side. On 5 August 1854, the *Moreton Bay Courier* wrote:

> The Darling Downs squatters were far, far above everybody else in the Moreton Bay districts: as high above them as Haman's gallows was above all other gibbets—or as the Downs was above the sea.

Oscar de Satge, a Swiss-born squatter and politician spoke of that first wave of squatters, describing them as having 'industry, courage, and honesty of purpose'. Their 'word was their bond', their agreements seldom to be found on paper, their servants and animals well cared for, their homesteads opulent and open to all, financed and built with generous lines of credit and with 50 per cent of every wool clip a clear profit. In fact it was Katie Hume who left one of the more vivid descriptions of one of the Downs' grandest homesteads, Westbrook Hall:

> It is of hewn stone, dark grey, quarried on the Run—coins of light brick—walls 2 ft thick—fireplace in every room, that's the way to be comfortable in this climate of extremes! It is one storey only—rooms 15 ft high—verandah round it 12 ft broad—dining room 30 ft long and other rooms in proportion including billiard room, library etc . . .

The majority of Queensland's squatters may have been less openly 'aristocratic' in their aspirations than their namesakes on the Downs, but their status was nevertheless unmistakable. Squatters in the northern country of central Queensland's Burnett district, for instance, which had its first runs taken up in

1849 in the wake of the new Waste Lands Act, were considered by most 'hard workers of the land'. The region away from its rivers and streams was drier than the Downs, sandy and scrub-filled, although some runs along the tributaries of the Burnett River gave one overseer, B.J. Bertelsen, cause for joy, describing the grasses there the equal of any in Europe and certainly to any in the Darling Downs. Mostly, though, the Burnett lands were only able to support either a single head of cattle or four or five sheep per acre, which is why the runs there had an average size of 900 square kilometres and also why the region was one of the continent's loneliest. In 1851, there was just one pioneer for every 47 square kilometres in what was a less than welcoming, often hostile land. Even though the Burnett squatter tended to rise out of the lower ranks through their industry and perseverance, their hospitality still seemed warmer to those carrying letters of introduction and with a healthy bank balance, than to the casual passer-by of lesser means.

The original inhabitants of the Burnett district, including the Yarmbura clan and the Thibura clan, the Nukunukubura around Mount Perry, the Warbaa around Monduran, and the Yawai of Walla, numbered in the thousands prior to European encroachment. In just over 30 years that number dwindled to around 150, most being killed during the frontier wars, either trampled by horses, or shot, or poisoned with strychnine or arsenic, or dying from introduced diseases such as measles, tuberculosis and smallpox.

For the large Indigenous population that inhabited Queensland—up to 40 per cent of the pre-contact population of the entire continent—the frontier wars, that were fought everywhere that European settlement extended, reach their brutal zenith. There were more reports of shootings and massacres in Queensland than in any other colony. The Queensland Native Police Force killed, it is estimated, in excess of 20,000 Indigenous men, women and children. It is thought that as many as 65,000 Aboriginal deaths occurred in the early decades of settlement. The three bloodiest massacres of white settlers also took place there.

One of the darkest chapters in the history of confrontations between Aborigines and settlers in Queensland was the Hornet Bank Station Massacre when, early in the morning of 27 October 1857, eleven settlers, including eight members of the Fraser family, were slaughtered at their sheep station on the Dawson River in Central Queensland by members of the local Jiman tribe.

There were several possible reasons for the killings. It may have been retaliation for the death of twelve Jiman people, shot by settlers for spearing their cattle. Or because the two older Fraser boys, William and John, habitually raped local Aboriginal girls. Their mother, Martha, had even asked the commander of the local Native Police to speak to the Jiman, in an attempt to calm the awful feeling in her stomach that nothing good would come of what they'd done. It's also been claimed, though since fiercely debated, that a Christmas pudding laced with strychnine had been given to the Jiman by someone in the Fraser family, and the time had come for the Jiman to take their revenge.

Squatters had begun settling Jiman lands in 1847 in the wake of an expedition through the region two years earlier by the explorer Ludwig Leichhardt, and their presence was deeply resented. Land was settled without so much as a nod given to negotiations, customs were disrespected, and acts of cruelty intensified as the Jiman were denied access to the lands they'd always known. This increased level of violence and disregard for Aboriginal rights can be traced back to 1842–43, when outbreaks of violence increased across the entire frontier, from the Port Phillip District in the south through New South Wales to southern Queensland, a culmination of mistreatment and mutual distrust dating back 50 years.

The massacre at Hornet Bank was, by all accounts, gruesome,

carried out by the light of a quarter moon with the assistance of an insider who knew where each member of the Fraser family slept (and was also known to the Frasers' dogs, who were killed first). Fourteen-year-old Sylvester Fraser was attacked in his bed but fell down in the darkness between the bed and the wall and escaped further injury. His six-year-old brother James, thinking Sylvester dead, scrambled out a window but was captured and killed. The family's tutor, James de Lacy Neagle, John Fraser, 23, and his brother David, sixteen, who were both sleeping on the verandah's skillion, were bashed to death by *nullah-nullahs* (hunting sticks). The angry mob, which Sylvester, the sole survivor, would later estimate at around a hundred, then moved through the house towards the bedroom of Sylvester's mother, Martha.

Martha Fraser begged with the mob to spare her and her children, in particular pleading with Baulie, a Jiman who had worked for the Frasers. 'You have been a brother to me for a long time', Martha said through the bolted bedroom door. 'I have given you much food and many blankets. Please, not me, not the girls'.

Induced to go outside, Martha and her elder girls, Elizabeth, nineteen, and Mary, eleven, were raped and then battered to death. Then Jane, nine, and Charlotte, three, were killed. The fact that Martha, Elizabeth and Mary were raped points to the guilt of her sons in their own treatment of Aboriginal women, as the Jiman believed in an 'eye for an eye' system of justice.

After the last attackers had left, after hearing the shrieks of his family being butchered, poor Sylvester climbed out from under his bed, his head gashed, his arms and legs aching from the multiple blows he'd sustained. He found the body of his brother James lying between the kitchen and the house, and then those of his mother and sisters. On the verandah lay the naked bodies of John and David. Also killed were two shepherds, and the family's Aboriginal houseboy, Jimmy.

Sylvester walked 16 kilometres to the nearest town, Eurombah, and told his story to the authorities. The next day his family was buried—his mother and daughters together in one grave, his brothers in another. And then fourteen-year-old Sylvester Fraser entered the pages of Queensland folklore by riding 500 kilometres to Ipswich to tell his older brother William of the tragedy. It's claimed he covered the distance in a mere three days, a not impossible feat given that he had no serious injuries, and certainly fresh horses would have been offered him along the way. Some claim he went accompanied by Pollet Cardew, the owner of Eurombah Station, but there is no evidence of that. A reporter for the *Queensland Times*, who interviewed William in 1909, wrote that William was adamant the ride took his younger brother just three days. As impressive a feat as it was, Sylvester's suffering had only just begun, and he went on to lose his sanity. He also developed uncontrollable fits, and died a broken man.

William had taken over the management of Hornet Bank the year before, after the death of his father John, and had left the station only days prior to the massacre, freighting wool to Ipswich, then known as Limestone Hill. When Sylvester told him of the massacre, William became filled with grief and rage. The brothers returned to Hornet Bank, and standing over the graves of his family, William raised a tomahawk in the air and vowed he'd not rest until he'd sunk it into the skulls of their killers.

The settlers in the district became united in their sorrow for the victims, but also with a hatred for the ferocious treachery of the 'savages', who they felt had turned on them. Armed patrols set out across the Dawson and Auburn districts, and a 'squatter's crusade' threatened to erupt if the authorities didn't respond. Twenty settlers had been killed on the Upper Dawson in the previous twelve months, and tensions were high. The *Moreton Bay Courier*, however, urged caution:

> Leaving Christianity out of the question, we pride ourselves on being a highly civilised people, governed by policy and laws in the highest degree of perfection. As such, we ought to know that

the blow of retributive justice should fall with discrimination, and on the guilty only.

The fruits of the massacre for the Jiman people would be the eventual destruction of their society. William Fraser went on to become one of Australia's worst-ever mass murderers, killing by most estimates over a hundred Jiman, as the authorities stood idly by. The total number of Jiman killed numbers in the hundreds. Those left simply scattered to the four winds, with the last known members dying in the 1940s, their culture and language forever lost.

The Hornet Bank Massacre and other massacres such as Myall Creek, where 28 unarmed Aborigines were slaughtered near the banks of New South Wales' Gwydir River, were common throughout the frontier. In the end how many settlers died as a result of white settlement? In his 1987 book *Frontier*, author Henry Reynolds estimates 3000 settlers lost their lives, with an additional 3000 suffering some kind of serious bodily wound. And Aborigines? Two hundred thousand killed, either through violence or by diseases such as smallpox, is most commonly suggested, assuming that the figure of 250,000 being present prior to the arrival of the First Fleet is deemed to be accurate.

In 1859, when all the land that forms present-day Queensland was at last removed from the Colony of New South Wales, the Colony of Queensland had 3.5 million sheep, 500,000 head of cattle and 30,000 settlers. Seventy per cent of its revenue and 94 per cent of its exports came from squatting. There was a pottery, a steam-driven flour mill, two tanneries, two salt works and just a handful of sawmills. But in the absence of selectors, pastoral stations could be as large as the new colony's horizons and the deep pockets of disgruntled southern squatters could make them. By 1860, more than three and a half million sheep and a half a million cattle were grazing over a quarter of Queensland's landmass and close to three-quarters of the colony's revenues and 90 per cent of its exports were derived from pastoral activities. Pastoral growth became the yardstick by which the colony's prosperity would be measured. The generous allowances of the colony's land regulations, combined with the re-investing in Queensland property by cashed-up Victorians, laid the foundations for a boom era that would last until the economic downturn of 1866. This prosperity, however, was the result of more factors than we might care to acknowledge.

By the mid-nineteenth century, a small percentage of Australians had some of the highest incomes *in the world,* thanks in no small part to the exploitation of convict and Aboriginal labour. Just as with African-American slaves in the United States, the rural aristocracy owed much to unpaid labour. Whether assigned to small-scale croppers or large-scale pastoralists, convicts, as well as South Sea islanders taken from their homes across the South Pacific in the practice known as 'blackbirding', and tens of thousands of Aborigines were made to work in kitchens, laundries, woolsheds and in the fields of pastoral stations across the length and breadth of Australia. Wages were rarely, if ever, paid and to this day Australians have little idea of the great debt they owe to the legions of Indigenous peoples who, against their will, helped build a nation right over the top of their own traditional lands.

Aborigines may well have been perceived as a threat to many an isolated homestead, but they were their saviours, too. With Indigenous resistance all but broken in the Darling Downs by the late 1840s, Aboriginals were 'allowed' into the region and employed as shepherds and farm hands. It was in the northern regions of the state, however, where Aboriginal workers would be most used and valued. In 1863, Bowen Downs Station was established with the assistance of a small number of Aboriginal stockmen, while in 1867 a town hall meeting in Bowen took a vote and elected to allow Aborigines to work at selected stations.

A number of northern Queensland squatters, however, had long since taken matters into their own hands and initiated cooperation with local Aborigines. Robert Christison was a Scottish pastoralist who arrived in Victoria in 1852. A jockey and accomplished horseman, Christison worked for Niel Black for a time, before arriving in Bowen in 1863, then journeying west to the Suttor River in the Flinders district where he established his pastoral property of Lammermoor on Towerhill Creek, on land that belonged to the local Dalleburra people. Christison won over the cooperation of the Dalleburra with 'fearless courage, followed by a spirit of justice and kindness', the fruit of a diplomatic approach that was 'extraordinarily vigorous and accurate'. Christison told the hated Native Police that 'if you molest my blacks, I'll run you in for assault to Bowen'.

The primary account of Christison's life comes from *Christison of Lammermoor*, a book published by his daughter Mary Bennett twelve years after his death in 1915. Most of what we know of him comes from this book, a romantic and biased work that paints a picture of a democratic oasis in the midst of a dangerous and unpredictable land. Christison's own letters and diary entries, however, shed a broader light on the man. He was a pragmatist, and 'allowing the blacks in' gave him access to cheap labour. There is no evidence that he ever advocated publicly for Aboriginal rights, nor is there anything to show that he actually spoke up against the violence of the Native Police.

Yet there remains little that is damning in the man's treatment of his Aboriginal labourers, and Christison remains the archetype of the successful northern squatter. He is the 'pioneer as patriarch', a man bent to succeed in a hostile land. Clearly never a brute, he behaved in ways that shamed many of his contemporaries. And while it is prudent to always be a little sceptical of narratives written by dutiful daughters of their pioneering fathers, it is safe to say that the frontier wars that darken our bloody history would have had fewer chapters to write if there'd been more men like Robert Christison.

◄O►

With Aborigines hardly in a position to negotiate wages in an atmosphere that smacked of slavery, pastoral empires continued to grow, and with them disputes between workers and owners. Shearers were increasingly fed poor rations, were paid by the sheep (17 shillings and 6 pence per 100 sheep) which saw disputes over pay rates increase, and could be dismissed for whatever reason their employees thought fit. Australia's first unions were formed to fight for shearers' rights, rights they were badly in need of. The shearer's life was hard. Squatters were under no obligation to pay for sheep they considered to have been badly shorn. Sheds were poor environments too for such hard work, often being oppressively hot, and if sheep were wet instances of illness among shearers increased, a phenomenon that couldn't be explained but was never doubted by the shearer.

Shearers had to work according to the terms set out by the squatter, most of which were reasonable but which could easily be weighted in the squatter's favour. Shearers absent from the shed during working hours or using obscene language could be fined 'a score of sheep'. It was examples like this that led to the founding of shearers' unions.

Paid according to the number of sheep shorn, competition between shearers to shear the most was rife. Whoever sheared the most in a day earned the title 'ringer', a title he kept until it was bettered. The shearer who consistently sheared the most in a day was a 'gun'. As the late 1800s wore on, some truly remarkable shearing figures were achieved, and most of them in Queensland because the wool wasn't as thick as in New South Wales and Victoria, and the sheep were lighter.

One shearer, Jackie Howe, sheared 327 ewes in just 7 hours and 40 minutes at Alice Downs Station near Blackall using blade shears (hand shears, not machine shears). It's a record that still stands today. The week before that he set a weekly record—1437 sheep in 44 hours and 30 minutes.

Howe was born in 1861 near Warwick, Queensland, and was one of the most famous shearers of his day, breaking records everywhere he went. He was also an active trade unionist, a member of the Queensland Shearers' Union until leaving shearing behind to become a publican in 1900. A giant of a man, he weighed 114 kilograms, had a 127-centimetre chest, hands the size of a small tennis racquet, and it was said could run 100 yards (91 metres) on a grass track in 11 seconds in bare feet. His mere presence in a shearing shed lifted tallies far above what they would have otherwise been. Howe died in 1920 at the age of 58.

The more successful shearers like Howe travelled the country by horseback, but most walked. In the 1890s, the invention of the bicycle with a new pneumatic tyre patented by the Scottish-born inventor John Dunlop, however, wrought something of a revolution in the life of the average shearer. They now became mobile. A bicycle was cheap, didn't have to be fed, was light and could go over any terrain. Shearers could now cover vast distances, the kind that would see city dwellers contemplating the purchasing of compasses and field glasses. No longer were they so dependent upon individual stations; they could at last cast a wider net. The 1890s also saw the emergence of another device that would radically and forever alter the shearer's world: the machine shear.

The first large-scale commercial application of the new mechanical shears took place at Dunlop Station near Louth in New South Wales in 1888. 184,000 sheep had been assembled, but when the shearers saw the equipment they refused to have anything to do with it and set up camp across the Darling River. The standoff continued for three weeks, broken only when the machine's inventor, John Howard, agreed to the shearers' demand that he swim across the river, a feat he performed twice. The experiment began, and the fact was the machine, though not faster, enabled the wool to be cut closer to the skin thus giving the squatter a greater yield. Shearers adjusted their positions to keep themselves close to the machine, and squatters across the nation looked forward to an era of increased prosperity.

—◄O►—

At the beginning of the 1860s, the Queensland government turned its gaze to the vast expanses of its far north and began to formulate an approach to land distribution that initially saw large tracts of land given over to a small number of squatters, who headed north with their sheep under the mistaken impression that the soils and grasses there would be good for the growing and production of fleece. Such naivety soon gave way to harsher realities, however, such as footrot, fluke, lung worm, dingoes and speargrass, all of which combined to wreak havoc on sheep populations. Speargrass, in particular, earned the ire of Robert Gray of Hughenden Station near the Flinders River in Central Queensland, who wrote:

> . . . the sheep become covered with its barbed seeds, like hedgehog spines which penetrate the body of the animal and cause death. This grass is so intermixed with the better kinds that sheep cannot possibly be grown in this country . . .

Queensland's initial land reforms were crafted to avoid the sort of rampant speculation that had occurred in the southern colonies, which the Queensland government saw as counterproductive to the growth of rural communities. Land that was purchased had to be stocked, not just purchased and kept idle.

Settlers with cattle fared better than those with sheep, and it wasn't long until North Queensland became the heart of Australia's beef trade, with the mobility of cattle allowing settlers to cover large areas of ground and claim good lands under Queensland's 'right of occupancy'. The northern Queensland squatter of the 1860s bore little resemblance to those early squatters of the southern colonies, venturing forth with either the backing of business partners or their own moneyed-up families.

Most cattle farmers operated on shoestring budgets and stocked their land using the principles of the 'open range', which meant no fences and little in the way of herd management.

Homesteads were primitive, and only those outbuildings that were needed were built, such as a stockyard, a saddle room, workers' quarters and a paddock or two by the homestead for the keeping of horses and stud cattle. Times would not get easier. In 1866, a financial crisis hastened the downward trend in the price for wool and stock. In 1869, four times as many runs were abandoned as in the previous year. New legislation that took effect in 1869 lowering rents and extending leaseholds came too late for many squatters, and those who managed to stay on were denied bank loans.

In the 1870s, cattle numbers increased, which was a problem as there were only so many that could be sold locally for meat, while exports of tinned meat were not considered good enough for sensitive English palettes. When William Hann and the geologist Norman Taylor discovered gold in the sandy bed of the Palmer River in Far North Queensland in 1872, however, a second wave of pastoral expansion took place. Often starved for meat, and with rations so small some miners were forced to cut up their own horses for food, cattlemen quickly converged upon the region. By 1875, bullocks were fetching unheard-of prices of up to £17 per head.

The Palmer River mines continued to be the primary market for North Queensland cattle throughout the 1870s, and, incidentally, provided further examples of Aboriginal labour proving an indispensable ingredient to the survival of many remote properties. William Chatfield of Natal Downs used Aborigines for sheepwashing, and would later recall that 'if it were not for Aborigines doing nearly all my work during the late rush to the Palmer (Goldfields), while white labour was not to be had, my losses would have been simply ruinous'. By 1876, the 400 Aboriginal workers on Queensland's northern stations made up 40 per cent of the region's workforce, the isolation inherent in the far north working to their benefit and allowing them to stay on their traditional lands in a way that was simply not possible in the southern colonies.

◄○►

In the 1860s, the Kennedy district inland from present-day Bowen, an area of which almost nothing was known, saw masses converge upon the region in the hope of securing good, well-watered land. They were squatters from Scotland, England and Ulster, former British Indian Army officers, ex-diggers with pockets full of money gleaned from the gold fields, and agricultural labourers. The Commissioner for Crown Lands, George Dalrymple, was overwhelmed with lease applications, and by the middle of 1862 had issued 454 leases comprising 81,585 square kilometres. Two of the best documented squatters of the Kennedy district were Joseph Hann and his son William.

Ignoring talk that all the best land in the district had already been taken, Joseph and William rode to the northern area of the district and selected ten runs along the Basalt River and Maryvale Creek, both tributaries of the Burdekin River. (The maximum area of any one run was limited, but there were no limits on the number of continuous runs one could purchase.) After purchasing sheep, cattle and horses on the Darling Downs, they drove them 1280 kilometres to their station on the Basalt River. Along the way fellow squatters took them in, including the Stuarts of Oxford Downs and the Archers of Rockhampton. By 1863, the Hanns had built additional homesteads at Maryvale and Red Bluff.

The frontier's mortality rate, however, was high, and sickness an ever-present danger, with settlers suffering endless bouts of fever. For the Hanns the pioneering life that began so full of promise ended in disaster. In 1864, William Hann's week-old son died, his mother passed away at Red Bluff after a debilitating illness, and Joseph Hann drowned in an attempt to cross the flooded Burdekin River.

In the 1850s and 1860s, the settling of Queensland's vast districts gathered pace. Central Queensland's Peak Downs district, 320 kilometres west of Mackay and Rockhampton, was traversed by

Ludwig Leichhardt in 1845 and again in 1846 and impressed the explorer to the point that he thought if they could be adequately watered they'd be some of the finest pastures on the continent. Indeed, in time the land around the Peak Range was considered to be second in quality only to the Darling Downs. The Maranoa district in south-west Queensland, 480 kilometres west of Brisbane, became home to its first squatter with children in 1858, when Mary McManus's father Stephen Spencer took his family to a deserted station on Muckadilla Creek. They lived under a canvas tent until a slab hut could be erected, had no servants, and rebuilt the stockyards. The first wheat ever grown in the district was grown by Mary's father, and not just wheat. The district's first figs, peaches and apricots were all planted by the Spencer family. The district's first sheep were theirs, too. By 1862, hundreds of settlers were flooding into the region. Wages were high, work easily procured, and the demand for draught horses so great that saddle horses were being attached to drays. The economic activity being generated in the new colony even helped shield it against some of the worse aspects of the general economic downturn of the late 1860s. They were, indeed, exciting times. So exciting, in fact, that in London it made the selling of Queensland to prospective settlers a relatively straightforward affair.

If you were living in London in 1868, and wanted to inquire about emigrating to Queensland in the wake of the Land Act of 1868, your first stop was 32 Charing Cross, where the government of Queensland had established an office. There wasn't a question its representatives couldn't answer, or a picture so bright they couldn't paint it. Queensland was, they said, a land of unlimited pastures, its flocks and herds increasing at a rate its pastoralists and shepherds could barely keep up with. New forays and opportunities were continually being made into the interior, the climate was healthy, there was food in abundance, and its soils were the equal of anything to be found in India or Europe. The land was open to all people regardless of religion, or whether they be English, Irish, Welsh or Scot. Its grass was superior to all others and ideal for the fattening of stock, with sheep growing to an average of 27 kilograms and cattle to 363 kilograms. The soil of its tablelands could grow plums, oranges, lemons, oats, wheat, maize, ginger, peaches, coffee, tea, cotton, linseed, apples and more besides, including lucerne which could yield six to eight cuttings a year.

If you wanted to cut timber all you needed do was pay a small fee to the government and you could chop down all the Moreton Bay pine, red cedar, iron bark, blue and red gum, myrtle and silky oak you desired. There were no wild beasts you needed be wary of, and emigrants were told they could travel hundreds of miles without seeing a snake. There were kangaroos, emus, wallabies, dingoes, swans, turkeys, duck and geese to hunt, while its rivers were overflowing with mullet, whiting, bream and perch.

The Land Act of 1868 was crafted to render the colony as attractive as possible to would-be emigrants. They would have to travel there at their own expense, but once there they were entitled to a land order that made them eligible for selected runs available either by grants, purchase or lease—40 acres for every adult, and 20 acres for each child between the ages of one and twelve in settled districts adjacent to market towns, and far greater allotments—up to 640 acres at 15 shillings per acre for land deemed agricultural, and up to 2560 acres for first-class pastoral land at 10 shillings per acre. Payments could be deferred for ten years at zero interest. Much of the land was thinly timbered and needed only the plough to be put to its soils. As regards sheep, prospective farmers were encouraged to purchase second-class pastures at a lower price, as primary pastures made sheep grow too fat and produce wool of inferior quality to those raised on poorer, 'leaner' land. Either way it was guaranteed there would be ample timber available for fencing, a reliable telegraph and frequent mail services for communication, and an effective police force to keep the peace.

It must have sounded too good to be true. Once you arrived you'd be met by a government representative who would advise you of the best localities in which to live, and where employment could be found, and free passage on the colony's expanding rail network was guaranteed for one month, allowing one to gauge where to settle. New arrivals were reminded of the advantages squatters had in Queensland in comparison to other colonies. For instance, squatters had greater rights to preemptive purchases, and if ever part of their land was withdrawn for sale or selection, any improvements made by the squatter would be fairly valued and compensated for. Squatters on new selections would, however, have to venture further inland and therefore have to pay higher wages for labour and greater land carriage costs too, and because of this people were encouraged to stay closer to settled districts if they had no prior farming experience.

A squatter in 1860s Queensland was very different to those who went, often naively and woefully ill-prepared, beyond the Limits of Location in 1820s New South Wales. In Queensland, a generation on, a squatter was considered an educated man with capital. They were respectable members of the community, even Justices of the Peace, and could be found throughout the elected legislature. Squatters' residences were the centrepieces of small villages with large numbers of employees; so many, in fact, that some even had schoolhouses built for the employees' children. Homesteads had spare rooms for travellers, and were surrounded by gardens and orchards. Squatter families also provided the means by which young emigrants, called 'new chums', would be given years of training in what was called the 'colonial experience', that is, knowledge of station life gained the only way such knowledge *could* be gained— through hard work. These young men, usually from wealthy English families, were sent here only as a last resort, having shown no aptitude for family businesses back home. They were shipped out not to be squatters, so much, but to have whatever it was that was negative or destructive in their characters exorcised by the rigours of station life.

In 1859, while leading an expedition of three men and fifteen horses to the border of South Australia and the land that would one day be known as the Northern Territory, the explorer John Stuart stumbled upon a beautiful natural spring, which he described in his journal thus:

> I have named this The Spring of Hope. It is a little brackish, not from salt, but soda, and runs a good stream of water. I have lived upon far worse water than this. To me it is of the utmost importance, and keeps my retreat open. I can go from here to Adelaide any time of the year and in any sort of season.

The Scottish-born Stuart was one of the nation's most indomitable inland explorers, and his journeys would result in the annexation of massive tracts of country for the South Australian government. But not even he could have guessed that his 'Spring of Hope' was part of a vast ocean of water that lay beneath his feet.

The discovery of the Great Artesian Basin—that ocean of subterranean water that lies beneath 23 per cent of the Australian continent—would have to wait until 1878. Coupled with the almost parallel perfecting of the mechanics of refrigeration, these discoveries were the twin events that combined to transform the Australian cattle industry. Refrigeration brought foreign markets to Australia's doorstep, and fresh artesian water meant new stations could be established on lands that were previously unsuitable for grazing.

The first flowing bore was struck at Kallara Station near Bourke in New South Wales in 1878, a shallow bore struck at a depth of just 43 metres. But the benefits of the Great Artesian Basin were felt most in Queensland, beneath which the majority of the basin sat, particularly in the marginal lands of the state's far west where settlements advanced in good years, only to recede when the rains failed. Because of the high cost of drilling, the first bore wasn't drilled in Queensland until 1888, spurred by a prolonged period of drought. By 1897, the number of bores either drilled or in the process of being drilled was approaching 550.

The discovery of the Great Artesian Basin helped to sustain life along dry stock routes and encouraged pastoralists to push ever westward, digging thousands of kilometres of drains to properties that would not have otherwise existed. It helped squatters who had lost their lands in the selection acts of the 1860s, 1870s and 1880s to move much further inland than they would ever have otherwise contemplated in the search for land, and captured the imagination of farmers, scientists and even poets. In 1895, Banjo Paterson visited Dagworth Station near Winton in north-west Queensland where he wrote the lyrics to *Waltzing Matilda*. It's long been thought he was inspired by the 1016-metre well that was dug there, the water from which came out at 196 degrees Fahrenheit (91 degrees Celsius), close to boiling point, and yielded in excess of 1,250,000 gallons (5,687,500 litres) a day. One bore drilled at Charleville in 1889 emerged with such force it brought with it the remnants of fossilised ferns.

In 1876, the author and adventurer David Kennedy Junior wrote *Kennedy's Colonial Travel*, an account of his travels through Australia, New Zealand and, eventually, Canada, in which he described a squatter he met in Rockhampton, the capital of the far north frontier. The squatter, Kennedy wrote, had just ridden into town from his property '200 miles upcountry'. Years earlier a number of Aborigines had attacked his family and killed his father, and the son now ran the station. The son thought station life dull, with not a lot to do each evening other than read a book or a magazine or visit his distant neighbour. One day a travelling circus stopped by and, with the station owner's permission, set up their tent within sight of his homestead.

In addition to his 45,000 sheep, the squatter owned 100 horses and broke in 40 colts every year. He described in colourful language to Kennedy how the colts would back up, plunge forward, rear and buck—whatever the horse could do to get the thing that was riding it off its back. Vicious young colts were called 'buck-jumpers' and would invariably splay out their forelegs, place their head between them and then, once its back was sufficiently arched, spring into the air, sending the rider flying into the dirt. The aim was to stay in the saddle until the animal exhausted itself, a feat easier said than done. The Aborigines, it seemed, fared better. 'The black man', Kennedy wrote, 'makes a good rider; he clings to the stirrup solely with his big toe, and seems to have excellent foothold, for he sits securely and gracefully'.

The two men talked for the better part of the afternoon, and by the time the squatter was done there was barely an aspect of station life that Kennedy wasn't familiar with. In particular his idealistic notions of the shearer were dealt some severe blows when told that many of them, at least in this far flung region, were sometimes little more than town layabouts in need of work, or mere labourers turned shearer for the day. Sheep given over to such men were in danger of having their throats cut by shears or maybe receiving a stab in the ribs that would be covered over by a blob of tar.

Shearing was physical work, but the real work was in getting the sheep to market, which in this case meant a 1932-kilometre journey to Melbourne. There were never less than 10,000 sheep in a single drive, led by a 'boss' and just a handful of drovers. Travelling by compass they ignored the roads, where possible taking the straightest, most direct line, with the sheep feeding on various squatters' runs as they went. To avoid lingering on roads or devouring too much of other farmers' grasses, the law stipulated they must travel at least 9.6 kilometres a day, which in this particular squatter's case meant a gruelling journey of nine months.

In the end, the wealth of the Shepherd Kings and the Grass Dukes—their quail hunts, horse-racing and cellars of fine wines—would not last. The second half of the nineteenth century brought changed political attitudes and the introduction of various land acts designed to limit their holdings and give priority to the 'selector' settlements of the southern colonies. Profits from wool and cattle, that had been consistently high until 1866 turned into five years of depressed prices before a six-year upturn in 1871 preceded a period of droughts, floods and increasing costs to production. Some pastoralists saw the bad times coming and diversified into agriculture. Others either sold off their land or lived off the money they'd borrowed.

By the end of the 1890s, the glory days of the Darling Downs had faded into history.

Victoria River Downs Head Station, Northern Territory, 1891.
State Library of South Australia

7

'KINGS IN GRASS CASTLES': SETTLING THE TOP END

'Cattle kings ye call us, then we are
Kings in Grass Castles that may be
blown away upon a puff of wind.'
—Patrick 'Patsy' Durack, 1878

In 1849, the British government's confidence in their dominion over the *whole* of Australia was so entrenched, and their claim to its territories deemed so secure from foreign threats, that the settlement at Port Essington on the Cobourg Peninsula, established in 1838, was abandoned without qualm. Not only that, but no thought was given to the establishment of *any* new settlements anywhere along the Northern Territory coastline. The worldwide gaining of territory and expansion of British interests was, of course, still a priority, but a fundamental shift in policy as to the method of acquisition had occurred. In 1849, old navigation Acts, designed to give tariff protection to British goods, were repealed in favour of free trade and the pursuit of new trade agreements (backed by the threat of British naval might).

So what did this new form of 'indirect' colonialism mean? What it meant for the Northern Territory and northern Australia in general was simple: facilitating settlements in the Top End was a cost the British government was no longer interested in meeting. If the lands there were ever to be settled, we'd have to do it on our own.

Among the vast array of explorers and pioneers whose epic journeys and visions fill the pages of our first hundred years, few can match the calibre, the determination and the epic achievements of two men: Patrick Durack, the eldest son of an immigrant Irish family, and the legendary drover and inveterate wanderer, Nathaniel 'Bluey' Buchanan.

Patrick Durack was born in County Clare, Ireland, in 1834, the first of eight children in a family that would struggle heroically in the 1840s famine. Emigrating to New South Wales in May 1853 in search of a better life, tragedy soon struck when just weeks after their arrival Patrick's father, Michael, was accidentally killed. Not yet twenty years old but keenly aware of his new responsibilities, Patrick set out on his own to the Ovens River diggings in Victoria, where he earned over £1000 in just eighteen months, enough money to enable him to return to New South Wales and purchase a small holding at Mummel near Goulburn, a place that his mother Bridget and his family could call home.

In 1863, consumed by a hunger for new land, Patrick, together with brother Michael, brother-in-law John Costello (Patrick had married John's sister Mary in July 1862) and William Landsborough, the first explorer to complete a north–south traverse of the continent, set out for south-western Queensland with horses and a small herd of cattle, all of which perished on the journey. After surviving an appalling drought on the way which nearly took their lives, and well might have were it not for the kindly intervention of Aborigines, the men went on to peg out an astonishing 44,000 square kilometres of land. In 1868, they built their first homestead at Thylungra Station entirely from rammed earth. The single-storey homestead, with its thatched roof and wide verandahs, remained the station's primary dwelling for more than 70 years. Within eleven years of establishing Thylungra they had amassed over 30,000 head of cattle, purchased from shrewd land sales and the profits from a series of hotels, constructed out of little more than mud and spinifex. Patrick, however, was always restless, always looking to new horizons to expand his ever-increasing holdings. And in 1879, a government surveyor named Alexander Forrest set out on a journey that would give Patrick Durack the new horizons he was looking for.

Forrest led a pioneering expedition of eight men from the De Grey River in the Pilbara region of Western Australia to the Kimberley in February 1879. Assisted by Aborigines, who on more than one occasion helped them find supplies of fresh water along the way, by early April they'd reached Beagle Bay on the west side of the Dampier Peninsula near Broome, passing over what was mostly poor and unspectacular land. The group skirted the coast on their way to the Fitzroy River, which they followed for almost 400 kilometres until mountains forced them to take a southerly detour (the mountains would later be named the King Leopold Range, after King Leopold of Belgium, who was the expedition's patron). They crossed a river which Forrest named the Ord on 24 June, and arrived at the Victoria River on 18 August.

With the group's rations almost exhausted and running low on water they reached the telegraph line (the Australian Overland Telegraph Line, the 3200-kilometre line connecting Darwin to Port Augusta, completed in 1872) where they found ample reserves of water in storage tanks kept for line repairers). Forrest and his team then continued on from the telegraph line and discovered large tracts of good pasture—the extent and quality of which, it is fair to say, he somewhat exaggerated—which Forrest named the Nicholson Plains. And it was

Forrest who gave the region its name—the Kimberley—named in honour of John Wodehouse, the First Earl of Kimberley and Secretary of State for the Colonies. Forrest went on to become a successful entrepreneur, reinventing himself as a land agent and leasing more than 51 million acres of land in 1883 alone.

By 1880, almost all of the remaining pastoral country in Queensland had been taken up, and so when Patrick heard of Forrest's discoveries he decided he had to see the land for himself. In 1882, thanks to the financing of a Goulburn banker named Solomon Emanuel, Patrick's brother Michael took horses and provisions aboard a ship in Brisbane and sailed to King Sound and Cambridge Gulf on the Western Australian north-west coast. Michael's favourable report back to his brother—of grassy plains stocked with emus, dingoes and pelicans, and its rivers filled with bountiful barramundi—suggested the Duracks should acquire land on the Ord River, and the Emanuel family on the nearby Fitzroy River. Upon receiving his brother's news, Patrick began making plans for what would become the longest cattle drive the continent had ever seen: taking 200 horses and almost 8000 head of cattle on a 4828-kilometre journey from south-west Queensland to the Kimberley's Ord River.

The mammoth undertaking would take more than two years. Several of the men who accompanied him died on the way, as well as half the cattle, and the cost of the exercise was estimated at more than £70,000. They arrived in the dry season, and while the men had no knowledge or experience of the sort of flooding that can occur when wet season rains come, they noticed that brushwood and native grasses indicated where the high water marks were, and that there were no signs of inundation over the surrounding plains. In contrast to the stunted scrubby landscape of western Queensland, here was a land filled with spreading wild figs, pines and trees with broad healthy trunks and good foliage.

Nothing they saw suggested this was a land that suffered all of the usual scourges. How could they have known they had arrived in the midst of a rare period of healthy rains and minimal flooding? They could not have foreseen that in years to come soil degradation, clouds of mosquitoes, floods, droughts and infestations of cattle ticks would all combine to decimate cattle farming in the East Kimberley. Patrick's driving ambition overwhelmed his concerns about the region's intense isolation. He dreamt of a time when the land would draw settlers by the thousands, much like Victoria and New South Wales before it, that he would create a dynasty that would have no end, with generations of Duracks thriving off the fat of the Kimberley grasses.

When the wet season did arrive, as it was destined to, work on the station came to a virtual halt as engorged rivers transformed the plains into sticky bogs and made it nearly impossible to muster cattle. Attention would turn to other matters, such as repairing boots and saddlebags, preparing fresh inventories and repairing fence lines.

The 1882 Durack cattle drive, and the many that followed, were audacious journeys into one of the last frontiers of European exploration, and helped to open up the East Kimberley to a new breed of pastoralist and further the final chapter in our nation's pastoral expansion. And Patrick Durack was always there, at the forefront of every drive, facing the same obstacles as his beloved cattle. As Patrick himself once wrote after crossing a swollen river:

The drover of cattle (as of sheep) has to know his business here especially when streams are flooded. Sometimes the leaders will not go straight across, but will begin to turn midstream, forming a 'ring' when many are likely to drown. It is at times advisable to take a few over first, so that the rest will then swim across to them. But in a big mob there are always recognised leaders . . . but at times it is necessary for some of the men to ride their horses in and swim with the cattle, someone each side, in order to keep them going straight across, often handling the swimming beasts to turn to direct them. Once a few have reached the far bank all is well for the rest to follow.

Overlanders who were the first to bring cattle to the Kimberley were referred to as 'first footers', the phrase given to the region's first wave of white settlers who used stock and helped establish pioneering stations such as Argyle Downs Station and later Ivanhoe Station and Carlton Reach. The Duracks also brought with them their own labour force, which included a number of Aborigines from western Queensland as well as family members and their acquaintances. The Aborigines would go on to become what Patrick once called his 'trusted Lieutenants', with more than a dozen continuing to work on Argyle Downs for decades to come. But the trust that existed between the Duracks and their transplanted Aboriginal labourers was sadly lacking when it came to local Kimberley Aborigines. And for good reason.

The Duracks pegged out lands from the mouth of the Ord all the way east into the Northern Territory, and over the next six and a half decades would either manage or lease some 3 million hectares (7,413,161 acres) of land and establish some of the greatest cattle stations the colonies had ever seen. And all on ancient Aboriginal lands. With an arrogance sadly typical of European colonisation, the Duracks settled the fertile land around the Ord and gave the land's traditional owners a choice: either work for us, or stay out of our way. Many Aborigines retaliated by spearing livestock, and common was the sight of Aboriginal people being led to prison chained neck to neck, their only crime to resist starvation as best they could in a world they no longer could call their own. For those able to compromise, their bush skills and knowledge of the land became valuable commodities. Patrick's grand-daughter Mary saw this uneasy alliance first-hand, and coined the phrase 'mutual exploitation' to describe it. And to the Duracks' credit, they were viewed by the Aborigines as fairer employers than many of their white settler counterparts.

In 1885, Patrick Durack retired to Brisbane and left the family company in the hands of his sons. He returned with his wife in 1887 and began mining the Kimberley gold fields before being recalled to Brisbane on business. During his absence the family's financial situation deteriorated and he again returned to Argyle Downs where his wife Mary tragically died at the age of just 51 after contracting malaria.

After Patrick's own death in 1898 the Durack's influence on the Kimberley region continued well into the twentieth century. Kim Durack, Patrick's grandson, went to the Kimberley region in 1936 to continue the family traditions, after years of study at Muresk Agricultural College in Perth, but soon realised that distant markets combined with a severe ongoing economic depression meant that a new 'scientific' approach to the land was needed. The soil was declining in value—in 1900 it sustained one animal for every 20 acres, now in the 1930s it was one for every 80 acres. Kim began experimenting, sowing the soil with grasses and various cash crops. By the 1940s, he was growing sorghum and millet, irrigated with water from his own pumping system, and for the remainder of his life was a proponent for large-scale irrigation of northern Australia.

As impressive and historic as the 1882 Durack cattle drive was, the longest cattle drive in Australian history began on 26 March 1883 by the overlanders and pastoralists William and Charles MacDonald—some 5600 kilometres from Goulburn, northwest across the outback and over the Top End into the East Kimberley. The drive took three and a half years. Upon reaching Katherine, Charles fell ill and had to return home, leaving William to continue alone. They'd started with two teams of bullocks, two wagons, 60 horses and 670 head of cattle, of which 343 died along the way. They also lost 47 horses and one of their wagons, with the remaining wagon now commonly accepted as being the first wheeled vehicle to cross the continent. When William finally arrived at the confluence of the Victoria and Margaret rivers on 3 June 1886, he immediately took up land and established what would become Fossil Downs Station. By the early 1950s, Fossil Downs had grown to encompass more than a million acres, and was the largest privately owned cattle station in Australia.

◀◦▶

The Durack's attempt to get stock into the region wasn't the first. In 1864, around a hundred settlers arrived with a boat load of sheep in Camden Harbour, to the south of present-day Broome, and there was a later arrival of sheep at Roebuck Bay. Both forays failed, however, and sheep wouldn't be successfully introduced to the region until Yeeda Station, 40 kilometres south of Derby, took its first herd in 1881. The sheep thrived on the station's grasses and produced 200 lambs in the first year.

The land that became Yeeda Station was first leased by the Murray Squatting Company in 1880, and its homestead with its bark roof and walls of iron and wood is widely considered to be the first house built anywhere in the Kimberley. (Earlier that same year the Murray Squatting Company illegally depastured stock in the Kimberley, in the hope of forcing the Western Australian government to grant them the sort of pre-emptive rights that squatters in the eastern colonies were once able to procure. They were unsuccessful.) Yeeda became a point of departure for the recently discovered Kimberley gold fields, but, like most stations in the Kimberley, its isolation must have seemed overwhelming. Its nearest neighbour, De Grey Station, was 160 kilometres away in the Pilbara.

The Pilbara region along the north-west coast was first explored by Francis Gregory in 1861. Gregory, an English-born explorer, entered the employ of the Western Australian government as a surveyor in 1841 and was an early advocate of opening up the north-west to grazing and agriculture. In 1861, with government backing, Gregory reached Champion Bay and from there led an eight-man party inland, following the Fortescue River before turning south-west to trace a line down the Hardey River. Returning to their departure point at Champion Bay they then set off again, this time in a north-easterly direction. When the party finally returned to Perth in December, Gregory estimated he'd seen somewhere between 2 and 3 million acres of grazing lands. In government ranks, interest in the region was high. The American Civil War starting in 1861 had cut off supplies of cotton to Britain's textile industry, and it was hoped areas suitable for cotton growing might be developed.

The first settlements in the Pilbara began to appear in the 1860s along the Harding River, De Grey River, and the area around the present-day town of Roebourne, and one of the first families to settle the region was that of John and Emma Withnell. Emma had heard from her cousin, explorer Francis Gregory no less, that there was land aplenty in the north and that she and John should consider leaving John's farm in the York district, which they'd been struggling to make profitable, and make a fresh start. So they did. In 1864, they took their two children, as well as Emma's sister Fanny and John's brother Robert, chartered the three-masted schooner *Sea Ripple*, filled it with their belongings and their livestock, and voyaged towards the Pilbara. Emma and her sister were the first white women to set foot there.

They nearly didn't make it. Emma was pregnant with their third child when she and her companions were forced to make camp at Nickol Bay after losing all but 83 of their sheep in a ferocious storm off the coast of present-day Cossack, which blew them 320 kilometres to the north. Repairing their stricken ship they returned to Cossack, and from there walked 13 kilometres inland with makeshift wooden clogs on their feet before making camp on the banks of the Harding River. A week later Emma gave birth to Robert, the first white child born in the north-west. John and Emma took up 30,000 acres beneath the summit of Mount Welcome, named by Emma because of the pools of fresh water they found there.

In late 1864, John and Fanny travelled to Perth and secured a 100,000-acre lease on the land at Mount Welcome and a further 100,000 acres on the Sherlock River. Within two years the population around them had grown to over 200, and their property had become the hub of a growing community that would become known as the Harding River Settlement. On 17 August 1866, it became the north-west's first gazetted town, named Roebourne in honour of John Septimus Roe, Western

Australia's first surveyor-general. John Withnell was the first person in the Pilbara to recognise the potential of canvas for carrying water, and in no time Emma found herself sewing a canvas swathe into a bag with a bottle neck and an accompanying strap, the strap allowing it to be hung on a verandah post and stay cool in the night breezes. John possessed an innate inventiveness that was necessary if one were to prosper in such a harsh environment. He even made a flat-bottomed boat to ferry passengers between Cossack and Roebourne and negotiated lucrative contracts for the privilege.

The growth of the settlement on the Harding River took place amid difficult times. In 1865, a smallpox epidemic killed many Aborigines and threatened the settlers. In 1867, the coastal trading ship, *Emma*, named after Emma Withnell, with its 42 passengers and one of the Withnell's own wool clips in the hold, disappeared without a trace. In 1868, John realised the diving abilities of the local Aborigines and would often spend time on the coast organising pearling forays with other pastoralists, in an effort to diversify their interests. In the early 1870s, a cyclone all but levelled their community, prompting John to build a larger, stone homestead.

Yet in spite of all their hardships, Emma Withnell persevered. Both she and John treated the local Ngalama Aborigines with kindness, with Emma tending to their wounds and personally vaccinating many during the smallpox epidemic. Through their dedication in forging deep ties with the local Boorong and Banaker peoples they were welcomed into their daily lives and could move throughout the region without hindrance, with John even permitted to witness an initiation ceremony—a rare honour for any settler. Seeing other people was a great comfort particularly to Emma, who at times felt overcome with loneliness, a weight she sometimes described to friends as unbearable.

In time, the Withnells became one of the north-west's great pioneering families. In 1874, Emma was elected to the district's first Board of Education, and although they sold their Mount Welcome Station in 1879, they would spend the next eleven years still in the Pilbara at their station on the Sherlock River, before leaving in 1888 to live in Guildford, now a Perth suburb.

Over a 24-year-period, from 1864 to 1888, the Withnells raised eleven children and established eleven stations, which were in time either owned or managed by their sons or sons-in-law. Their son Jimmy is credited with starting the Pilbara gold rush, which began two years after the great rush for gold in the Kimberley. At Mallina Station in January 1888, while splitting logs for a humpy, Jimmy picked up a rock to throw at some bothersome crows when he noticed it shone with glistening flecks of yellow. The telegraph did the rest. In no time prospectors, their skills forged in the Kimberley fields, were everywhere. Officially more than 20,000 ounces (566 kilograms) were taken from the Pilbara by the beginning of the 1890s, but the true figure will never be known.

John Withnell died in Perth in 1898 at the age of 74. Twelve months later Emma, who was only 57, built a house on the banks of the Avon River 100 kilometres from Perth, but she made several journeys back to the north-west in the ensuing years to visit her children and grand-children. Emma, who had by this time long earned the title 'The Mother of the North West', died in her sleep on 16 May 1928.

As late as the 1870s, no successful British settlement had been established in the far north-west. In fact, from its very inception the population of the entire Western Australia colony had been painfully slow to develop. Its primary settlement, the Swan River Colony, was established in 1829 with some 400 civilian and military settlers who arrived aboard the ships HMS *Sulphur* and *Parmelia*. By 1832, the population stood at a miserly 1500. In 1833–34, a total of twelve ships left the colony, taking with them almost 1400 settlers, around as many as were left behind. Ongoing difficulties in clearing the land for crop production saw the population crawl its way upwards to 5886 by 1850. Also, the colony was seen as a 'free settlement' without the feared 'convict stain', much in the vein of South Australia. This meant convict labour was officially not an option and couldn't be used to further the colony's development. (The colony would eventually be constituted a 'penal settlement' in 1849.)

Throughout the 1840s, illegal squatting on Crown land had become so widespread, just as it had in the colonies to the east, that the Western Australian government was forced to introduce land leases. In 1851, land was divided into Class A and Class B. Class A was defined as land within either 5 kilometres of a town or 3 kilometres of the coast or source of permanent water, while Class B was everywhere else. Sheep were the preferred stock of the south-west, although flock sizes were considerably smaller than those in the east, with average numbers in the west between 2000 and 4000 head rather than 10,000 or more—modest numbers which in turn meant the large squattocracies that developed in the east would not evolve here. There was still a sprinkling of large pastoralists, but they worked closely with more town-centred owners of small flocks and the holdings of local agriculturalists. There was also a greater sharing of flocks, and of the labour used to maintain them.

The pastoral industry in the colony's south-west was very different to what evolved in the north, where the pastoral visions that characterised the great cattle stations of Queensland would one day be transplanted and realised. It must have seemed a monumental task, considering the distances and obstacles involved. To drive cattle from Queensland to the barely known landscapes of the Kimberley and the Northern Territory's Top End would require planning, perseverance and, above all, some kind of dependable route along which one could travel.

And one mighty track, the Old Gulf Track, made it all possible.

◄O►

You won't find the Old Gulf Track on any historical maps; due to its sheer remoteness, a lack of agreed markers along the way and its short history it managed for the most part to avoid being documented. Yet while its existence was brief—just 40 years from 1879 to not long after the end of World War I—it made possible the pastoral settling of a vast swathe of Australia. It was our equivalent of America's Oregon Trail, an immigration highway trodden by the hooves of tens of thousands of cattle. And while the economic hardships of the 1890s, and a lack of local markets, might have seen many of those cattle retrace their paths back along it to more dependable southern pastures, for those who stayed the trail provided a new way of life in a previously unknown land.

As to precisely where the track started and the route it took, there is still conjecture. Some say it began east of the Queensland border at Turn Off Lagoon on the Nicholson River, while others claim it originated at Settlement Creek to the west in the Northern Territory. Whatever its origins, it wound its way westward between the Barkly Tableland and the Gulf of Carpentaria until reaching the Roper River Valley, where it continued past Old Elsey Station before turning north along the Overland Telegraph to Katherine. A variety of stock routes continued further north to Darwin and from there turned westward and on to Western Australia.

Pioneered by the explorer Ludwig Leichhardt in 1844–45, the trail was first used to herd cattle in 1872 when Wentworth D'Arcy Uhr, the noted gold prospector, Queensland police officer and cattle driver, took 400 head of cattle from Charters Towers to Roper Bar on the Overland Telegraph. A man with a fearsome reputation for violence, it's said that he shot any Aborigines that got in his way and whipped one of his own men who had dared to cross him.

Yet Uhr's journey was considerably less eventful than others who attempted the crossing. Men would desert their posts, cattle would wander off only to be speared by local Aborigines, progress would be slowed for weeks by flooded rivers, and drovers would be laid low with bouts of fever. Despite the dangers, by 1877 vast regions of the Northern Territory had been leased by settlers who had arrived in the southern colonies too late to find any decent land there. And so it fell to men like Patrick Durack to play their part in the carving out of a new chapter in our pastoral history. And, of course, legends like Nat Buchanan.

—◀○▶—

Nat Buchanan, recognised by the 1988 Australian Bicentennial Committee as one of the 200 people who made our nation great, was a mythic figure of the Australian bush. Poems and songs have been written about him. Another Irishman, Buchanan was born in Wexford, and arrived in Australia with his father Charles, mother Anne and four brothers in 1837 when he was eleven years old. The family settled in the New England district of New South Wales, and Nat had an unremarkable upbringing. As an adult he spent time prospecting for gold, and in 1859 moved to Rockhampton in Queensland.

Along with explorer William Landsborough, Buchanan was the first European to explore Queensland's central west, establishing Bowen Downs Station in 1862 and putting 3000 head of cattle on its 3885 square kilometres. In 1867, he abandoned the station after a period of prolonged drought, but became the first person to pioneer a stock route from the station north to the Gulf Country. He was the first European to traverse the Barkly Tablelands, succeeding where others had failed and paving a new route into the Top End.

Buchanan set a droving record in 1880 when he took more than 20,000 cattle along the Old Gulf Track to Glencoe Station, a 1609-kilometre journey with no predefined route and no settlements along the way. He was the first to establish a station, Wave Hill, in the Northern Territory's Victoria River District, and was one of the first men to take cattle into the East Kimberley when he took 4000 head to Ord River station in 1883 on a route followed three years later by gold prospectors desperate to get to the gold fields around Halls Creek. Buchanan described the Ord River landscape as being 'very good, basaltic and limestone plains with bald hills, well watered with creeks and springs, timber rather scarce, and herbage—chiefly Mitchell grass'.

Buchanan was an explorer at heart, and most of his adventures went unrecorded. No doubt they were similar to the one described in this verse about the dreaded Murranji Track.

> Wild dogs howl and hedge-wood groans,
> A night wind whistles in semi-tones,
> And bower birds play with human bones
> Under a vacant sky.
> The drover's mob is a cloud of dust,
> The drover's mob is a sacred trust,
> Where devil says 'Can't!' and God says 'Must!
> Out on the Murran-ji.

Due to the extreme isolation of stations across the Top End, droving routes assumed a level of importance like nowhere else. The Canning Stock Route is probably the most famous and least used of them. The Old Gulf Track was the first, but one other cannot pass without a mention. It went by several names over the years. The first to cross it before it even became a route called it the 'Death Track' and sometimes the 'Suicide Track', but eventually it came to be known as the Murranji Track, the 'Ghost Road of the Drovers'—a torturous path through a region of 'sinister, soundless scrub' successfully traversed for the first time in 1886 by none other than that most indomitable of early explorers and drovers, Nathaniel 'Bluey' Buchanan.

The Murranji was short in comparison to other droving routes—just 240 kilometres in length. But the land through which it passed tested the nerve of all who entered it, filled with dense stands of lancewood and bulwaddy scrub that made it just about impossible to prevent cattle attempting to wander off or being spooked when branches rubbed together in the wind. Once a stampede started it was impossible to contain, with long hours spent rounding up cattle that went off in more directions than a compass. Pleas from drovers to the government to clear the land of the scrub went unheeded, and the track passed through some of the most drought-affected lands in the country, which proved a great obstacle until the digging of the first bores. George Farwell, the English-born traveller and prolific author of life in colonial Australia, who arrived in Sydney from London in 1935, described the landscape of the track, which hadn't changed any in the decades since the droving days ended:

> No one who has not seen the bullwaddi can appreciate its savage nature. It spreads its very many upward growing limbs very close to the ground, and is so tough you can never bend it, and can break it only when it is close to dying. Its branches have spikes like iron that cut deep into flesh and can impale a beast rash enough to collide with it at speed. It is not a tree, but something of a medieval torture chamber. The lancewood, despite its name, is not so aggressive. It is a thin, straight growing acacia, almost as slender as a tribesman's spear, but again it grows so thickly as to make the passage of a mob of cattle difficult.

Buchanan discovered the first waterhole in the Murranji's flat, parched terrain, but it wouldn't be the curious historical footnote it is were it not for its prickly, wretched undergrowth. Take that away and all you're left with is just another stock route. That Buchanan dared to penetrate it at all is remarkable enough. Unlike the much-hyped Canning Stock Route, which in its entire history saw the movement of just a few thousand cattle, it's estimated a million of the beasts were driven, reluctantly, through the diabolical Murranji maze.

Although Buchanan was the first white man to cross it, others came close. In 1855–56, Augustus Gregory, an English-born surveyor, explored the west and north of the region while following the Victoria River but failed to encounter its scrub. In 1861, John Stuart, in his second unsuccessful attempt to cross the continent from south to north, encountered what he described in his journal as a 'small leaved tree much resembling the hawthorn, spreading out into many branches from the root' as he tried to make his own way towards the Victoria River. He described it as being 'as thick as a hedge', and indeed the plant was known for a time as 'hedgewood' before being given the name 'bulwaddy'. Stuart failed to pass through what he called 'the thickest scrub I have ever had to contend with'—his horses refused to enter it, and after repeated attempts to skirt around it, having had 'our hands, faces, clothes . . . saddlebags . . . all torn to pieces', he returned to Adelaide.

Nat Buchanan never chose to put down roots and become a pastoralist. Being sedentary was never in his nature. Instead it was his gift to open the way for others. Throughout his life he acquired little by way of possessions, and we are left to guess at the many wonders he must have seen. And it is very likely, as was claimed by the *Bulletin* on 9 July 1881, that even with eighteen years of exploring still ahead of him, Nathaniel 'Bluey' Buchanan had already helped facilitate the settling of more land than any other single person in our nation's history.

The Kimberley was not just cattle country. There were those who took sheep there too, in no small part due to the report compiled by Alexander Forrest who estimated the valleys he'd seen on his 1879 journey were capable of 'depasturing a million sheep'. In 1881, the explorer and pastoralist George Julius Brockman, born in the Swan River Colony in 1850, arrived in Beagle Bay with 500 sheep. Before ever setting foot in the Kimberley, Brockman had led a colourful and adventurous life. At age sixteen he left home with all he possessed on his saddle and rode over 600 kilometres to Busselton, where he hunted wild cattle on the Donnelly River. He became foreman at a couple of sheep stations, but soon tired of that and sailed a teak log with chaff bags for sails north to Shark Bay to try his hand at pearl fishing. Later, in the Pilbara region, he managed De Grey Station, the colony's first pastoral lease. Brockman stocked 100,000 acres along the Meda River with 1100 ewes before acquiring the 800,000-acre Minilya Station from his brother in 1884.

In 1881, a pastoral boom the equal of anything in the southern colonies occurred in the upper regions of the Northern Territory in the region known as the Gulf Country, an area of some 223,600 square kilometres comprising 17 per cent of the territory. It was administered by the colonial government in Adelaide, as from 1863 to 1911 the territory was part of South Australia. The lease on the first station to be established there, Elsey Station on the Roper River, was taken up by Abraham Wallace in 1879. (Jeannie Gunn, the Australian author and teacher, arrived there with her husband Aeneas in 1902 and her classic book on life in the outback, *We of the Never Never*, published in 1908, is an account of her time at the station.)

The stations in the Gulf Country were massive, with 16,000 square kilometres shared between just fourteen land owners. Upon taking up leases, land owners had three years to comply with legislation on mandatory minimum stock levels and by the middle of 1885 all fourteen stations were fully stocked.

Tragically, the conquest of the Gulf Country came at enormous cost to the nineteen Indigenous language groups that had called the region home for at least 35,000 years. No one can know for sure, but it's estimated between 600 and 800 Aboriginal men, women and children were killed between 1881 and 1910 in as many as 50 massacres, made all the more incomprehensible considering six out of the original fourteen stations failed, and were abandoned within a decade. Only two of the original fourteen stations, Eva Downs Station and Walhallow Downs Station, had a policy of 'not shooting blacks'. Interestingly, they were also the only two stations that were small in scale, and not owned by wealthy investors or partnerships.

Throughout the region, settlement was achieved at the point of a gun. And what guns they were. Either the .57-calibre Snider rifle, designed to bring down an elephant on the African savannah, and the even more powerful .45-calibre Martini-Henry that could kill at a distance of more than a kilometre. On 14 November 1885, with the news of the killings in the north beginning to filter through to the streets of Adelaide, the *South Australian Register* wrote a scathing denunciation: 'Down in South Australia good men try to civilise them with the Bible; elsewhere we civilise them with the Martini-Henry rifle'.

In the Kimberley region, too, massacres were not uncommon. Charles Dashwood, the South Australian-born judge and public servant known for his fair and humane treatment of Aborigines, noted that some travellers were shooting them 'for sport', while others had heard tales of a race of 'warlike savages' that existed to the west of the border and killed them on sight more or less out of fear. Dashwood wrote that during the years of the Kimberley gold rush prospectors and drovers 'shot the blacks down like crows'. The slaughter became so widespread, even the pro-settlement *Northern Territory Times* spoke out against its 'indiscriminate' nature, saying there 'ought to be a show of reason in the measure of vengeance dealt out to them', a point of view at odds with its sentiments just weeks earlier after the death of a prospector in Arnhem Land when it editorialised to no one in particular: 'Shoot those you cannot get at, and hang those that you do catch on the nearest tree as an example to the rest'.

In the Kimberley in 1883, a survey of the valleys around the Fitzroy, Mena and Lennard rivers counted eight stations with a total of 22,000 sheep. But there were problems. Sheep were not as hardy as cattle. Footrot and scab were rife along the coastal plain where rainfall was heavy. The Kimberley's natural grasses grew to enormous heights in the wet season, as high as 1.8 metres, and when the dry season came were of little use

as 'nibbling' grass for sheep. And local Aborigines were increasingly fond of mutton so sheep needed constant shepherding, not
just to protect them from Indigenous appetites but also from
dingoes and even toxic plants.

Early flood events tended to go unrecorded, yet floods
would regularly come and go and in their wake decimate sheep
flocks. Despite this, the speculative land boom took hold in
the Kimberley from the mid-1880s, and by 1900 there were
seven stations along the Fitzroy River alone, with as many as
14,000 sheep transported to Fremantle every year. By 1899,
there were over 230,000 sheep in the Kimberley, but after
1910 sheep numbers began a gradual decline which continued
until the land was almost bereft of them. The tropical north
was always going to be too wet for sheep to thrive, and when
the ground wasn't too wet it proved far too harsh, better suited
to hardy cattle than vulnerable sheep. Although you'd have
been hard-pressed telling that to the greatest cattle baron our
nation has ever produced—Sidney Kidman.

Sidney Kidman was born in Adelaide in 1857 to George and
Elizabeth, a farming couple who sent their son to be educated
at private schools, the influences of which proved insufficient
to prevent him from leaving home with 5 shillings to his name
and a one-eyed horse at the age of thirteen and riding off to
join his brothers who were droving sheep and herding stock in
the Barrier Ranges in the far west of New South Wales.

Even from a young age, Kidman possessed a level of acumen
and enterprise that made his relentless acquisition of wealth
almost inevitable. His first horse deal, made while working at
Mount Gipps Station in the heart of the lower Barrier Ranges,
was the purchase a poorly conditioned horse for 30 shillings from
an itinerant drover. With good feed and nurturing the chestnut
colt's constitution rebounded so dramatically that Kidman
decided to keep it. Realising an ability to quickly turn around an
animal's fortunes and make a quick profit, he set about purchasing a second such horse, returning it to health, and even when
unable to sell it, managed to exchange it for two more horses.

Kidman liked to sit around campfires and listen to stories told by passing drovers, stories that described a great flood plain in Queensland's Three Rivers country, of epic journeys along the Lachlan River, and one particular night a story about a place called Cobar where, it was said, prospectors had begun to find large deposits of copper. Kidman, upon hearing this, made an impulsive and very Kidman-like decision: he would leave Mount Gipps, strap his swag to his saddle, and ride his chestnut colt east—*400 kilometres east*—to Cobar.

Arriving in Cobar, a mining town so new it was still in the stages of being developed, he guessed where the main street would be, began to cut down some saplings, and made himself a shed. He'd decided that mining wasn't for him, but feeding people who were miners might be. So he determined to become a butcher. Kidman purchased some bullocks from a cattle station almost 50 kilometres away, returned with them to Cobar, slaughtered them, and sold out of meat in just a few hours. The next day he returned to the cattle station and negotiated a better price on ten bullocks. Then he purchased a bullock wagon and won the contract to transport the copper ore to Bourke.

The business grew in value, and a year later he was offered £1000 for it by a Sydney businessman, which he accepted. Kidman never forgot those stories of a great flood plain in the south-west of Queensland, and it was cattle that was in his blood, not business. He travelled north and bought 500 head of drought-affected cattle, drove them to some well-grassed pastures along the Bullo River in New South Wales, and when they'd recovered drove them on into Broken Hill and sold them at a premium. Combine this windfall with an inheritance he received at the age of 21, and there was no stopping him. He purchased a fourteenth share of the Broken Hill Proprietary Company (BHP), and in 1886 purchased his first station, Owen Springs, west of Alice Springs. Although Kidman established stations throughout the country, his daring approach to unlikely acquisitions made the Kimberley a particularly attractive target, and his stations there, which sat on some of the most unpromising horizons on the continent, persevered through bad times that saw others walk off the land.

Many consider Kidman's greatest achievement was realising the potential of the flood plain around the Three Rivers area in south-west Queensland—what would soon become known as the Channel Country. Kidman could spot the potential for green pastures where others only saw barren landscapes, and he knew that when it rained up north in the Gulf Country the waters would eventually come here, regardless of the absence of local rains.

It was in the overlooked 'middle-ground' of the continent that Kidman began purchasing land which would, in time, guarantee him access to water and make possible the great cattle drives from his northern stations to southern markets. He established two links of interdependent stations— one stretched from the Gulf of Carpentaria down through western Queensland and western New South Wales to South Australia, and the other from the Fitzroy River in the Kimberley and Victoria River Downs in the Northern Territory all the way to the Flinders Ranges. Kidman believed that his supply chain—which centred on the Three Rivers country of south-west Queensland and included stations spread throughout the back country of the Northern Territory, Queensland, New South Wales and South Australia like Carcoory Station, Dubbo Downs, Glengyle and Victoria River Downs—gave him the strategic edge to survive any drought. The 1901 drought tested his theory, but he prevailed. One million out of the four million cattle in Queensland died that year, while Kidman lost only a 'modest' 50,000 head.

Kidman's cattle drives were the stuff of legend. Some began in the Barkly Tableland down through Kidman properties fed by the Georgina and Diamantina rivers and down Cooper Creek into South Australia. Others began at his Kimberley properties Victoria River Downs and Fitzroy Downs and headed south towards Alice Springs down the Oodnadatta Track and into the Flinders Ranges. Kidman became a larger-than-life figure, known throughout the land. When a rodeo was organised at Jubilee Oval in inner-city Adelaide to mark his 75th birthday, 40,000 people turned up. Fences were crushed, people fell off rooftops, while others climbed trees to view the events. One hundred people were injured. When Sidney Kidman died in 1935, at the age of 78, he owned 68 stations covering almost 68,000 square kilometres, stocked with 250,000 sheep and 200,000 cattle. He owned more pastoral land than anyone else in the world, his achievements so remarkable they were reflected upon in obituaries the world over, from New York to London.

Pastoralists like Patrick Durack and Sidney Kidman, famous and influential as they were, were hardly representative of the sort of men who came to the north and attempted to settle it. More common were those prospective settlers with limited means who fell midway on the spectrum between the penniless stockman and the pastoral capitalist. Men like Thomas Kilfoyle.

Born in Ireland in 1842, Kilfoyle arrived in Australia in June 1855. Hardly anything is known of his two decades spent as a drover, but in her book *Kings in Grass Castles* Mary Durack noted he was employed at her father's Thylungra Station in south-west Queensland in 1875, where his skills, even then, were viewed by her pioneering father as almost indispensable:

> Tom Kilfoyle, one of the best bushmen in Australia, was doing the carrying for Thylungra. He'd been through a few dry gullies in his time and he knew the ropes and all the tricks of the stockman's trade. Your Grandpa (Patrick) used to reckon he'd sooner have him on his books than his borders. Every time he'd pay him he'd say: 'And here's a bonus, Tom, to keep ye from taking up the block next door'.

Thomas Kilfoyle used his time in Queensland to amass £400
of savings, which he invested in 1881 in a bout of 'speculative
grazing'—the practice of using maps to buy land 'sight unseen'
to be used as leverage in the acquisition of the land he *really*
wanted. In 1882, Kilfoyle joined a Durack expedition into the
East Kimberley district to explore the lower reaches of the Ord
River, and in 1887 began building his own station, which he
named Rosewood, running from the eastern Kimberley region
east into the Northern Territory. On 3 October that year, he
wrote in his diary that he was 'at home all day digging the
well in the morning', the next day 'getting thatch to cover in
the harness room, fetching thatch for the house' and 'getting
rafters for the house, putting on the battens for the house'. Two
more days were spent collecting thatch, and finishing a slab
over the well. It took the entire month of November to collect
enough timber to fence his modest homestead. When the rains
came he'd spend his time indoors repairing pack saddles.

By March 1888, he had sunk another well, squared up his
kitchen posts, cut timber for a new work shed, and made a
list of things he wanted to buy: flour, sugar, tobacco, mustard,
vinegar, trousers, matches, carrots, boots, chaff, oats and clay
pipes. It took anywhere from four to ten days, depending on
the rains, to make a return journey to Wyndham for supplies.
On 28 June 1888, at the second running of the Wyndham Cup,
his horse *Saladin* won the Handicap Hurdle over 1½ miles
(2.4 kilometres). His other entry, *Shamrock*, came second. And
Thomas Kilfoyle was 25 sovereigns and £76 to the good.

Such was the lot of the 'average' Kimberley pastoralist.

Dancing at a picnic at Boulia, Queensland, 1920.
State Library of Queensland

8

AUSTRALIA FELIX

'I have been fighting the desert all my life; and I have won.'
—James Tyson, cattle baron, 1895

Those squatters and pastoralists who, in the 1880s, sat as ageing patriarchs over vast swathes of our nation, had benefited from the roll of the dice. When they took their first steps into the great unknown, it must have seemed as though everything conspired against them. They saw their animals perish in floods, in droughts and in fires, and from diseases they often failed to comprehend, much less contain. They fought Aborigines, who resisted as best they could the forcible taking of their ancient lands. They came here with little knowledge of the continent's climate and its soils, not knowing whether a river that was low was that way because it was *always* low, or would soon be high again. When bad times came, as they inevitably did, many squatters fell, and never rose again.

Only the strong-willed, the competent, and the lucky survived to see their runs evolve into homesteads, homesteads into stations, and stations into dynasties. Hardship was a kind of winnowing which in time bred a pastoral elite, the product of decades of hard work, a generational commitment by families who saw children and grand-children benefit only because of the vision and dedication of those who came before them. John Macarthur's Camden Park didn't attain the status we now accord it until the mid-1850s, twenty years after his death. Pastoral empires didn't emerge overnight.

By the 1870s, most of the good pastoral and grazing lands had long since been settled by squatters and entrepreneurial pastoralists, while various Selection Acts designed to encourage the growth of new communities mostly failed to fulfil their promise when prospective buyers realised they needed more land than the Acts often allowed for in order to eke out a living. As already discussed, squatters survived the era of 'selection' largely unscathed, and even thrived in spite of it by using the law to buy back their own lands under false names, or through the application of other questionable methods.

By the 1880s, the homesteads of many of Australia's great stations were as much symbols of the squatters' determination not to surrender their lands as they were a home. Pastoralists often employed as many as 60 or 70 men, which together with their families meant a station's population could easily reach to well over a hundred. Men slept in barracks, while women often lived in purpose-built cottages built in rows to resemble a suburban street. There were workshops, woolsheds, shearers' quarters, stables, barns and a station store from which everyone could purchase everyday items without having to travel into towns that were often too far away to contemplate. The pastoral homestead was the centre of daily life for station hands and their families, with multiple generations often being in the employ of the same family. And over it all loomed the squatter—the King of his Grass Castle, the Shepherd Kings, the Diamonds of Empire. Masters of all they surveyed.

Power and influence on such a scale often led to arrogance

and autocratic rule, though acts of benevolence were not uncommon. It's easy to see how squatters may even have begun to dream of a future Australian aristocracy, with themselves at the helm—although any such thoughts were banished when a proposal for hereditary peerages was put to London's House of Commons in the 1850s, and met with howls of derision. Another impediment to any dreamt-of aristocracy was the control the British government maintained over the Australian civil service. The privileged children of squatters found themselves unable to enter influential public positions, and had to content themselves with private professions. The frustration many squatters felt at being locked out of public office saw some divert their energy into the building of some *very* big houses, saying in brick and mortar what a peerage did on paper.

In 1875, a paper was presented to the Agricultural Society of New South Wales by English-born pastoralist Thomas Mort and French-born engineer Eugene Niccolle. Entitled *The Preservation of Food by Freezing and the Bearing it will have on the Pastoral and Agricultural Interests of Australia*, it was another step forward in the decades-long quest to develop the means to transport frozen carcasses to Britain, and thus establish an export market for cattle. Various experimental concepts would follow until eventually, on 29 November 1879, the SS *Strathleven* sailed from Sydney with a compressed air system in its hold designed to keep beef chilled on long voyages. The *Strathleven* arrived in London in February 1880, its cargo intact, and new horizons for the exporting of meat and dairy products to Britain transformed the cattle industry.

As the 1880s progressed, the colonies left behind their pioneering phase and had about them a growing maturity, with an ensconced squattocracy making fortunes so vast they were the envy of the dominions. And few associations could boast such an exclusive membership. In New South Wales in 1883 there was in excess of 8 million acres of colonial land under the ownership of just 96 individuals, a rural clique of immense influence and means. By 1895, more than 320 pastoral properties, each of them extending over a minimum 20,000 acres, spread far and wide across the state, their combined acreage constituting an area larger than Ireland. By the late 1890s wool prices, which had been in the doldrums for five years thanks to depression and drought, remained low despite the wool clip compensating for the lower price due to an increase in the weight of the average fleece.

When the speculative land boom of the 1880s peaked in 1888, banks which had lent heavily and operated in an era devoid of government-provided deposit guarantees began to close their doors in the face of rising bankruptcies. The closures were infectious—in August 1891, the Van Diemen's Land Bank; in September, the Mutual Provident, Land, Investing & Building Society; in February 1892, the Toowoomba Deposit Bank; in July 1892, the Victoria Mutual Building & Investment Society— and became a full-blown crisis when in January 1893 the Federal Bank closed. By May, almost a dozen more banks across the country had suspended trading.

The crisis in the nation's banks would be largely resolved by 1894, but in 1893 the effects of a worldwide depression proved far more difficult to shake. It was not a uniform calamity—its epicentre was Victoria while, by contrast, Western Australia rode on something of a boom in the 1890s due to the discovery of gold with the Cue, Coolgardie and Kalgoorlie gold rushes of 1891–93. For most of the continent, however, there was no quick bounce back from the effects of the depression, with many economic indicators not showing any real improvement until the early 1900s. During this time there was an almost complete halt in foreign investment, a crucial factor considering it was foreign money that had financed something like 40 per cent of all domestic investment during the boom years of the 1880s. And if all that man-made chaos weren't enough, Mother Nature then entered the game with the devastating Federation Drought.

The Federation Drought of 1895–1903 was the longest period of below-average rainfall to have occurred since European settlement began. A series of three separate El Niño events, its timing couldn't have been worse, coming in the wake of a banking crisis, falling commodity prices and a savage depression. It wasn't the only drought in Australian history that set back colonial progression and decimated sheep and cattle numbers, but it was without doubt the most ruinous. In 1896, oven-like temperatures saw Bourke in outback New South Wales suffer three continuous weeks of temperatures over 44 degrees Celsius and 150 of its inhabitants died from heat and disease. Banjo Paterson in *Song of the Artesian Water* (1896) put it simply enough:

> If we fail to get the water then it's ruin to the squatter,
>   For the drought is on the station and the weather's growing
>   hotter.

The drought decimated livestock in New South Wales, with sheep numbers falling from almost 57 million in 1894 to 36 million by 1899. In 1897, in towns across eastern Australia, the heat combined with an increase in typhoid to push up mortality rates by more than 20 per cent. Dust storms and bushfires raged across the landscape, killing unknown numbers of livestock. They were particularly fierce in Gippsland in eastern Victoria, where smoke turned day into night. In 1898, the drought and choking dust caused the South Australian pastoralist Thomas Pearse to write to the *Burra Record* in despair:

While I am writing this the dust is blowing in clouds; no lambing for the last three years, and a bad prospect for one this year; high rents and wild dogs galore; three parts of this country blown further east . . . It will take three good seasons for the country in question to be of the same value as it was before the drought set in.

Another South Australian pastoralist, Robert Bruce, who went on to achieve fleeting fame as an author in 1902 with the publication of *Reminiscences of an Old Squatter*, described the drought in words that are uncompromising and brutal:

My doleful theme is long protracted drought,
That robs the landscape of its verdant charms,
The anxious squatter of his nightly sleep,
His flocks of life: that swells his overdraft,
Till, like invading host, it sweeps away
His cash, his credit, all his dreams of wealth.

Neither man, beast nor plant were spared its ravages. Vegetation became scarce, and stock values as well as the quantity and quality of wool clips plummeted. Lambs were slaughtered to increase the chances their mothers, spared the task of weaning, might survive. By the time the drought finally broke in 1903 cattle numbers across the colonies had fallen by some 40 per cent (and by two-thirds in Queensland), while sheep numbers halved to 54 million and it would take until 1926 to return to pre-drought levels. Selectors, less able than pastoralists to withstand bad economic times, defaulted on loans. Unemployment among labourers and station hands skyrocketed. The cost of meat fell as farmers were forced to sell animals they were unable to feed, while the cost of scarce crops and grains increased.

Western Queensland was laid waste. One reporter who travelled through the region in 1902 for the *Bulletin* described the apocalyptic effects. The grass was 'withered', the bullocks staggering around 'bleary-eyed'. Sheep were 'mere bones, holding up a pelt', stranded in a landscape with 'not a tree or a shrub for miles; nothing but dust and desolation'. The air smelled 'fetid'; settlers with little to do but lounge on their verandahs 'stupefied with liquor'. And every day ended the exact same way, with the sun going down on the horizon like 'a ball of fire'.

The effects of the drought prompted nationwide discussions on how best to store and distribute water, including plans for the more equitable use of river water in the Murray–Darling Basin and other prominent rivers, improving general irrigation and the building of dams. It can even be argued that the need for a national, unified approach on water was a powerful driver for the 'Yes' vote on Federation that was soon to come.

In South Australia in the mid-1890s, despite decades of what were considered fairly liberal land Acts, the wheat yield remained at a modest 5.2 bushels (0.35 tonnes) per acre and there was little evidence to support the view that better farming methods were making any inroads into the state's challenging soils, or indeed if methods had improved over time at all. When seasons were good, however, South Australia's farmers were able to deliver considerable yields and more than one season saw the colony exporting wheat to markets in Victoria and New South Wales.

Determined to realise the land's potential, the South Australian government began working hard at diversifying its economy and securing the quality of its pastoral industry as well as its emerging industries of dairy, wine and others, with a view to increasing the exports of produce such as eggs, beeswax, honey and butter to Britain. The Central Agricultural Bureau, set up in 1888 with just six private sector members and four public servants, set about advising farmers and pastoralists about approaches to horticulture and land management, and by 1895 had expanded to over 80 branches throughout the state. Specialist agricultural staff conducted experiments in research and development on new crops and potential new fertilisers. The focus was intense and helped bring workers to rural areas. The 1901 census recorded that in excess of 34,000 people were working as farmers on 2,370,000 acres, which translated to one person for every 70 acres, twice the number as in New South Wales and Victoria.

In Tasmania, the 1893 depression affected all the colony's industries with the exception of mining, which had long buttressed the colony's economy, with discoveries of tin at Mount Bischoff in 1871, followed by discoveries along the Ringarooma River, Derby, Bradshaw's Creek, Cox Bite, Stanley River, Gladstone, Coles Bay and countless others. In 1894 alone, the Mount Lyell copper mine produced a staggering 853 tons of copper and silver ore. Beyond the mining sector, however, all was not so shiny. In an effort to stem the loss of non-mining labour—men who were in their prime going to the mainland in search of work— the government passed legislation allowing any person upon reaching their eighteenth year, if they had not already purchased Crown land, to select a single parcel of land of between 15 and 50 acres for the modest sum of 26 shillings and 8 pence per acre. The legislation was a form of selection, and came with some generous financial terms. No deposit was required, and only one-fifteenth of the purchase price was required to be paid annually, beginning after three years. The owner, however, was required to reside habitually on the land for eighteen years, the term of the repayments a big ask for land that was purchased in an unimproved state. In the wake of the 1893 depression almost as much land returned to the Crown via defaults as was sold. Selectors and settlers fell into arrears with creditors and legislation again was passed, this time to allow the postponement of repayments for up to five years.

Despite the effects of the depression still hanging like a cloud over the island colony, the population loss had been arrested by 1894–95. Numbers of stock depastured and the amount of land under pastoral lease also increased, and by 1899 the amount of domestic produce being exported reached a record

£2,577,000. In spite of a history of favouring pastoralism over agriculture—a mostly practical approach given that heavy rains, mountainous terrain and a bitterly cold interior climate made cultivation difficult—the shipping of apples to Great Britain in the 1880s had been a great and ongoing success, and by the 1890s land clearing in the north-east and north-west unlocked the potential of volcanic soils to make the humble potato the island's primary agricultural export. But problems remained. The mineral boom which had brought such great wealth to the island's economy was over, the nascent timber industry was poorly structured and organised, soil exhaustion was becoming evident in some early settled areas, in the north-west potato blight was savaging crops, and restrictive trade policies adopted by the mainland colonies were adversely impacting Tasmania's secondary industries. As the new century dawned, the peculiar challenges that this economically vulnerable colony would face time and again in the decades ahead were beginning to surface.

The 1880s saw the emergence of a 'tropical squattocracy' in Western Australia's Kimberley region. In 1880, the Murray Squatting Company built the region's first homestead with walls of wood and iron and a bark roof. Large stations, such as the Rose family's Parkfield Station with its 30,000 acres of freehold and leased lands, produced meat and salted butter for the Perth market from their herds of beef cattle and champion dairy cows.

Homesteads throughout north-west Western Australia were often separated by distances of over 150 kilometres, and in an attempt to populate these areas and other remote regions a Homestead Act was passed in 1893 which allowed for the granting of homestead leases on very agreeable terms. The Act also allowed for the setting aside of land within 64 kilometres of a railway line on which homesteads no larger than 160 acres could be established without a deposit, by males over the age of eighteen and women who were acting as the sole head of a family, providing they were not already the owners of a property in excess of 100 acres. The framers of the Act were hopeful its generous terms would create interest in previously neglected areas of the colony, foster mixed farming and agriculture and prevent the formation of large freehold stations. But they were destined to be disappointed.

For many, the gold fields still held the lure of more lucrative returns, and, it was hoped, for far less effort than station life on what were considered marginal lands. The problem that Western Australia had grappled with ever since the establishment of the Swan River Colony showed no signs of abating: a tiny population spread so thin you could barely see it made the rapid development of agriculture all but impossible. But in time, ironically, the answer presented itself—new markets that came into being on the back of the discovery of gold. In 1894, the colony had 21,500 acres of land under wheat; by 1898, it was 78,000 acres. In the same period, for oats, barley, and in fact in all of the staple crops under harvest, production outstripped population growth. The colony's croppers were able to defy the vagaries of a dry, harsh land. Sadly, the same could not be said for its pastoralists.

By the end of the nineteenth century, newly established stations in the western Kimberley were monopolising the supply of beef to Perth, and those in the east began looking at developing a stock route that would increase their access to the state's south-west. The government, keen to open up competition and thus lower meat prices, was happy to oblige and in 1905 proposals for a route across three of Western Australia's harshest deserts—the Gibson Desert, the Great Sandy Desert and the Little Sandy Desert—began to gain traction. The man selected to survey the new route was a young and unheralded surveyor named Alfred Canning, and the route he created—with the help of eight men, two horses and 23 camels—was the aforementioned Canning Stock Route.

Stretching from Hall's Creek in the Kimberley to Wiluna in the state's mid-west, the route was surveyed in less than six months in 1906. It was completed in April 1910, after the digging of the last of 54 troughs and water wells, local water sources he likely would not have found were it not for the Martu Aboriginal men who Canning captured, chained and forced to work at his behest. And the wells were designed without a thought given to the needs of the Aboriginal people. Aborigines often could not use them, as the water was too far submerged and couldn't be accessed without a camel to haul it up on the windlasses. Thirsty Aboriginal men, women and children died in their attempts to access the water, some falling into the wells and others injuring themselves on the heavy windlasses. Aboriginal hatred of the wells grew so fierce that they even began to set fire to the timber buckets and handles so that local drovers couldn't use them. By 1917, only a fraction of the wells were still in operation.

The route was 1850 kilometres long, the longest stock route in the world, made longer than it needed to be because of Aboriginal attempts to make its construction as difficult as possible by directing Canning to water sources that were not always in the most direct line. Commercial use of the route began in 1910, with small groups of horses and bullocks at first, but it wasn't until September of 1911 that cattle made the first successful crossing. Conflicts with Aborigines along the route, combined with a high number of damaged wells, saw just eight cattle drives between 1911 and 1931 when Canning was again hired to carry out repair work on the wells. With the wells opened, cattle drives resumed, but the route proved unworkable for very large herds, and over the next 28 years there were just 21 drives along Australia's most mythic stock route.

In Victoria, the era of Marvellous Melbourne and its associated land boom which characterised the 1880s, came to an end, replaced by an urban unemployment rate of 20 per cent. Briefly the second-largest city in the British Empire after London, Melbourne had built 'out' rather than 'up', the precursor of the Australian suburban sprawl, serviced by an expanding network of railways and tram lines. Land speculation, which had been rife, resulted in a spectacular crash which saw Melbourne at the epicentre of the Australian depression of 1893. Growth and investment came to a halt with the exception of the construction of the city's underground sewerage system, and its early 1890s population of 490,000 remained stagnant for the next fifteen years.

Rural Victoria fared little better. By the 1890s, all of the great gold mining towns were faint reflections of their early prosperity, their populations decimated. Robert Croll, a resident of Stawell in western Victoria, lamented how the population had decreased by 2000 in a decade, with entire houses being moved off their stumps leading to 'gaps in the streets that made Stawell look forlorn indeed'. The 1890s saw government attempts to increase population densities in the country through the establishment of small-scale agriculture, seen as necessary to overcome a stagnant population that hadn't increased since the early 1860s.

The policy of closer settlement is thought to have made 1890s Victoria considerably more efficient than New South Wales when it came to wool production, but in terms of overall production the movement of sheep numbers from Victoria to New South Wales could hardly be more striking. In 1860, Victoria produced over 40 per cent of the nation's wool and New South Wales 19 per cent. By the 1890s, Victoria produced only 14 per cent and New South Wales 59 per cent. The early economic dominance of Victoria, which saw Melbourne briefly reign as the nation's capital after Federation, was laid waste in the final decade of the nineteenth century.

In Queensland, the 1893 depression combined with low cattle prices and dwindling markets to deliver many large stations into the hands of receivers, and the further north you went, the greater the sense of loss. Many of the older squatters went under and their properties were in the hands of the banks. Often unable to sell the stations they acquired, banks instead set about improving them, investing in new fencing and water storage. Even expensive artesian wells were occasionally dug, and in the years after Federation the quantity of wells in the Gulf and Etheridge districts was such that cattle loss in dry seasons was drastically reduced.

Demographic and social change also came to northern Queensland in the 1890s with the advent of the 'grazing selector': settlers encouraged onto properties that had been resumed from large stations and came with 30-year leases. This resulted in the establishment of closer settlements, and began to chip away at the north's pervasive sense of isolation. The carving up of large northern stations even had the support of some pastoralists. Edward Palmer, a cattleman whose own station Canobie was repossessed in the early 1890s, felt that most stations in the north were simply too large to manage effectively, with too much rent being paid for unused land and breeding animals often weakened by lack of water.

Perhaps the most revolutionary change to the northern cattle stations, and cattle stations everywhere, was the introduction of refrigeration and the construction of regional freezing facilities. In 1892, the Queensland Meat Export Company began trading in Townsville, and freezing facilities at Bowen and Burdekin among others soon followed, financed in part by a tax placed on stock under the *Meat and Dairy Produce Encouragement Act 1893*. Now, at last, the world's markets were at Australia's doorstep (although a British preference for Argentinian beef contributed to poor prices for Australian meat in London markets and made the export of meat to Britain at times an unprofitable exercise).

Despite the opening of new markets, Queensland and Northern Territory cattle farmers still faced all of the usual farming hurdles. A cattle tick crossed over from the Northern Territory into North Queensland in 1891 and over the next five years decimated northern herds. In 1894, the entire Gulf Country was quarantined, but even this failed to prevent stock losses of up to 60 per cent. Add to this the Federation Drought, which caused untold losses of its own, coupled with increased demand from domestic markets to the south, and it's easy to sympathise with frustrated meat exporters who would lament that they had gone from an era of no markets and an excess of stock to having too many markets but little or no stock.

And yet the continual expansion by Queenslanders, west through the Maranoa and Warrego districts and north along the Fitzroy, Burdekin and Flinders rivers, lured by the prospect of inexhaustible supplies of artesian water, the source of which was still a mystery, saw Queensland approach the new century with unbridled optimism. In the years to come its cattle stations would be the largest in the country, its herds the most numerous and its pastoral potential unrivalled.

In the Northern Territory in the early 1900s, taking advantage of increased prices for cattle, small settlers began taking up leases and grazing licences alongside older, established stations. But much of the Territory was still wild country, particularly the Victoria River District, which even today is something of a blank space on the map but which in 1900, despite the first settlers arriving in the 1830s, was still a no-man's-land populated by a motley assemblage of woolly stockmen, horse thieves, madmen and dreamers. Much of the region, its history either lost or at best poorly recorded, remained effectively closed to outsiders well into the twentieth century, its lands 'locked up' within the fence lines of some of the nation's largest cattle stations. The climate and isolation, however, made most who came here eventually return to live in other more populated regions, a reason why pastoral dynasties in the Victoria River region are today hard to find.

As the 1890s drew to a close, the land holdings of some pastoralists were so immense they almost defied comprehension. James Tyson, the 'millionaire squatter', was born near Narellan in New South Wales in 1819, the son of William Tyson, who had arrived as a convict in 1809. James established a butcher shop in the Victorian gold fields in the 1850s, sold it for £80,000 and by 1898, the year of his death, he owned more than 5.3 million acres on seventeen stations throughout Queensland and New South Wales. He was Australia's first great cattle king and the nation's first native-born, self-made millionaire. Banjo Paterson even wrote a poem about him after his death, which he titled, appropriately and triumphantly, 'T.Y.S.O.N.' and which read, in part:

What tales there'll be in every camp
By men that Tyson knew;
The swagmen, meeting on the tramp,
Will yarn the long day through,
And tell of how he passed as 'Brown',
And fooled the local men:
'But not for me—I struck the town,
and passed the message further down;
That's T.Y.S.O.N.!'

When he died, childless and without a will, James Tyson's estate was worth a staggering £2.35 million dollars, around $10 billion in today's terms. Called 'Hungry' by some for his ravenous desire for pastoral property, the man was barely ill a day in his life. He was tall and broad-shouldered, paid for everything in cash, and dressed in ordinary clothes which allowed him to pass through towns unrecognised. An astute businessman, Tyson was also a hands-on pastoralist, as much at home on a cattle drive as he was in a board room, and enjoyed telling people how he'd spent his life fighting the desert:

I have been fighting the desert all my life; and I have won. I have put water where there was no water and beef where there was no beef. I have put fences and roads where there were no roads. Nothing can undo what I have done, and millions will be happier for it after I am long dead and forgotten.

By the end of 1901, the year of Federation, many of the great pioneers of the Australian pastoral industry were gone. The squatter and prolific author Edward Curr died at Alma House in Melbourne on 3 August 1889, only days after retiring from his position as Victoria's Chief Inspector of Stock. Nathaniel 'Bluey' Buchanan, the tamer of the dreaded Murranji Track, the man who opened up more of outback Australia to settlement than any other and who finally settled down himself at his property Kenmuir on Dungowan Creek outside Tamworth in New South Wales, was gone too.

Patrick Durack died on 20 January 1898, and was buried alongside his wife Mary at the family plot in Goulburn. The original Durack Homestead still survives, but not in its original location. When the creation of the Argyle Dam in the 1970s threatened to flood the historic property it was dismantled stone by stone and moved to the hill on which it now sits. The relocated homestead, 85 per cent true to the original, now sits peacefully among boab and gum trees on the edge of Lake Argyle, its gun barrel hallway still funnelling the Kimberley's cooling evening breezes.

Sidney Kidman was 43 years old when Australia became a nation on 1 January 1901, and with his purchase of the Northern Territory's 21,000-square kilometre Victoria River Downs—'The Big Run'—the previous year, his empire was showing no signs of shrinking. In 1901, the much-lauded Top End bushman Thomas Kilfoyle was still involved in the butchering of meat, in applying for slaughterhouse licences, constructing cattle yards, and, of course, going to race meetings.

The 1890s witnessed the last phase of expansion into the marginal inland areas of the continent and the consolidation of decades of toil and struggle. It was also a period of increased self-awareness, of coming to an understanding of what it meant to be Australian. Quite apart from its contribution to the nation's economy, the era of the pastoral squattocracy did much to foster that spirit of independence that has since permeated so much of Australian society and given rise to that wandering spirit that is still best seen in what Robert Knopwood, writing in Van Diemen's Land in 1805, first referred to as 'the bush'.

And yet through drought and flood and depression and fire, the notion of *Australia Felix*, of 'fortunate Australia', that name given by Thomas Mitchell in 1836 to the verdant, knee-high grasses of Victoria's Western Districts, has never waned. Australians have always felt lucky. At no time in the economic history of a nation had so many economic, political and demographic factors combined to create wealth on the scale wrought by our early pastoralists. We fought, tooth and nail, against the climate and the landscape, and, for the most part, just like 'Hungry' James Tyson, we won.

With Federation we took our disparate colonies and territories and achieved a bloodless union. Yet thirteen years later, the sons and daughters of our pastoralists, our shearers and our swagmen, our labourers, our boundary riders and our stockmen, took their horses, if they had one to call their own, and went to fight in a dreadful war. Our rural and outback stations—our families—suffered irreplaceable losses.

But in the early 1900s, the first hints of war were still many years away, and as the new century unfolded there seemed no gulf wide enough to keep us from what we aspired to. The *Sydney Morning Herald* summed up what life was like in rural Australia, the Federation Drought by then a memory, in the article 'On the Land, Farm and Station' on 8 September 1906:

> There is no rural picture more alluring than a pastoral holding in
> a country fitted for agriculture where droughts come but rarely,
> flocks multiply in profusion, money flows freely, temperatures
> observe considerate averages, and life is close to the idyllic.

For the time being, at least, with the sons and daughters of farmers safely by their sides, working the soils and tending the livestock of Australia Felix, all seemed well.

NOTES

CHAPTER 1

'comfortable hut . . .' from Edmund Perrin and Terry Kass, 'Liberty Plains' in *The Dictionary of Sydney*, 2008

'he wore habitually Hessian boots . . .' from Edward Curr, *Recollections of Squatting in Victoria*, 1883

'the best watered Country . . .' from William Lawson, *Journal of an Expedition across the Blue Mountains*, 11 May–6 June 1813

'the smallest scrap of paper . . .' and 'following Mr Whyte's ploughed line' from Stephen H. Roberts, *History of Australian Land Settlement*, p. 179

'To see a windmill on the plains . . .' from Grace Hendy-Pooley, *Early History of Bathurst and Surroundings*, 1908, p. 231

'from the early part of 1822 to the end of 1825 . . .' from Henry Dangar, *Index and Directory to Map of the Country Bordering Upon the River Hunter*, 1828, p. 39

'A state of affairs arose which was unprecedented . . .' from C.J. King, 'Squatting and the 1847 Orders-in-Council', *Review of Marketing and Agricultural Economics*, vol. 25, issue 3, 1957, p. 45

'a gem, and not' and 'a memorial to the zeal' from John F. Brock, *A Tale of Two Maps—NSW in the 1830s by Mitchell & Dixon: Perfection, Probity & Piracy!*, 1906, p. 8

'stock of every description . . .' from *Sydney Gazette*, 17 October 1829

'following Mr Whyte's ploughed line . . .' from S.H. Roberts, *History of Australian Land Settlement*, 1924, p. 179

CHAPTER 2

'a waterside town scattered wide over upland and lowland . . .' from Alexander Harris, *Settlers and Convicts, or Recollections of Sixteen Years' Labour in the Australian Backwoods*, p. 6

'immense downs and forests partially wooded' from John Molony, *The Native Born*, 2000, p. 106

'I could not avoid noticing that Major Mitchell's roads . . .' from Louisa Meredith, *Notes and Sketches of New South Wales*, 1844, p. 73

'Not all the armies of England . . .' and 'a perverse rejection of the bounty of Providence' from Julian Howard, *Building a New Nation: History for Form III*, 1964, p. 46

'improper occupiers of waste lands', 'must lead every reasonable man . . .' and 'held by no better title' from Samuel Sidney, *The Three Colonies of Australia*, 1852, p. 107

'robber of the rich . . .' from Jane Wilson, 'Bushrangers' in *Australian Dictionary of Biography*, 2015

'an object of first importance', *Lithgow Mercury*, 29 September 1905

'The bullock drivers are almost the best-paid . . .' from Rachel Henning, *The Letters of Rachel Henning*, 2014

'You may as well have attempted . . .' from Alastair Davidson, *The Invisible State*, 1991, p. 28

'Nine out of ten of these squatters . . .' from Thomas Banister and Mossman, Samuel, *Australia Visited and Revisited*, 1853, p. 70

'He is the biggest chuckle-headed ass God ever created . . .' from John Robertson and Russel Ward, *Such Was Life: Select Documents in Australian Social History*, vol. 2, 1851–1913, 1978

'rarely varied meal of tea, mutton and damper made
its appearance on the table . . .' from Edward Curr,
Recollections of Squatting in Victoria, 1883, p. 126

'We get hold of a fashion when we go to Sydney . . .' from
Margaret Maynard, *Fashioned from Penury: Dress as
Cultural Practice in Colonial Australia*, 1994, p. 177

'The same old story, get up, dress the children . . .' from Mary
Braidwood Mowle, 'Papers of Mary Braidwood Mowle
1832–1881'

'A new man coming along . . .' from Roberts, 1924, p. 179

'The residence at Goonoo Goonoo . . .' from *Newcastle
Chronicle*, 22 October 1870

CHAPTER 3

'complete savages' and 'smelled like foxes' . . . from Flinders
Ranges Research, 1996 <www.southaustralianhistory.com.
au/ki.htm>

'The paths which they had made' . . . from Charles Bonney,
'Account of the Hawdon and Bonney trek with cattle from
New South Wales to Adelaide 1838', in Kevin K. Kain, *The
First overlanders, Hawdon and Bonney*, 1991, p. 73

'Altogether the scene was picturesque enough . . .' from Curr,
1883, p. 65

'a firm reddish soil . . .' and 'exceedingly well behaved'
from Edward Eyre, *Autobiographical Narrative of
Residence and Exploration in Australia 1832–1839*,
1984, p. 155

'the arts of civilisation', 'civilising and Christianising', and
'habits of useful industry' from Peter Read (ed), *Aboriginal
History Journal*, vol. 13, 1989, p. 18

'if the government had from the first . . .' from John Wrathall
Bull, *Early Experiences of Colonial Life in South Australia*,
1884

'a little cold lead . . .' from Robert Foster and Amanda
Nettelbeck, *Out of the Silence*, 2012, p. 71

'A new pastoral country . . .' from *South Australian Register*,
7 June 1951

'The rabbit has come to stay . . .' from 'The story of John Conrick, pioneer' in *The News*, 31 July 1923, p. 11

'enduring every privation . . .' and 'All in all, it is a horrible life . . .' from Leith MacGillivray, 'We Have Found Our Paradise', *Journal of the Historical Society of South Australia*, no. 17, 1989

'the whole country was so cavernous . . .' from MacGillivray, 1989, p. 29

'There is little joy . . .' from Leith MacGillivray, *Land and People: European Land Settlement in the South East of South Australia 1840–1940*, 1982

'a wretched place to live . . .' from MacGillivray, 1989

'I doubt that New Holland is a fit place . . .' from MacGillivray, 1989

'Its chief importations are spirits . . .' from MacGillivray, 1989, p. 30

'wouldn't mind seeing 100,000 of them' from Charles Price, *German Settlers in South Australia*, 1945

'make gold with the plough' . . . from David Hunt, *True Girt: The Unauthorised History of Australia*, 2016, Ch 10

'We are afraid that some of the fleeces . . .' from *Adelaide Examiner*, 4 February 1843

'10 lb (4.5 kg) tobacco boiled in 15 gallons . . .' in W. Stephen Smith, *The History of Sheep Scab in South Australia*, scholarly paper, 1975, p. 4

CHAPTER 4

'the bush' from Robert Knopwood, *The Diary of the Reverend Robert Knopwood 1803–1838*, 1977, p. 69

'by no means uncommon . . .' from Sharon Morgan, *Land Settlement in Early Tasmania*, 2003, p. 67

'Van Diemen's Land had not a great reputation . . .' from Anthony Trollope, *Australia and New Zealand*, 1873, p. 182

'our starving countrymen . . .' and 'grumble excessively . . .' from William Williamson, in James Boyce, *Environmental*

History of British Settlement in Van Diemen's Land, 2006,
　p. 212
'no less than 120,000 weight . . .' from K.R. von Stieglitz,
　A Short History of Cressy and Bishopsbourne, 1947
'a very large head . . .' from Ted Henzell, *Australian
　Agriculture: Its History and Challenges*, 2007, p. 58
'At that time there was no thought . . .' from James Boyce,
　Van Diemen's Land, 2008, p. 70
'Wool is in general greasy and badly managed by settlers . . .'
　from Morgan, 2003, p. 64
'more adapted for slaughter than for the dairy' from Edward
　Curr, *An Account of the Colony of Van Diemen's Land*,
　1824, p. 84
'Large tracts of closely matted scrub . . .' from Henry Hellyer,
　'Field Journal, 1827', *Henry Hellyers's Observations:
　Journals of life in the Tasmanian Bush 1826–1827*, edited
　by Bertram Thomas, 2011
'the lower order of settler considers . . .' from Boyce, 2008,
　p. 69
'driving through a park', 'hills . . .' and 'oaks . . .' from
　Augustus Prinsep, *The Journal of a Voyage from Calcutta
　to Van Diemen's Land*, 1883, p. 102
'making use of their money . . .' from Morgan, 2003, p. 26
'Everything in Tasmania . . .' from Steve Harris, *Solomon's
　Noose*, 2015, Ch 21
'The beautiful appearance of a hedge' from Curr, 1824, p. 119
'Marvellous Melbourne' from George Sala, 'The Land of the
　Golden Fleece' in *The Argus*, 8 August 1885

CHAPTER 5
'I stuck a plough . . .' from Henty, Edward, et al, *The Henty
　Journals*, edited by Dr Lynette Peel, 1996
'It has become known to me . . .' from Noel F. Learmonth,
　The Portland Bay Settlement, 1934, p. 103
'The inhabitants . . .' from *Portland Guardian and Normanby
　General Advertiser*, 14 January 1843

'most eligible place . . .' from Joy Braybrook, *John Batman*,
　　2012, p. 35

'lovely stream', 'six miles up river' and 'This will be the place
　　for a village' from Braybrook, 2012, p. 35

'There is no money, no credit, no trade . . .' from A.G.L.
　　Shaw, *A History of the Port Phillip District*, 2003, p. 169

'without education, intelligence, or knowledge of society'
　　from Shaw, 2003, p. 133

'Miss Newcomb, who is my partner . . .' from Anne Drysdale,
　　*Miss D & Miss N, an extraordinary partnership: The
　　Diary of Anne Drysdale*, edited by Bev Roberts, 2009

'blue serge suits with cabbage tree hats', 'belts supporting
　　leather tobacco pouches' from Curr, 1883, p. 5

'I traversed plains thousands of acres in extent . . .' from
　　Maggie MacKellar, *Strangers in a Foreign Land*, 2008,
　　p. 98

'no such thing as a market price for anything' from
　　MacKellar, 2008, p. 136

'drag back the horses hooves like snow' from MacKellar,
　　2008, p. 94

'More beautiful than the finest park land I ever saw at
　　home . . .' from MacKellar, 2008, p. 121

'The best way to procure a run . . .' from Ian Clark, *Scars in
　　the Landscape*, 1995, p. 1

'abandoned land', 'melancholy exodus' and 'Belle Époch'
　　from Richard Zachariah, *The Vanished Land*, 2017

'The blacks are very quiet here now . . .' from Henry Meyrick,
　　letter written to his relatives in England, 30 April 1836

'the work of an amateur . . .' from Duncan Cooper, *The
　　Challicum Sketch Book 1842–53*, edited by Philip L.
　　Brown, p. 24

'Nothing, I think, gives a surer proof . . .' from Trollope,
　　1873, p. 24

'Here also the rust tinged . . .' from John McQuilton,
　　The Kelly Outbreak 1878–1880, 1987

CHAPTER 6

'The Darling Downs will never grow a cabbage' from
    Maurice French, *A Pastoral Romance*, 1990, p. 237
'It is now the case . . .' from Kay Saunders, *Workers in
    Bondage*, 1982
'surrounded by good neighbours . . .' from Maurice French,
    'Squatters and Separation: A Synoptic Overview',
    Queensland History Journal, no. 20, 2010, p. 816
'Take that immense tract of country . . .' from Valerie Donovan,
    From Queensland Squatter to English Squire, 1994, p. 67
'the pastoralists of the Darling Downs . . .' from French,
    2010, p. 809
'These gentlemen live in . . .' from Robert Macklin, *Dragon
    and Kangaroo*, 2017, p. 62
'over, never to return . . .' from Margaret Kiddle, *Men of
    Yesterday*, 1961
'We rode a few miles' from Anna Kate Hume, *Katie Hume
    on the Darling Downs, A Colonial Marriage: Letters of a
    Colonial Lady 1866–1871*, edited by Nancy Bonnin, 1985,
    p. 29
'It is of hewn stone . . .' from Hume, 1985, p. 70
'You have been a brother to me for a long time . . .' from
    Gordon Reid, *A Nest of Hornets*, 1982, p. 63
'3000 settlers lost their lives . . .' from Henry Reynolds,
    Frontier, 1987, p. 30
'. . . the sheep become covered with its barbed seeds' from
    Anne Allingham, 'Pioneer Squatting in the Kennedy
    District', lecture, University of Queensland, 1975
'if it were not for Aborigines . . .' from Dawn May, *Aboriginal
    Labour and the Cattle Industry*, 1994
'I have named this The Spring of Hope . . .' from John
    McDouall Stuart, *Explorations in Australia: The Journals
    of John McDouall Stuart During the Years 1858, 1859,
    1860, 1861 & 1862*, 1865
'200 miles upcountry' and 'dull' from David Kennedy,
    Kennedy's Colonial Travel, 1876, pp. 98, 65
'The black man . . .' from Kennedy, 1876, p. 99

CHAPTER 7

'Cattle kings ye call us' from Mary Durack, *Kings in Grass Castles*, 1959, p. vi

'The drover of cattle . . .' from Geraldine Byrne, *An Analysis of the Social Profile of the Kilfoyles of Rosewood Station*, 1995, p. 47

'very good, basaltic and limestone . . .' from Darrell Lewis, *A Wild History*, 2012, p. 12

'Wild dogs howl and hedge-wood groans . . .' from Bobbie Buchanan, *In the Tracks of Old Bluey*, 1997, p. 109

'No one who has not seen the bullwaddi . . .' from Darrell Lewis, *The Murranji Track*, 2007, p. 4

'small leaved tree . . .' from McDouall, 1865, p. 288

'depasturing a million sheep' from Michael Pearson and Jane Lennon, *Pastoral Australia*, 2010, p. 88

'not shooting blacks' from Tony Roberts, 'The Brutal Truth: What Happened in the Gulf Country', *The Monthly*, November 2009

'for sport' and 'warlike savages' from Roberts, 2009

'shot the blacks down like crows' from Roberts, 2009

'indiscriminate', 'ought to be a show of reason . . .' and 'Shoot those you cannot get at' from Roberts, 2009

'Tom Kilfoyle, one of the best bushmen in Australia . . .' from Byrne, 1995, p. 9

'at home all day', 'getting thatch to cover' and 'getting rafters for the house' from Byrne, 1995, p. 64

CHAPTER 8

'While I am writing this the dust . . .' from Don Garden, 'The Federation Drought of 1895–1903, El Niño and Society in Australia' in *Common Ground: Integrating the Social and Environmental in History*, 2010, p. 276, originally published in the *Burra Record*, 25 May 1898, see also *South Australian Register*, 7 June 1898

'My doleful theme is long protracted drought . . .' from Garden, 2010, p. 281

'withered', 'bleary-eyed', 'mere bones, holding up a pelt', 'fetid' and 'stupefied with liquor' from Garden, 2010, p. 281, originally published in *The Bulletin*, 21 June 1902

'gaps in the streets . . .' from Graeme Davison and Marc Brodie (eds), *Struggle Country: The Rural Ideal in Twentieth Century Australia*, 2005, Ch 4, p. 3

'What tales there'll be in every camp . . .' from A.B. Paterson, 'T.Y.S.O.N.', first published in the *Australasian Pastoralists' Review*, 15 December 1898

'I have been fighting the desert all my . . .' from Orison Marden, *Wisdom & Empowerment*, 2017, Ch 5

BIBLIOGRAPHY

Alexander, Alison (ed), *The Companion to Tasmanian History*, Centre for Tasmanian Historical Studies, University of Tasmania, Hobart, 2005

Allingham, Anne, 'Pioneer Squatting in the Kennedy District', lecture, University of Queensland, Brisbane, 1975

Banister, Thomas and Mossman, Samuel, *Australia Visited and Revisited: A narrative of recent travels and old experiences in Victoria and New South Wales*, Addey & Co., London, 1853

Braybrook, Joy, *John Batman: An Inside Story of the Birth of Melbourne*, Xlibris, 2012

Beckett, Gordon, *A Collection of Essays on the Colonial Economy of New South Wales*, Trafford Publishing, Victoria, BC, 2012

Bennett, Mary, *Christison of Lammermoor*, Alston Rivers, London, 1928

Binney, Keith, *Horsemen of the First Frontier (1788–1900) and The Serpent's Legacy*, Volcanic Production, Sydney, 2005

Bischoff, James, *Sketch of the History of Van Diemen's Land*, John Richardson, London, 1832

Black, Maggie, *Up Came a Squatter: Niel Black of Glenormiston 1839–1880*, New South Books, Sydney, 2016

Bonney, Charles, 'Account of the Hawdon and Bonney trek with cattle from New South Wales to Adelaide 1838' in Kevin K. Kain (ed), *The First Overlanders, Hawdon and Bonney: Their accounts of the first cattle drive from New South Wales to Adelaide 1838*, K. Kain in association with Gould Books, Adelaide, 1991, p. 73

Boyce, James, *Van Diemen's Land*, Black Inc., Melbourne, 2008

—— *'Environmental History of British Settlement in Van Diemen's Land'*, thesis, University of Tasmania, 2006

Brock, John F., 'A Tale of Two Maps—NSW in the 1830s by Mitchell & Dixon: Perfection, Probity & Piracy!', paper 5, available at: http://xnatmap.org/adnm/conf_06_11/c06/aPaper%2005.pdf

Buchanan, Bobbie, *In the Tracks of Old Bluey: The Life Story of Nat Buchanan*, Central Queensland University Press, Rockhampton, 1997

Buckridge, Patrick and McKay, Belinda (eds), *By the Book: A Literary History of Queensland*, University of Queensland Press, Brisbane, 2007

Bull, John Wrathall, *Early Experiences of Life in South Australia*, E.S. Wigg & Son, Adelaide, 1884

Byrne, Geraldine, *'An Analysis of the Social Profile of the Kilfoyles of Rosewood Station'*, thesis, Edith Cowan University, Perth, 1995

Chang, Claudia and Koster, Harold, *Pastoralists at the Periphery: Herders in a Capitalist World*, University of Arizona Press, Tucson, 1994

Clark, Ian, *Scars in the Landscape: A Register of Massacre Sites in Western Victoria*, Australian Institute of Aboriginal and Torres Strait Islander Studies, Aboriginal Studies Press, Canberra, 1995

Connell, Robert and Irving, Terence, *Class Structure in Australian History*, Longman Cheshire, Melbourne, 1980

Cooper, Duncan, *The Challicum Sketch Book 1842–53*, edited by Philip Brown, National Library of Australia, Canberra, 1987

Cryle, Mark, 'A "Fantastic Adventure": Reading Christison of Lammermoor', paper presented to Professional Historians Association, Queensland, 2009

Curr, Edward, *An Account of the Colony of Van Diemen's Land: Principally Designed for the Use of Emigrants*, George Cowie & Co., London, 1824

——*Recollections of Squatting in Victoria*, George Robertson, Melbourne, 1883

——*The Australian Race*, John Ferres, Melbourne, 1887

Dangar, Henry, *Index and Directory to Map of the Country Bordering Upon the River Hunter*, Joseph Cross, London, 1828

Davidson, Alastair, *The Invisible State: The Formation of the Australian State*, Cambridge University Press, 1991

Davison, Graeme and Brodie, Marc (eds), *Struggle Country: The Rural Ideal in Twentieth Century Australia*, Monash University ePress, Melbourne, 2005

Donovan, Valerie, *From Queensland Squatter to English Squire: Arthur Hodgson and the Colonial Gentry 1840–1870*, University of Queensland Press, Brisbane, 1994

Drysdale, Anne, *Miss D & Miss N, an extraordinary partnership: The diary of Anne Drysdale*, edited by Bev Roberts, Australian Scholarly Publishing, Melbourne, 2009

Durack, Mary, *Kings in Grass Castles*, Constable & Robinson, London, 1959

Eyre, Edward, *Autobiographical Narrative of Residence and Exploration in Australia 1832–1839*, Caliban Books, London, 1984

Fenton, James, *A History of Tasmania from its Discovery in 1642 to the Present Time*, J. Walch & Sons, Hobart, 1884

Flinders Ranges Research, *Kangaroo Island*, 1996, available at: www.southaustralianhistory.com.au/ki.htm

Foster, Robert and Nettelbeck, Amanda, *Out of the Silence: The History and Memory of South Australia's Frontier Wars*, Wakefield Press, Adelaide, 2012

Franklin, Jane, *This Errant Lady: Jane Franklin's Overland Journey to Port Phillip and Sydney*, edited by Penny Russell, National Library of Australia, Canberra, 2002

French, Maurice, *A Pastoral Romance: The tribulation and triumph of squatterdom*, University of Southern Queensland Press, Toowoomba, 1990

French, Maurice, 'Squatters and Separation: A Synoptic Overview', *Queensland History Journal*, no. 20, 2010, pp. 804–19

Garden, Don, 'The Federation Drought of 1895–1903, El Niño and Society in Australia' in G. Massard-Guilbaud and S. Mosley (eds), *Common Ground: Integrating the Social and Environmental in History*, Cambridge Scholars Publishing, Newcastle upon Tyne, 2010, available at: http://climatehistory.com.au/wp-content/uploads/2009/12/Garden_Book_Chapter_2010.pdf

Gunn, Aeneas, *We of the Never Never*, Hutchinson, London, 1908

Harris, Alexander, *Settlers and Convicts, or Recollection of Sixteen Years' Labour in the Australian Backwoods*, C. Cox, London, 1847

Harris, Steve, *Solomon's Noose: The True Story of Her Majesty's Hangman of Hobart*, Melbourne Books, Melbourne, 2015

Heinrich, Dorothy, *The Man Who Hunted Whales*, Awoonga, 2011

Hellyer, Henry, 'Field Journal, 1827', *Henry Hellyer's Observations: Journals of life in the Tasmanian bush 1826–1827*, edited by Bertram Thomas, North Down Press, 2011

Hendy-Pooley, Grace, *Early History of Bathurst and Surroundings*, Royal Australian Historical Society, Sydney, 1908

Henty, Edward, et al, *The Henty Journals: A Record of Farming, Whaling and Shipping in Portland Bay 1834–1839*, edited by Dr Lynette Peel, Miegunyah Press, Melbourne, 1996

Henning, Rachel, *The Letters of Rachel Henning*, The
University of Adelaide Library, 2014, available at:
https://ebooks.adelaide.edu.au/h/henning/rachel/
letters-of-rachel-henning/

Henzell, Ted, *Australian Agriculture: Its History and
Challenges*, CSIRO Publishing, Melbourne, 2007

Heywood, Benjamin, *A Vacation Tour at the Antipodes*,
Longman, Green, Longman, Roberts & Green, London, 1863

Hodgson, Christopher, *Reminiscences of Australia: With
Hints on the Squatter's Life (1846)*, Kessinger Publishing,
Whitefish, 2010

Howard, Julian, *Building a New Nation: History for
Form III*, Shakespeare Head Press, Sydney, 1964

Hume, Anna Kate, *Katie Hume on the Darling Downs,
A Colonial Marriage: Letters of a Colonial Lady
1866–1871*, edited by Nancy Bonnin, Darling Downs
Institute Press, Toowoomba, 1985

Hunt, David, *True Girt: The Unauthorised History of
Australia*, Black Inc., Melbourne, 2016

Jackson, R.V., *Australian Economic Development in the
Nineteenth Century*, Australian National University Press,
Canberra, 1977

Johnson, Murray and McFarlane, Ian, *Van Diemen's Land:
An Aboriginal History*, University of New South Wales
Press, Sydney, 2015

Kennedy, David, *Kennedy's Colonial Travel: A Narrative
of Four Year's Tour Through Australia, New Zealand,
Canada etc.*, Edinburgh Publishing Co, 1876, available
at: https://archive.org/details/kennedyscolonial00kenniala

Kiddle, Margaret, *Men of Yesterday: A Social Hitory of the
Western Districts of Victoria 1834–1890*, Melbourne
University Press, 1961

King, C.J., 'Squatting and the 1847 Orders-in-Council',
Review of Marketing and Agricultural Economics, vol. 25,
issue 3, 1957, p. 45, available at: http://ageconsearch.umn.
edu/bitstream/8960/1/25030045.pdf

Knopwood, Robert, *The Diary of the Reverend Robert Knopwood 1803–1838*, Tasmanian Historical Research Association, Hobart, 1977

Lawson, Henry, 'The Hero of Redclay', *Over the Sliprails*, Angus & Robertson, Sydney, 1900

Learmonth, Noel F., *The Portland Bay Settlement: Being the history of Portland, Victoria from 1800–1851*, Historical Committee of Portland, 1934

Lewis, Darrell, *The Murranji Track: Ghost Road of the Drovers*, Central Queensland University Press, Rockhampton, 2007

Lewis, Darrell, *A Wild History: Life and Death on the Victoria River Frontier*, Monash University Publishing, Melbourne, 2012

MacGillivray, Leith, '*Land and People: European Land Settlement in the South East of South Australia 1840–1940*', thesis, University of Adelaide, 1982

——'We Have Found Our Paradise', *Journal of the Historical Society of South Australia*, no. 17, 1989

MacKellar, Maggie, *Strangers in a Foreign Land*, The Miegunyah Press, Melbourne, 2008

Macklin, Robert, *Dragon and Kangaroo: Australia and China's Shared History from the Goldfields to the Present Day*, Hachette Australia, Sydney, 2017

Marden, Orison, *Wisdom & Empowerment: The Orison Swett Marden Edition*, Musaicum Books, 2017

Massard-Guilbaud, Genevieve & Mosley, Stephen (eds), *Common Ground: Integrating the Social and Environmental in History*, Cambridge Scholars Publishing, 2011

May, Dawn, *Aboriginal Labour and the Cattle Industry: Queensland from White Settlement to the Present*, Cambridge University Press, 1994

May, Dawn, 'The North Queensland Beef Cattle Industry: An Historical Overview' in B.J. Dalton (ed), *Lectures on North Queensland History*, no. 4, James Cook University, Townsville, 1984, pp. 121–59,

available at: http://www.textqueensland.com.au/item/
chapter/9b938237e189a1274770d0d2e94209ad

McHugh, Evan, *Outback Pioneers: Great Achievers of the
Australian Bush*, Penguin Books Australia, Melbourne, 2008

McLean, Ian, *Why Australia Prospered: The Shifting Sources of
Economic Growth*, Princeton University Press, 2013

McQuilton, John, *The Kelly Outbreak 1878–1880: The
Geographical Dimension of Social Banditry*, Melbourne
University Press, 1987

Meredith, Louisa, *Notes and Sketches of New South Wales
During a Residence in that Colony*, John Murray, London,
1844

Mitchell, Thomas, *Three Expeditions into the Interior of
Eastern Australia*, T. & W. Boone, London, 1839

Molony, John, *The Native-Born: The First White Australians*,
Melbourne University Press, 2000

Munro, Colin, *Fern Vale; or, the Queensland Squatter:
A Novel*, T.C. Newby, London, 1862

Morgan, Patrick, 'Gippsland Settlers and the Kurnai Dead',
Quadrant Magazine, vol. 48, no. 10, October 2004, pp. 26–8

Morgan, Sharon, *Land Settlement in Early Tasmania:
Creating an Antipodean England*, Cambridge University
Press, 1992

Morgan, James, *The Premier and the Pastoralist*, Wakefield
Press, Adelaide, 2011

Mowle, Mary Braidwood, 'Papers of Mary Braidwood
Mowle 1832–1881', National Library of Australia,
Canberra (unpublished)

Ostapenko, Dmytro, '*Growing Potential: Land-Cultivators
of the Colony of Victoria in the late 1830s–1860s*', thesis,
La Trobe University, Melbourne, 2011

Parsonson, Ian, *The Australian Ark: A History of Domesticated
Animals in Australia*, CSIRO Publishing, Melbourne, 1998

Pearson, Michael and Lennon, Jane, *Pastoral Australia:
Fortunes, Failures and Hard Yakka*, CSIRO Publishing,
Melbourne, 2010

Perrin, Edmund and Kass, Terry, 'Liberty Plains' in *The Dictionary of Sydney*, 2008, available at: https://dictionaryofsydney.org/entry/liberty_plains

Poiner, Gretchen & Jack, Sybil, *Limits of Location: Creating a Colony*, Sydney University Press, 2007

Powell, Alan, *Far Country: A Short History of the Northern Territory*, Melbourne University Press, 1982

Price, Charles, *German Settlers in South Australia*, Melbourne University Press, 1945

Prinsep, Augustus, *The Journal of a Voyage from Calcutta to Van Diemen's Land*, Smith, Elder and Co., London, 1883, available from: http://handle.slv.vic.gov.au/10381/200252

Read, Peter (ed), *Aboriginal History Journal*, vol. 13, Australian National University, Canberra, 1989

Reid, Gordon, *A Nest of Hornets: The Massacre of the Fraser Family at Hornet Bank Station, Central Queensland, 1857, and related events*, Oxford University Press, 1982

Reynolds, Henry, *Frontier: Aborigines, Settlers and Land*, Allen & Unwin, Sydney, 1987

Richardson, John, *The Lady Squatters*, Drysdale, Victoria, 1986

Roberts, Stephen H., *History of Australian Land Settlement, 1788–1920*, Frank Cass & Co. Ltd, London, 1924

Roberts, Tony, 'The Brutal Truth: What Happened in the Gulf Country', *The Monthly*, November 2009

Robertson, John, *Such Was Life: Select Documents in Australian Social History*, vol. 2, 1851–1913, Alternative Publishing Cooperative, Sydney, 1978

Reeder, Stephanie, *The Vision Splendid*, National Library of Australia, Canberra, 2011

Satgé, Oscar de, *Pages from the Journal of a Queensland Squatter*, Hurst & Blackett Ltd, London, 1901

Saunders, Kay, *Workers in Bondage: The Origins and Bases of Unfree Labour in Queensland 1824–1916*, University of Queensland Press, Brisbane, 1982

Shaw, A.G.L., *A History of the Port Phillip District: Victoria Before Separation*, Melbourne University Press, 2003

Sidney, Samuel, *The Three Colonies of Australia: New South Wales, Victoria, South Australia*, C.M. Saxton, Barker and Co., New York, 1860

Slocomb, Margaret, *Among Australia's Pioneers: Chinese Indentured Pastoral Workers on the Northern Frontier, 1848 to c.1880*, Balboa Press, Sydney, 2014

Smith, Pamela, 'Station Camps: Legislation, Labour Relations and Rations on Pastoral Leases in the Kimberley Region, Western Australia', *Aboriginal History*, vol. 24, 2000, pp. 75–97, available at: http://press-files.anu.edu.au/downloads/press/p72891/pdf/article0518.pdf

Smith, W. Stephen, 'The History of Sheep Scab in South Australia', scholarly paper, Adelaide, 1975, reproduced in 2006 by Primary Industries and Regions South Australia, available at: http://history.pir.sa.gov.au/__data/assets/pdf_file/0003/16275/sheep_scab_history_bon_web.pdf

Stieglitz, K.R. von, *A Short History of Cressy and Bishopsbourne*, Evandale, 1947, available at: http://handle.slv.vic.gov.au/10381/185094

Taylor, Charles, *The Literary Panorama and National Register*, Cox, Son & Bayliss, London, 1807–1819

Taylor, Peter, *Australia: The First Twelve Years*, Allen & Unwin, Sydney, 1984

——*Station Life in Australia: Pioneers and Pastoralists*, Allen & Unwin, Sydney, 1988

Tench, Watkin, *A Complete Account of the Settlement at Port Jackson*, University of Adelaide, 2014

Trollope, Anthony, *Australia and New Zealand*, G. Robertson, Melbourne, 1873, available at: http://digital.sl.nsw.gov.au/delivery/DeliveryManagerServlet?embedded=true&toolbar=false&dps_pid=IE3869431

White, J.C., *Queensland the Progressive: An Account of the Colony; its Soil, Climate, Productions and Capabilities*, S.W. Silver & Co., London, 1870

Zachariah, Richard, *The Vanished Land: Disappearing Dynasties of Victoria's Western Districts*, Wakefield Press, Adelaide, 2017

INDEX